The Framlingham Branch

by
Peter Paye

THE OAKWOOD PRESS

© Oakwood Press & Peter Paye 2008

British Library Cataloguing in Publication Data
A Record for this book is available from the British Library
ISBN 978 0 85361 678 8

Typeset by Oakwood Graphics.
Repro by PKmediaworks, Cranborne, Dorset.
Printed by Cambrian Printers, Aberystwyth, Ceredigion.

Dedication

*To the late Doctor Ian C. Allen, revered by local railway staff as
'The unofficial shedmaster of Framlingham depot'.*

By the same author:
  The Snape Branch (Oakwood Press, 2005)
  The Hadleigh Branch (Oakwood Press, 2006)

Much of the rolling stock used on the Framlingham branch was also used on the Hadleigh and Snape branches. For this reason the plans published in the author's earlier titles have not been repeated in this volume.

Title page: 'B12/3' class 4-6-0 No. 61561 is deputising for the allocated branch locomotive as she reverses a two-coach branch set and a Gresley corridor coach into the platform at Framlingham in June 1951. The signal box is to the left and goods shed to the right.
The late Dr Ian C. Allen

Front cover: 'J15' class 0-6-0 No. 65389 performs shunting duties at Framlingham on 11th February, 1960.
Colour-Rail

Rear cover: A morning down mixed train crossing River Ore underbridge No. 1105 at 90 miles 18 chains from Liverpool Street and approaching Framlingham hauled by 'F6' class 2-4-2T No. 67230.
The late Dr Ian C. Allen

Published by The Oakwood Press (Usk), P.O. Box 13, Usk, Mon., NP15 1YS.
E-mail: sales@oakwoodpress.co.uk
Website: www.oakwoodpress.co.uk

Contents

'J15' class 0-6-0 tender locomotive No. 65467 spins along the branch between Parham and Framlingham with the 1.40 pm mixed train ex-Wickham Market on a fine and sunny 11th October, 1952. *G.R. Mortimer*

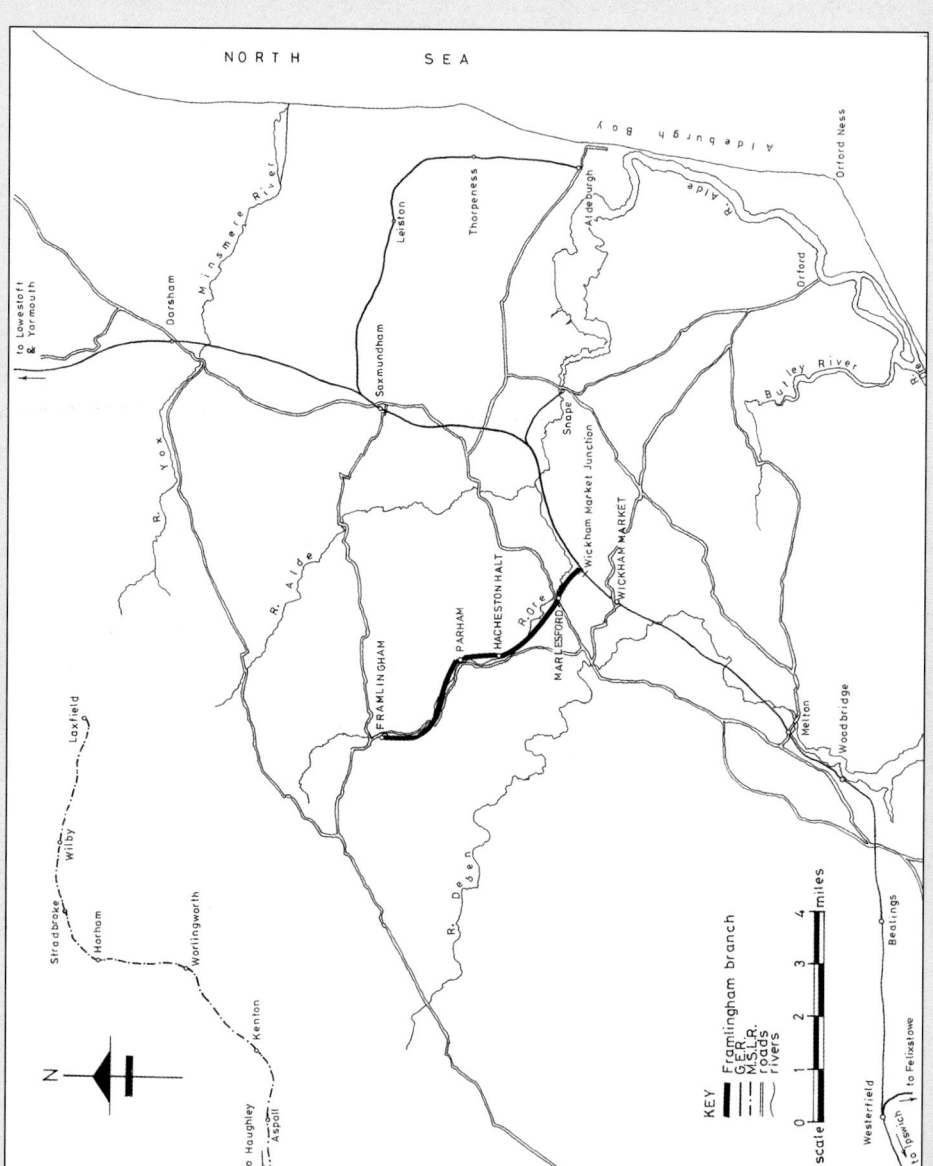

Map of the Framlingham branch and surrounding railways.

Introduction

The county of Suffolk, sandwiched between metropolitan Essex to the south and the emptier open Norfolk to the north, has a rolling landscape stretching 50 or so miles from the flat fenlands of Cambridgeshire in the west to the eastern shingle shores facing the North Sea between Lowestoft and Felixstowe. At the time of Domesday, Suffolk was the most populous of the English Counties with over 400 churches established in close-knit settlements dotted across the countryside. The topography was chiefly of a boulder clay plateau away from the coast, with sandy clay loams in the north-east, clay loams to the west and sands and gravels to the south. East Suffolk consisted of sandy hills, with fertile areas between, bisected by small streams, such as the Rivers Alde, Ore and Deben which led to muddy inlets and the natural harbours of Lowestoft, Southwold, Aldeburgh and Woodbridge.

The cultivation of the land by the plough had for generations been the main industry but agriculture was dependent on good transport for the farmers and growers to get their produce to markets. The old Suffolk tracks and roads were gradually improved and in the late 18th and early 19th century turnpike roads were soon established. Carriers' carts, however, were slow and ponderous on their journeys, with many delays incurred during wet or adverse weather. Often produce rotted *en route* and earned poor prices at Ipswich, Norwich or other provincial markets. The advent of the railways in East Anglia brought drastic improvements and after initial scepticism there was the urgent desire for towns to be served by the new lines.

East Suffolk initially benefited with the building of the Halesworth, Beccles and Haddiscoe Railway, opened to passenger traffic on 4th December, 1854 and worked by the Eastern Counties Railway (ECR). Its original focus was a link with the existing Norwich to Lowestoft line, connecting it directly with Norwich and Great Yarmouth but no sooner was the original plan nearing completion than there was clamour for a southwards extension towards Ipswich. The title of the company was altered to the East Suffolk Railway (ESR) by Act of Parliament on 3rd July, 1854, the statute authorizing the company to build a line from Halesworth to Woodbridge, to connect by an end-on junction with the Eastern Union Railway (EUR) extending thence to Ipswich. The chief promoters were Sir Samuel Morton Peto for the ESR and Richard Cobbold, the Ipswich brewer and banker, for the EUR. To engender further trade and traffic, the Act also authorized the building of branches from Saxmundham to Richard Garrett's Engineering Works at Leiston, later extended to Aldeburgh, Snape Junction to Newson Garrett's maltings at Snape and from Wickham Market to the ancient market town of Framlingham. The path of the main line had originally been routed via Framlingham but the Duke of Hamilton had objected to the railway passing through his estate at Easton and the Framlingham townsfolk were naturally concerned at the possible loss of trade. The main line and branches were ultimately opened for traffic on and from 1st June, 1859 worked by the ECR.

Framlingham served as the railhead for a considerable area of rural East and Central Suffolk. Plans were mooted for the Mellis & Eye Railway, opened in 1867, to be extended to Framlingham but nothing came of the venture and so the branch continued to serve the locality for almost half a century under the

BR/Sulzer type '2' 1,160 hp diesel-electric locomotive, later BR class '24', No. D5040 trundles past the down platform at Wickham Market with the Framlingham branch goods train. Note the removal of the facing points leading from the up main line giving former access to the goods yard. In the background is overbridge No. 438 which carried the road from Campsea Ash to Wickham Market over the railway. The station nameboard denotes Wickham Market for Campsea Ashe, with an 'E', which was the original spelling when the East Suffolk line first opened but was then discarded for many years.

The late Dr Ian C. Allen

aegis of the ESR/ECR, then from 1862 by the Great Eastern Railway before the opening of the Mid Suffolk Light Railway in 1904 for goods traffic, and 1908 for passenger traffic. Even then the loss of traffic was minimal and the Framlingham branch continued under the London and North Eastern Railway (LNER) from 1st January, 1923 and finally British Railways, Eastern Region from 1st January, 1948. Unfortunately the 1930s were lean years and after World War II much traffic transferred to the road. Passenger traffic was especially poor so that such services were withdrawn on 1st November, 1952. Thereafter farmers and growers quickly transferred their custom to road transport and freight facilities were withdrawn from the branch on and from 19th April, 1965 and the line closed completely. On closure of the branch passenger service in 1952 the late Doctor Ian C. Allan, who freely donated many of the photographs for this volume and who practised in Framlingham, was of the opinion 'the town lost its heart'.

This then is the fascinating story of the Framlingham branch from conception to closure. I have attempted to trace the history of the line and details have been checked with available documents, but apologies are offered for any errors, which might have occurred.

Peter Paye
Bishop's Stortford

Note: The spelling of Campsea Ash has been used throughout the text for clarity although it is also known as Campsea Ashe, Campsey Ashe and Campsey Ash.

Chapter One

The Coming of the Railway

The ancient Suffolk town of Framlingham, linked with Boadicea, is situated on the side of a low hill on the banks of the River Ore and some of its ancient houses and shops have a mellow beauty enhanced by red pantiled roofs. Its market charter goes back to 1276 and the triangular market place at the top of the rise from the mill brook is still the heart of the community, whilst spiritual needs are catered for in the parish church of St Michael, a noble Gothic building of cut flint, with a 96 feet-high tower. Over the centuries Framlingham has been associated with the names of royal and noble personages who have taken active and prominent roles in the development of English history. Most have been associated with the great castle set to the north of the town, of which considerable remains exist under the guardianship of English Heritage. Redwald, King of the Angles, is said to have established a castle on the site in the 7th century, but the existing impressive structure dates from the reign of Edward II when it was completed by Thomas de Brotherton, Earl of Norfolk and Marshal of England. Thereafter it passed through various ownerships including the Bigod's, Ufford's, Mowbray's and the Howard's. One of the most exciting times in its long history involved Princess Mary. In 1553, Edward VI gave Framlingham Castle to his sister Mary. However, on the death of the king she was at Hunsdon in Hertfordshire and her first impulse was to go to London to claim the throne, but following advice, she removed her court back to Framlingham where she had easy access to the coast. Following many trials and tribulations she was ultimately crowned Queen. Later in the time of Elizabeth I the castle was used as a prison for recusant priests before being returned to the Howard family in 1613. The glory of Framlingham was over and the castle and the town thereafter entered a solemnity, which continued until the upheaval caused by the coming of the industrial revolution and the advent of the railway. The leading personalities of the town wondered if they were to be included on any of the proposed routes, for failure to be incorporated might lead to economic stagnation and a drift of the populace away from the community.

The coming of railways into East Anglia began in earnest with the incorporation of the Eastern Counties Railway on 4th July, 1836. With a share capital of £1,600,000, the company was granted powers to construct a 126 mile line from Shoreditch in East London to Norwich and Yarmouth via Colchester, Ipswich and Eye. By September £58,100 of shares had been sold but there was great concern that only a twelfth of the capital raised was of local origin. Construction of the railway commenced in late March 1837 at the London end only, as incomplete negotiations with landowners prevented a start being made concurrently at Norwich and Ipswich. The problems continued when landowners along the proposed route demanded higher compensation, and by October 1838, with 40 per cent of the capital called, only nine miles of railway was under construction. With creditors urgently pressing, action was necessary to prevent total ruin and by April 1839 Lancashire proprietors, who had taken a majority stake in the undertaking, forced a decision to terminate the line at Colchester.

The first public trains ran from a temporary terminus at Mile End to Romford on 20th June, 1839, with extensions each end to Shoreditch and Brentwood opening for traffic on 1st July, 1840. Robert Stephenson was engaged by the ECR Directors to give engineering advice but he could only confirm that another £520,000 was required to complete the railway to Colchester. Mutinous shareholders were almost bludgeoned into meeting the calls for outstanding shares and application was made to Parliament for a further £350,000 share capital in 1840. With these assets and the added borrowing powers authorized by the 1840 Act, construction of the final section went ahead. Eventually the line was opened to Colchester for goods traffic on 7th March, 1843, and for passenger trains on 29th March. The 51 mile line, of unusual 5 ft gauge, had taken seven years to construct at a cost of nearly £2½ million, the works alone amounting to £1,631,000 had exceeded the original estimate for the whole project from London to Yarmouth.

The ECR Directors decision to terminate the project at Colchester was of particular concern to the merchants of Ipswich and Norwich, who were fearful of isolation from the railway network and probable loss of trade. Some ECR shareholders from Norfolk and Suffolk, alarmed by the slow progress and decision of April 1839, obtained a rule nisi in the Bail Court to force the fulfilment of the company's contract with the public, but this was overruled in 1840 when Parliament refused to extend the ECR's powers beyond July of that year. Local factions then decided to take action by planning a railway linking Norwich with Yarmouth and this received the Royal Assent in 1842, to be followed in the following year by a projected line from Norwich to Brandon. By now Ipswich traders and businessmen were fearful of economic isolation. The situation was aggravated by the ECR plan to join up with the Norwich to Brandon line at Thetford, with the main line by-passing Ipswich altogether and leaving the town at the end of a branch line from Hadleigh.

Objections were raised but ignored and so the traders and merchants of Ipswich produced their own scheme for a line linking the town with the ECR at Colchester. Plans were prepared by Peter Schuyler Bruff, who had already worked on surveys for the initial ECR route from London. The leading advocate of the Ipswich scheme was John Chevallier Cobbold, a member of the wealthy Ipswich banking and brewing family, who was a member of the original ECR board of Directors. As well as connecting Ipswich with Colchester, the promoters of the scheme also intended to continue with a line running north to Norwich, and the new company, entitled the Eastern Union Railway, was incorporated on 19th July, 1844.

In the meantime the ECR plans for a route to Thetford were abandoned but a group of businessmen in Bury St Edmunds were concerned that the town would also be isolated from the developing railway network. In February 1844, the ECR Directors received a deputation who wished to salvage their plans but were advised the company was unwilling to extend its line beyond Colchester. The townsfolk subsequently promoted their own line, the East and West Suffolk Railway and were advised the EUR would not oppose the railway provided the route went from Bury St Edmunds to Ipswich via Hadleigh and not interfere with the direct line from Ipswich to Colchester.

The development of railways in Norfolk and Suffolk was the subject of a special investigation by the Railway Department of the Board of Trade and, in a final report of 4th March, 1845, full support was given to the EUR scheme to Ipswich and for the extension to Norwich. The tract of land north-east of Ipswich towards Bury St Edmunds finally received the attention of railway developers with the passing, on 21st July, 1845, of the Act authorizing the construction of the Ipswich & Bury St Edmunds Railway. With an initial capital of £400,000 the new concern appeared nominally independent but was, however, an extension of the EUR, with no less than six EUR Directors appointed to a Board totalling 15 members. The Colchester to Ipswich section of the EUR was opened for goods traffic on 1st June and passenger traffic on 15th June, 1846, whilst the extension to Bury St Edmunds was opened to goods traffic on 7th December and passenger traffic on 24th December, 1846. In the same year Cornelius Welton, a land agent and surveyor from Wickham Market, produced plans for line passing through Ashbocking and Clopton from where a branch would run to Framlingham, but nothing came of the venture.

Meanwhile in the autumn of 1845 a proposed railway to Hadleigh , backed by the EUR, had effectively stemmed the competitive desire of the ECR to build a duplicate line from Colchester into East Anglia. Much to the annoyance of the Ipswich company, the ECR had not abandoned the goals of Norwich and Yarmouth, but had taken steps to reach Norfolk via an alternative route. On the same day the ECR was incorporated in 1836, a rival company, the Northern and Eastern Railway (N&E), received the Royal Assent to build a line over the 53 miles from Islington to Cambridge financed by a share capital of £1,200,000. The N&E like the ECR soon encountered financial difficulties and it was 1839 before construction commenced and even then only with the sanction of the ECR. To conserve finances the N&E route was diverted from Tottenham via Stratford, where running powers were permitted into the ECR Shoreditch terminus. Like the ECR the new line was built to a gauge of 5 feet, and despite abandonment of the route north of Bishop's Stortford by Act of Parliament in 1840, had reached the Hertfordshire market town on 16th May, 1842, at a cost of over £25,000 per mile. In 1843 the N&E secured an extension Act for a line to Newport, some 10 miles nearer Cambridge, but on 23rd December of the same year the ECR agreed terms on a 999 years lease for the company from 1st January, 1844. Once the lease was in force, the ECR lost no time in obtaining powers linking Newport to the Norwich & Brandon Railway at Brandon on 4th July, 1844. The N&E line, along with the existing ECR line, was converted to the standard gauge of 4 feet 8½ inches in the late summer of the same year and after a formal opening the previous day, the whole line from Bishop's Stortford to a temporary terminus at Norwich (Trowse) commenced public service on 30th July, 1845.

The southern railway approach to Norwich was surveyed by Joseph Locke and built by the EUR. It ran from a junction with the Bury St Edmunds line at Haughley, north west of Stowmarket and ran direct to the Norfolk capital via Diss. The line was opened in stages, initially for goods traffic to Finningham from 7th June, 1848, then to Burston for goods on 11th June and passengers from 2nd July, 1849, with completion throughout by 7th November of the same year. Thus while the main routes from London to Norwich via Cambridge and Ipswich were established, a vast acreage of East Suffolk was devoid of railways.

The genesis of the branch railway to Framlingham began in 1851 when a local venture, the Halesworth, Beccles & Haddiscoe Railway (HB&HR) obtained powers to construct a line connecting the river ports of Halesworth and Beccles with the Reedham to Lowestoft line of the Norfolk Railway. The following year it was empowered to enter into a working agreement with that company and subsequently opened to goods on 20th November and passenger traffic on 4th December, 1854. From the beginning the railway was operated by the ECR, which had leased the Norfolk Railway in 1848, and by June 1855 the company was able to show a modest profit of £528. In the meantime the HB&HR Directors, encouraged by the backing they had received, proposed a southward extension to Woodbridge to join up with the EUR. The EUR connection from Ipswich, originally proposed in 1847, was never built, and so these plans were also dusted down and resurrected in the hope the combined railways would provide a through route to the Suffolk capital and chief port of the county. At the same time it was proposed to re-title the HB&H undertaking, the East Suffolk Railway. Sir Samuel Morton Peto, who had ambitious schemes afoot to elevate the status of Lowestoft, immediately recognised the new line would provide a more direct access to London than the existing routes via Norwich. He quickly became the principal subscriber and subsequently offered to lease the whole line for 14 years on a cost not exceeding £10,000 per mile, with 3½ per cent paid during construction.

The original intention had been to route the Halesworth to Woodbridge extension via the town of Framlingham but the Duke of Hamilton had objected to the line passing through his estate at Easton and so the proposed railway was routed further to the east. The proposals for both the EUR and ESR schemes, together with plans and books of reference, were deposited with the Parliamentary Private Bill office on 30th November, 1853, with copies sent to parish councils affected by the planned railways. Included in the ESR proposal were branch railways to serve Richard Garrett's engineering works at Leiston, Newson Garrett's maltings at Snape Bridge and the town of Framlingham. As well as seeking authority for the main line from Westhall near Halesworth to Woodbridge, the Framlingham proposal sought permission to build,

a railway commencing via a junction with the said first mentioned intended railway at or near a field called White Walk belonging to Louisa Shaldon and Frederick William Schreiber and in the occupancy of Henry Tillett, situated in the parish of Campsea Ashe, on the south-east side of a road or lane, leading from Wickham Market by Blackstock Wood to Blaxhall and terminating at or near a field called Mill Field belonging to and in the occupation of Edmund Goodwyn, and situated in the parish of Framlingham in the said County of Suffolk, on the west side of the road leading from Framlingham to Wickham Market. Which said intended railway will pass from, in and through or be situate within the several parishes, townships and extra-parochial or other places following, or some of them. That is to say Campsea Ashe, Blaxhall, Little Glenham, Marlesford, Hacheston, Easton, Parham and Framlingham, all in the County of Suffolk.

The ECR Directors objected to the schemes and sent their General Manager to public meetings to argue against the proposals. The new line would in effect drain traffic from the Ipswich to Norwich main line via Haughley, which the ECR, after taking all steps to destroy when in EUR hands, now controlled. Realising they were losing the battle, the ECR officers then astutely altered their strategy and agreed to work the new East Suffolk line, but without the financial guarantees applicable to the original Halesworth to Haddiscoe section, thus ensuring a controlling power.

The vesting of all the assets of the Halesworth, Beccles and Haddiscoe Railway to the newly titled East Suffolk Railway was duly authorized by the East Suffolk Railway Act (17 and 18 Vict. cap. cxix), which received the Royal Assent on 3rd July, 1854. The statute also sanctioned the extension of the main line authorized in 1851 on to Woodbridge and the construction of three branch railways or tramways, the first from a junction at Saxmundham to Leiston with an extension on to the Manufactory of Richard Garrett in Leiston and the second from a junction on the main line in the Parish of Campsea Ash to Framlingham. The third branch railway or tramway commenced by a junction with the main line in the Parish of Farnham, in the County of Suffolk and terminated in the Hamlet of Dunningworth in the Parish of Tunstall near Snape Bridge. As with the other branches three years were permitted for the compulsory purchase of land for the Framlingham branch and five years for the completion of works.

The share capital of the new company for the new schemes was £450,000 formed of £150,000 shares of the former Haddiscoe company and £300,000 new shares. The company was authorized to borrow £50,000, once half of the original capital was actually paid up. The first Directors of the new company were Edward Leathes, Andrew Johnston, Richard Till, James Peto, Holland Thomas Birkett and George Teed. George Berkley of 24 Great George Street, Westminster, London and designer of Fenchurch Street station in the city was appointed company Engineer.

On 22nd February, 1855 Sir Samuel Morton Peto estimated the cost of the Halesworth to Woodbridge line at £194,686 2s. 6d., or £8,812 per mile, with the principal stations at Halesworth and Saxmundham and cheaply built minor stations at Melton, Campsea Ash, Snape and Bramfield. The 5 mile 52 chains Framlingham branch was costed at £8,064 per mile compared with £6,109 for the short line to Leiston and an exorbitant £10,601 12s. 7d. for the Snape branch. At a subsequent meeting of the Special Joint Committee of the ECR, the Norfolk Railway and the EUR held on 11th May, 1855 G.P. Bidder, the ESR Consulting Engineer, reported that the final costs of the proposed lines were not yet available. This, despite having submitted a written report from his office at 24 Great George Street, Westminster on 5th May, 1855, with the estimated cost of the line and three branches concurring with the figure given by Peto in February. The meeting considered the facts of the report.

The district served by the ESR was approximately 450 square miles bordered on the east by the coast, whilst 15 miles to the west was the EUR linking Ipswich with Norwich. At the northern extremity were the towns of Lowestoft and Bungay and to the south the River Deben. The land acreage was 493,471, whilst the population in the 1851 census was recorded as 104,760. Bidder considered it was an 'absolute condition' that only the main line should be considered as priority with the branches as an optional extra. The three members of the Joint Committee, R. Moseley, Charles Capper and A.G. Church begged to differ, and considered the main line would be best served by the feeder lines and all constructed together.

The ECR had initially considered taking over the ESR but at the ECR shareholders meeting on 13th July, 1855, Mr Bruce, a Director, opposed the idea saying the ECR shareholders would lose money if the takeover was made. He was

ANNO DECIMO SEPTIMO & DECIMO OCTAVO

VICTORIÆ REGINÆ.

****

Cap. cxix.

An Act for making a Railway in Deviation and Extension of the *Halesworth, Beccles, and Haddiscoe* Railway from *Westhall Low Common* to *Woodbridge,* and certain Branches therefrom, and for changing the Name of the Company to the *East Suffolk* Railway Company.

[3d *July* 1854.]

W HEREAS an Act was passed in the Session of Parliament held in the Fourteenth and Fifteenth Years of the Reign of Her present Majesty, called "The *Halesworth, Beccles, and* 14 & 15 Vict. *Haddiscoe* Railway Act, 1851," whereby the *Halesworth, Beccles, and* c. xxvi. *Haddiscoe* Railway Company were incorporated and authorized to make a Railway from the *Lowestoft* Railway at *Haddiscoe* in the County of *Norfolk,* by *Beccles,* to *Halesworth,* with a short Branch to the *Lowestoft* Railway in the Parish of *Haddiscoe,* and such Railway is now in course of Construction between the Terminus at *Haddiscoe* and a Place called *Westhall Low Common* in the Parish of *Westhall* in the County of *Suffolk:* And whereas the making of a Railway in Extension of the said Railway from *Westhall Low Common* aforesaid to near the Town of *Woodbridge* in the County of *Suffolk,* with Branch Railways or Tramways therefrom to *Leiston, Snape Bridge,* and *Framlingham,* would be of great public and local Advantage; and the said *Halesworth, Beccles,*

[*Local.*]   21 G   and

East Suffolk Railway Act of 3rd July, 1854, which amongst other things sanctioned the building of the Framlingham branch.

severely critical of the report made by the ECR officers on the prospects for the East Suffolk line saying they had omitted Aldeburgh and Snape when calculating the effects of local ports on the railway. He also claimed that the estimate of 104,760 persons in the catchment area of the railway was 15 per cent too high. David Waddington, the ECR Chairman, countered saying 'if they did not construct the line other parties would'. Mr Lewin, a shipper of flour from Woodbridge stated he had traded for the past 40 years and fully advocated the building of the railway. After further discussion Bruce won the day and the shareholders were sent further information on the line so they could reach a decision. The shareholders duly endorsed the doubts of Bruce and rejected takeover, leaving the ESR to finance the building of the line. The Directors of the Norfolk Railway also met on the same day and reported the cost of constructing the ESR would reach £10,000 per mile.

The ESR Company issued its Prospectus on 1st September, 1855 and estimated revenue of £48,014, by comparing the amount of trade in East Suffolk with that in other areas already served by railways. It stressed passenger revenue would be £22,261 and goods receipts £25,753, whilst operating costs were expected to be 46 per cent of receipts with debt interest on the construction of the line a mere 5 per cent. The initial working profit of 54 per cent was, however, to be largely swallowed up paying off miscellaneous debts. Local traffic alone was expected to pay a 5 per cent dividend. The ESR Prospectus still expressed the promoters' desire for the ECR to take over the concern but, because of the ECR shareholders' decision, the ESR Directors begged the ECR to help. The request was conveyed via an intermediary, J.C. Cobbold, the EUR Chairman, whose company was already controlled by the ECR. The ECR Directors, however, refused to contribute towards the construction of the ESR line and the local Directors were forced to raise the sum of £600,000, a figure £150,000 in excess of the share capital authorized by the 1854 Act.

The ECR authorities initially had no qualms with Sir Samuel Morton Peto's subscription to the ESR Woodbridge extension, but when in 1856 two newly-authorized companies backed by Peto, the Yarmouth & Haddiscoe Railway (Y&H) and the Lowestoft & Beccles Railway (L&B) accepted his proposal to lease them for 21 years at 6 per cent, their suspicions were aroused. At the same time Peto was showing interest in making a line from Pitsea, on the London, Tilbury and Southend Railway, which he already leased, to Colchester from where running powers would be sought over the EUR to Woodbridge. By such means it was possible for a competitive service to run from London to Yarmouth and Lowestoft in direct opposition to the ECR. Fortunately the Pitsea to Colchester line was never constructed, but the process of amalgamating the Y&H and the L&B with the ESR in 1856 was the start of grandiose plans. Later Peto revised his terms with the ECR so that the whole line would be leased for 21 years, with 6 per cent paid from 1st July, 1857, whether open to traffic or not, on the undertaking that double track was provided from Yarmouth to Woodbridge but leaving the Lowestoft to Beccles and Leiston, Snape and Framlingham branches as single lines. The contract for building the railway and branches was duly awarded to Peto, Brassey & Betts.

At the half-yearly meeting of the shareholders held on the last day of February 1857 at the Angel Inn, Halesworth, Berkley, the company Engineer, reported the main line was laid out and construction well advanced. Negotiations had commenced for the acquisition of land for the Framlingham, Snape and Leiston branches. In early June the *Ipswich Journal* reported that between two and three million bricks intended for the construction of various bridges and stations had been landed at Woodbridge. They had been purchased at Harwich and transported round the coast by barge, having originated from brickyards in the environs of London. At the beginning of July 1857, a 'highly finished' locomotive arrived at Halesworth from Birkenhead to be used on ballasting work on the main line between Saxmundham and Woodbridge and also the three branch lines.

Sinclair, the ECR Engineer and locomotive superintendent, reported on 7th July, 1857 that he had carefully examined plans for the proposed stations on the ESR at Wickham Market or Campsea Ash as well as Saxmundham and Yoxford and considered them to be 'skilfully laid out and sufficient for traffic'. At Wickham Market he

> should have preferred the goods shed to be placed parallel with the centre of the line and the same distance from it as the passenger station - an arrangement which would allow for the extension of the platform, should it be required.

By August 1857 all cuttings and embankments on the main line were completed and four-fifths of the bridges had been constructed. Nine miles of the formation had been ballasted and eight miles of track laid.

In September 1857 the *Ipswich Journal* reported that good progress was being made on the main line, and that a pile of bricks was in place near the site of Campsea Ash station waiting for bricklayers to start work. On 7th October, 1857 the *Suffolk Chronicle* reported a journey along the line when a reporter was conveyed in a horse-drawn wagon from Woodbridge to Ufford Bridge. Here, there was a break in the line as 'the land required for the railway had only just been purchased'. The journalist then walked the three miles to Campsea Ash where he joined another train, which took him on to Saxmundham.

At the half-yearly meeting of ESR shareholders held at the end of February 1858, George Berkley, the Engineer, reported the main line was nearly completed whilst rails were laid along the Snape branch. The other branches were not as advanced but the earthworks and bridges on the Framlingham branch were in a forward state, whilst permanent way materials had been delivered to the Leiston line. At the gathering the Directors optimistically announced the main line and branches to Snape Bridge and Leiston would open in July with the Framlingham line opening in the September 1858. Consistent flooding of the trackbed near Parham added to the delays on the Framlingham branch. To eliminate the problem the contractor's men re-directed the course of the river away from the railway.

The ESR Directors announced the main line would be opened for traffic in July 1858 but when the ECR Directors visited the various new works of the ESR on 3rd and 4th June, 1858, construction was far from complete whilst the connecting EUR line from Ipswich was also incomplete. The ECR Directors were accompanied by Owen, the Secretary and Robertson, the superintendent of the line, and on the first day travelled to Ipswich by the 4.30 pm express from Shoreditch, whence they journeyed by road to Woodbridge. The next morning the party travelled to see the partially built station at Campsea Ash and where the rails were laid before continuing to Snape. At the same time Peto asked the ECR Directors if the company could supply two old carriages so that workmen could be conveyed to site. The request was agreed subject to payment of a small amount and Moseley, the General Manager, was instructed to arrange choice of vehicles and transfer them as quickly as possible.

In the early months of 1859 rumour and counter rumour were rife on the opening date for the ESR main line and branches. On 5th February it was said the line would be opened completely at the beginning of March as station masters and other officials were appointed, but four days later 'Indignant Shareholder' complained to the *Ipswich Journal* that he understood the line was to be open for goods traffic only. By 19th February, 1859 the press prophesied 'much anxiety would be voiced' at the half-yearly meeting to be held at Halesworth on 25th February, as the railway would not open on 1st March, and June or July were the expected dates for opening to passenger traffic. 'Unless something satisfactory was announced', Sir Samuel Morton Peto would 'have to run the gauntlet of fierce determined opposition from shareholders'.

On Friday 25th February, 1859 as a prelude to the meeting, the company through Mr Lockey, the sub-agent of the contractors Peto, Brassey & Betts, arranged with the ECR to run a special train from Woodbridge to take shareholders and other interested parties to Halesworth. The special formed of an engine and 12 first class coaches, conveying amongst others Sir Samuel Morton Peto and Mr Wagstaff, the company solicitor, departed at 10.00 am, and stopped initially at Campsea Ash station before traversing the branch to Framlingham. After returning to the main line, the train made a momentary halt at Snape Junction so that passengers could view the completed goods line before continuing to Saxmundham and Halesworth. At the meeting, chaired by the Earl of Stradbroke, the Secretary W. Day announced the main line and branches were completed and ready for inspection. It was reported the ESR had cost £450,000 to construct and it was agreed the company should extend the Leiston branch to Aldeburgh as soon as possible. It was hoped that the line would open for traffic on 13th March. Notice had been given to the Board of Trade, and by 2nd March, 1859 arrangements were made for two heavy locomotives to be available for the inspecting officer's visit the following Thursday. Sinclair was also delegated to attend.

Captain H.W. Tyler conducted the official Board of Trade (BoT) inspection of the main line between Woodbridge and Yarmouth, together with the branches to Framlingham, Snape, Leiston and Lowestoft, on Thursday 7th March, 1859. The inspector noted the permanent way on the Framlingham branch was formed of bridge rails of a lighter weight than the double-headed rails used on the main line. The earthworks were standing well and Tyler noted the sharpest curve on the branch was of 18 chains radius near Framlingham Junction. The bridges and viaducts had no spans longer than 37 feet, and those constructed of timber spans on brickwork or cast-iron spans on brickwork were standing well. Some of the cast-irons spans were calculated to take only five times the weight of the rolling load instead of six times as recommended by the Iron Commission in 1849 and the inspector required these spans to be strengthened. The Captain required the auxiliary signal at Framlingham to be repositioned so that the signalman had means of knowing whether the signal was operational or not. Clocks were to be supplied at all stations and Tyler required the company to furnish him with a certificate advising the method of safe working of the single lines, including the Framlingham branch. Because of the incompleteness of works the opening of the lines offered for inspection was refused. Within days Berkley, working closely with the contractors, arranged for the remedial works to be put in hand.

At a special meeting between the Directors of the ECR and ESR on 8th April, 1859, Sir Samuel Morton Peto was handed copies of the proposed timetables and passenger fares lists, and noted the goods cartage rates would be available within a few days. It was agreed that ECR staff appointed to the new stations, including Marlesford, Parham and Framlingham, would take up their duties for the opening on 1st May, 1859. Indeed all men appointed as station masters, clerks, porters and signalmen were taken to the various stations by Mr Dutton, superintendent of the line, and advised of their future role. Although the ECR had taken action to staff the ESR stations, matters at Woodbridge were far from satisfactory, forcing the *Ipswich Journal* of 23rd April, 1859 to remark, 'It is now apparent the line will not open at the end of the month'.

Progress on the remedial works was so advanced that on 26th April, 1859 the ECR announced a special train would run the following day to deliver stores and furniture to all branch stations. Behind the scenes, however, many shareholders and local traders and businessmen were highly critical of the delay in opening the line as almost two months had passed since the BoT inspection. To quell the growing tide of complaints, the company took the unusual step of publishing the extract of a letter dated 3rd May from Berkley, the company Engineer, in the *Ipswich Journal*:

> Captain Tyler has today seen the slight alterations he required to be made to some of the signals have been completed. You will be aware that these were made nearly two months since but we waited until he was in the neighbourhood in inspecting the line from Ipswich to Woodbridge before they could conveniently be seen by Captain Tyler.

Captain H.W. Tyler had indeed re-inspected the East Suffolk main line and branch and in his report of 5th May, noted all the requirements made in his earlier report had been completed. He had received an undertaking signed by the Chairman and Secretary of the company that only 'One Engine in Steam' would be allowed on the single line branches at any one time. Having received this assurance the inspector duly sanctioned the opening of all lines, including the Framlingham branch.

Some time elapsed, however, and it was 27th May before the ECR announced that the ESR main line and branches to Framlingham, Leiston and Snape would be opened to traffic on and from Wednesday 1st June, 1859. On the Framlingham branch many local people took advantage of a journey but the *Ipswich Journal*, reporting the event, stated that 'after many postponements' the short notice of opening gave the local inhabitants no time to 'arrange suitable demonstrations or decorate the station' to celebrate the event. The bells of St Michael's church pealed at intervals throughout the day and a special cricket match was arranged. Tea was provided by John Pipe at the Crown Inn, a function attended by about 40 gentry and important inhabitants of the town. John Pierson presided over the junketing and the usual speeches promoting success to the railway were made. Unfortunately the day was marred by an accident to porter Edward Plantin at Framlingham station. As the 12.53 pm train from Wickham Market was approaching the platform at 1.10 pm, Plantin, for unknown reasons, stepped in front of the locomotive before it had halted. The engine driver reversed the locomotive but could not prevent the accident. Doctor G.E. Jeafferson, the town Surgeon promptly attended the injured man who was removed from under the locomotive before receiving attention. The concert arranged for 8.30 pm at the Corn Exchange was cancelled as a mark of respect, as Plantin was the leader of the instrumental performers. The following day Plantin had made a recovery but later died from his injuries. At the subsequent inquest held at the White Horse Inn it was reported to the Coroner, C.C. Brooke, that Plantin, employed by the ECR as a light porter, was required to uncouple the locomotive from the coaching stock so that it could run round the vehicles prior to recoupling for the return journey to Wickham Market. For some reason he had stepped in front of the locomotive before it stopped and the engine driver, with great presence of mind had reversed the locomotive. Had he not done so Plantin would have been cut in two. The Coroner duly recorded a verdict of accidental death and absolved the railway company from any blame.

The ESR Directors held a banquet at Lowestoft on Tuesday 14th June, 1859, to celebrate the opening of the railway. Sir Samuel Morton Peto chaired and conducted the proceedings, which followed the usual meal and complimentary speeches. Amongst those attending were the Earl of Stradbroke, Lord Paget MP, Horatio Love and J.C. Cobbold respective Chairmen of the ECR and EUR, together with the ECR Engineer Robert Sinclair and Peter Bruff, his counterpart on the EUR. Despite opening for traffic, considerable minor works had yet to be completed and on 22nd June, 1859, the ECR authorities agreed to convey all materials required for completion of the lines over their system free of charge. Richard Garrett and Sons provided a miscellany of items for the new railway from their Leiston works, including lamp posts, ironmongery, and general ironwork to the value of £4,300.

Once the railway had settled down to regular operation several deficiencies were revealed. The track layout at Wickham Market came in for severe criticism, for if stock was left in the horse dock siding it was impossible for an engine to clear the points. The track leading to the goods shed was of such lightweight rail that it was unsuitable to take the weight of locomotives. On 6th July, 1859 it was agreed to make the necessary track changes to allow engines to pass the horsebox siding without striking wagons, and for heavyweight rail to be laid in the goods shed road. Later in the same month it was discovered that the water supply at Framlingham station was unfit for human or animal consumption. On 20th July the problem was passed to Sir Samuel Morton Peto to resolve. At the same time the ESR Chairman was requested to arrange for the installation of the electric telegraph linking the branch stations.

Initially the neighbouring Snape branch was worked by one of three freight trains running between Ipswich and Yarmouth, but from 2nd September the main line goods service was reduced to two trains in each direction. The resultant reduction meant it was no longer economical for one of these trains to work the branch. It was suggested the engine allocated to work the Framlingham branch could work the Snape branch traffic to and from Wickham Market station goods yard. Wagons would then be transferred to and from the through Ipswich to Yarmouth goods trains at Wickham Market. This arrangement was tried for a few days but was apparently unmanageable and, at the meeting of the ECR and ESR Joint Committee on 24th September, it was agreed the Snape branch would revert to being worked by one of the two daily goods trains.

The expected transfer of parcels and freight traffic from road and sea to rail failed to materialize, as the rates charged by the ECR/ESR were considered exorbitant. The ESR Directors were so concerned that they called upon the operating company to reduce the tariff of charges to compete with the road carriers. At the meeting of the ECR and ESR Joint Committee on 24th September, 1859 it was agreed to reduce the parcel rates by 4d. and 6d., depending on distance. It was also agreed to reduce the charges for the conveyance of grain, oil cake and manure from Melton and Woodbridge to Marlesford and Parham from 3s. 4d. per ton to 2s. 6d. and to Framlingham from 4s. 0d. to 2s. 6d. per ton. Equally the rate for the conveyance of the same commodities from Snape to Wickham Market and Marlesford was reduced from 3s. 4d. to 2s. 6d. per ton.

By mid-September the electric telegraph had been installed on the Framlingham branch where the cost for operating the system was established at 6s. 0d. weekly, whilst a monthly payment of 12s. 0d. was also to be made to the ECR in lieu of initial payments made by that company to the Electric Telegraph Company so that work could begin. By 29th September, it was reported that the goods yard at Framlingham was in a 'dreadful state' and full of ruts. Sir Samuel Morton Peto was asked to arrange for urgent repairs to be carried out. Throughout the autumn goods traffic on the branch had been increasing, largely as a result of the reduction in goods rates, so much so that in mid-November 1859 a request was made for the temporary employment of additional staff to handle the commodities, especially at Framlingham. Authority was duly given on 23rd of the month, whilst three days later it was agreed to consider the fare structure to and from Framlingham, especially from Ipswich, where a reduction was introduced based on the rail mileage basis.

Mr Whatling of Saxtead was on his way home in his horse-drawn gig from Wickham Market in the evening dusk of a November day in 1859 when, approaching Broadwater level crossing, the animal was startled at the sound of an approaching train. Whatling was thrown to the ground suffering severe cuts and bruising and his gig damaged as the horse 'immediately started off at great speed' and galloped along the road to get to the crossing first. The impending disaster was averted as the gatekeeper had closed the gates and managed to catch and calm the beast. Whatling was recovered from the roadside and conveyed home for medical attention. In the same month the *Framlingham Weekly News* reported,

On account of the great increase of goods traffic on our branch line, an extra goods train runs daily. We understand the amount of business and number of receipts of the company have been beyond expectation; and the line bids fair to be a modern branch not only in beauty and the structure of its buildings, and picturesque views and landscapes, but also in the returns of business transacted and passengers carried.

A later report quoted, 'We understand upon good authority that the passenger and traffic receipts at our station are equal to those of Saxmundham and Woodbridge combined'.

The ESR Directors were disturbed by the anomalies in charges for goods traffic, especially when conveyed to or from ECR stations. At a meeting on 7th December, 1859 the Earl of Stradbroke suggested that from 1st June, 1860 to negate any dubiety all East Suffolk traffic returns should go to the Railway Clearing House for clearance and settlement of accounts with the ECR. At the same time reports were received regarding the conduct of Mr Brown the Framlingham station master. The complaints were upheld and at the same meeting it was agreed the officer be removed from his post, downgraded and transferred to the goods department. At the same gathering it was agreed the value of the railway buildings at Framlingham for insurance purposes would be fixed at £3,500, with goods in storage or awaiting transit at £100.

Despite the opening of the line much of the initial work was shoddy. As early as 4th January, 1860 complaints were being made regarding the condition of the approach road to Wickham Market station, which had turned into a quagmire with the winter rains. Ten days later the Framlingham branch train knocked down a lad clerk named Tillett as it entered Wickham Market station. He was crossing between the up and down platforms when the incident occurred. In the same month station master Edward Whitehead assumed the vacant position at Framlingham.

The Joint Committee decided on 28th January, 1860 that the public would be allowed to send telegraphs from stations on the branch, whilst the following month the ESR authorities were gratified to learn that the parish rates for the East Suffolk line and branches was to be reduced to £25 per mile per annum. A strange request was received in early May 1860 when Messrs Edwards and Edwards of 23 Southampton Buildings, London applied for a joint season ticket to Framlingham to be available on Friday afternoons for the down journey and Monday mornings for the up journey. The request was declined and the appellants were advised to purchase the normal return tickets.

At some time between Whitsunday and Monday, the evening of 2nd and 3rd June, 1860 it was discovered that £11 1s. 0d. was missing from Framlingham station booking office. It was immediately assumed the theft was an 'inside job' carried out by relief clerk Dow, who was in charge, and his fellow staff on duty, booking clerk Hammond and porter Kipps. After investigation the culprit was found to be Hammond, who had removed the money without the knowledge of his colleagues. He was dismissed as the result of his actions, whilst the company resolved that in future staff would not be permitted to retain the company's money overnight.

On 18th July, 1860 the subject of surplus lands was raised with the intention of selling off the property for a small profit. However, when the Framlingham branch was investigated it was found the site declared surplus at Wickham Market was for letting, with the possible right for a siding. Along the line at Marlesford there was no land declared surplus, whilst at Parham the spare land was reserved for the erection of a granary. At the terminus the investigators fared no better for the spare land was the site of a granary and plot for letting. During the inspection it was revealed that the sidings at Wickham Market were under ECR control and any arrangements made by the ESR officers had to be with the agreement of the ECR. This agreement was actioned in September when the local goods agent requested the provision of a 5 ton capacity fixed crane at Wickham Market to handle Messrs Whitmore's outgoing agricultural machinery. The provision of the crane was readily agreed by the ECR but was then passed to Sir Samuel Morton Peto for the necessary finance.

Early in October 1860 a letter was received from a Mr Jermyn Pratt complaining of the misunderstandings being caused by Campsea Ash station being so named, when the tickets showed Wickham Market. The original name of the station was decided by the ESR Directors as Wickham Market but following disagreement with the ECR officials it had initially been renamed and then reverted to Wickham Market. The matter was discussed at the meeting of the Joint Committee on 24th November, 1860 and passed to the ECR for a decision. Within a week the ESR officials were advised the Wickham Market title would remain.

On 23rd December, 1860 between 11 pm and 12.00 midnight, two men attacked and robbed the blacksmith in the village of Kettleburgh. After subsequent enquiries booking clerk Swann and lad porter Lawrence, both employed at Framlingham station, were arrested, charged with the offence and committed for trial, losing their jobs in consequence.

In May 1861 Messrs Gibbons of Ipswich arranged for a timber sale in the station yard at Framlingham and were charged £1 0s. 0d. for using railway property for the event. The event resulted in increased conveyance of timber to Framlingham and export from the station once the timber had been sold. Again because of the increase in goods traffic handled at Framlingham, on 9th October, 1861 the goods manager requested the provision of additional staff to load and offload the commodities to minimise delay especially to outgoing consignments. The following month it was announced that station master Edward Whitehead was unable to continue his duties at Framlingham because of ill health. The ECR Board awarded him six months' salary when he finished duties on 6th November, in recognition of his seven years' service with the company.

The problems over the siding at Marlesford were discussed at the meeting of the Joint Committee on 23rd April, 1862. Charles Capper, a Director, stated the siding had been constructed for a Mr Welton. He had not contributed towards the cost of installation but was willing to do so if the company conceded he had full ownership of the siding. Moseley, the General Manager, after investigating, found the siding was used as a public siding and the matter was put to the ECR for a decision. The following month the ECR Chairman of the committee complained that a warehouse had been built by Newson Garrett on the up side of the line opposite the booking office at Wickham Market station. The ESR Directors had sold the ground to Garrett and part of the building was being used as a dwelling house and small shops for the sale of tea and tobacco. Capper was duly instructed to bring the matter before the ESR Board to 'remedy the evil compliance'. On 18th June, 1862 the subject was under investigation by Wagstaff, the solicitor. Along the line at Framlingham Junction, authority had been given on 5th May, 1862 for the provision of an oven in the signalman's hut.

Chapter Two

Great Eastern Operation

Having leased or taken over the working of all the major railways in East Anglia, the ECR was the principal party to a scheme being prepared for the amalgamation of the Eastern Counties, Eastern Union, East Anglian, Newmarket and Norfolk Railways into a new undertaking to be known as the Great Eastern Railway (GER). The Act sanctioning the amalgamation - the Great Eastern Railway Act 1862 (25 and 26 Vict. cap. ccxxiii) received the Royal Assent on 7th August, 1862 but took effect retrospectively from July of that year.

With ECR officers taking over the leading positions in the new organization few initial changes were made to Framlingham branch services. As a result of the takeover, ESR proprietors were awarded £340,000 in GER 4 per cent debentures and £335,000 in 4½ per cent preference shares, as well as ordinary shares to the value deemed appropriate in future revenue expectations by Captain Galton of the Board of Trade. In return the GER was indemnified against £86,488 contract debt and other liabilities of the company.

In early March 1863 Mr Welton, Secretary of the proposed Albert Middle Class School and College near Framlingham (founded as Suffolk's memorial to the Prince Regent who died in 1861), wrote to the GER asking for a siding and points to be laid at Marlesford to enable the builders to procure sand and materials for construction. A supporting letter was received from Lord Stradbroke. Sinclair, the Engineer, was asked to investigate and reported back to the Traffic Committee on 1st April that the siding would have to be provided at a distance of nearly a mile from Marlesford station and would therefore have to be provided with the regulatory system of signals and signalmen to operate them. The estimated cost including signals was £350 and working expenses £150 per annum. It was agreed that the Secretary reply to Welton saying the siding would be installed providing the full cost was borne by the college. The question of the siding was deferred, however, pending authorization for the college. When the final decision was announced to allow the building of the college, subscribers who had been to Ipswich for a meeting, arrived at Framlingham to the ringing of handbells on the platform and a torchlight procession through the town led by the town band. The siding was never provided as the costs were considered prohibitive but some material was conveyed via the existing goods yard opposite Marlesford station. Other material was conveyed by road to Framlingham and the college took its first pupils in 1865.

Despite five years of branch line operation, horses were still being frightened by the steam engine and in April 1864 a locomotive shunting coaches in Framlingham station startled four horses. Fortunately George Eade managed to stop them before they galloped out of the yard and down the road. In another incident a horse was deliberately let loose on the railway at Kettleburgh Road level crossing 'for a lark'. The engine of the approaching train 'slowed but brushed its tail' before the animal was captured without incurring further injury.

Following the complaints made to the Traffic Committee on 17th August, 1864, regarding the lack of a waiting room on the up side platform at Wickham Market, Sinclair was asked to investigate. He reported back on 12th October stating that there was insufficient space on the up platform for the construction of a waiting room as there was no means of widening the platform without entirely remodelling the station yard, which could only be achieved at considerable cost. After discussion it was agreed to defer the provision of the building.

Early in November 1864 an application was made to the GER authorities for a flag station to be located mid-way between Parham and Framlingham for the benefit of people living in the locality. Robertson, the superintendent, was asked to investigate and, as he was of the opinion the two stations were adequate for existing and future traffic levels, the application was declined by the Traffic Committee on 23rd November. On being advised Mr Corrance, on behalf of the appellants, wrote asking for a reappraisal but was advised on 7th December that the Directors had upheld the decision.

During the summer of 1864 surveys were conducted for a short railway linking the Suffolk town of Eye with Mellis on the Ipswich to Norwich main line. Initially the promoters, including Sir Edward Clarence Kerrison Bart, MP and Lord Henniker, were supportive of the line extending beyond Eye to join up with the existing branch line at Framlingham. However, when the plans were deposited with Parliament on 30th November, 1864, the intended route terminated at Eye. The Mellis & Eye Railway Act was duly authorized on 5th July, 1865 (28 and 29 Vict. cap. ccxlix). In the meantime on the Framlingham branch, Sinclair had advised on 14th June, 1865 that the cost of providing an additional siding at Marlesford for building materials was £118 and authority was duly given for the work to be carried out.

The motive power provided for the branch services in the early years left much to be desired regarding availability. On one occasion the locomotive scheduled to work the first train on Monday morning failed and a large number of passengers were forced to wait until 12.05 pm to continue their journey! Two travellers, the Reverend W. Berlee and T.T. Buckmaster, a season ticket holder, created much mayhem and demanded a special train to get them to London. This was provided at a cost of £800 and departed soon after 10.30 am, with Buckmaster, a prosperous miller, determined to sue the GER for the costs of travel and inconvenience caused. The remaining passengers, however, were not invited to travel on the special train! Later on August Bank Holiday Monday 1865 the locomotive working the last down train to Framlingham failed at Parham. Some passengers alighted from the train and walked home, whilst others stayed on board until repairs had been made and the train subsequently reached the terminus soon after midnight. The next morning excursionists seeking a trip to the seaside boarded the train ready for the 6.50 am departure, but as it departed the coupling rod on the locomotive fractured 'leaving the air bitter with protests' of passengers. An official investigation was demanded and the recriminations included the overloading of the timetable, the inadequate supply of locomotives and mismanagement.

During the spring of 1867 the GER authorities were investigating the poor returns earned at some of their stations. In 1866 an annual saving of £85 had been achieved with the closure of five stations and in their search for further candidates for closure the intermediate station of Parham, located 2¼ miles east of Framlingham and 2½ miles west of Marlesford, was investigated. Fortunately with respectable earnings of £474 1s. 0d. in 1866, the station escaped the threat of closure.

After the Christmas holiday in 1867 the editor of the *Framlingham Weekly News* enthused on the benefits the branch was bringing to the town:

> The Great Eastern Railway Company have been reaping their Christmas fruits; for the trains have been very heavily laden with goods and passengers; and friends from the east, west, north and south have mustered beneath the thatch of the old homestead, and embraced each other under the mistletoe, and told of past experiences in front of the Christmas fire.

In April 1868 J.C. Cobbold wrote to the GER asking if the boundary fence separating his land from railway property near Framlingham could be realigned and straightened. The Engineer duly investigated and reported to the General Manager that if permission were granted the GE company would have to part with 1¾ poles of land. Neither the General Manager nor superintendent had any objections to the arrangement provided Cobbold made payment of £10 for the deal, and the sale was sanctioned on 22nd April. The transaction was verified on 3rd June when the cashier was advised to expect the £10 payment. The annual Suffolk Show in June 1868 was held on the Castle Meadow at Framlingham and 52,000 square feet of canvas was brought by rail for the marquees. The streets were decorated from the station to the Castle and over 12,000 people visited the event, many arriving and departing by train.

The subject of the restoration of the church at Campsea Ash was raised at the meeting of the Traffic Committee on 15th July, 1868 when the General Manager advised that the Reverend H.E. Knatchbull had written to the company asking for a subscription towards the repairs. The Secretary was directed to reply that the Directors had no funds available for such purposes. Early in July 1869 the Directors were surprised to receive another letter from the Reverend Knatchbull and his churchwardens, this time complaining of the 'improper conduct' of station master Frederick Short with the local schoolmistress at Wickham Market. On being advised of the charges the station master emphatically denied the allegations made against him and on 13th July the Directors advised the Reverend Knatchbull of their findings. At a subsequent meeting of the Traffic Committee on 27th July the General Manager advised the gathering that the Reverend Knatchbull had called to see him that morning and demanded further action. On being advised that the Directors could take no further action, Knatchbull advised there had been a previous misconduct of a similar nature and the character of station master Short required further investigation. This, the General Manager agreed to do and Robertson was asked to investigate. The superintendent duly visited Wickham Market and saw the schoolmistress who stated there was no foundation whatsoever in the allegations against Short. On 11th August, 1869 the GER Secretary formally replied to Knatchbull advising him of the findings.

In the early spring of 1870 complaints were made regarding the condition of the approach road to Parham station. A local tradesman, Mr Smith, offered to carry out the repairs free of charge if the GER company provided the ballast but on 30th March his offer was declined. The following month the superintendent requested the lengthening of the platforms at Wickham Market by 60 feet to obviate the increasing longer trains pulling up twice to allow passengers to alight. After discussion the Way & Works Committee deferred the works pending further investigation.

On the evening of 27th September, 1870 Mrs Stocker (aged 72) was knocked down by a train while crossing the line from one platform to another at Wickham Market. Unfortunately she died later from her injuries and at the subsequent inquest the jury recorded a verdict of accidental death. They also recommended that the GER pay proper attention to the well-being of persons crossing the line and, if practical, provide a footbridge between the platforms, after which no persons should be allowed to cross the lines. Within a week the Reverend Image wrote complaining of the dangerous state of the foot crossing linking the up and down side platforms at the station and also the necessity of a waiting room on the up side platforms. Both the Engineer and superintendent advised there was no room for a waiting shelter on the up side but there was room available on the down side platform. The Engineer did not see any need for alterations at the station but thought it desirable for part of the up side platform to be raised and confirmed that a small waiting shelter be provided at a cost of £25. The Traffic Committee tentatively agreed to such action on 9th November, 1870 but the expenditure was deferred at the meeting on 23rd November.

In May 1871 a Mr Cuthbert applied for the provision of a siding at Parham but, after questioning the station master and local goods agent, the superintendent advised the amount of traffic did not warrant the installation. Then in the autumn of 1871 the superintendent had urged the installation of the block telegraph on the East Suffolk line between Ipswich and Saxmundham to obviate pathing problems with express services, especially to Aldeburgh, which were being delayed by slower services. The Traffic Committee raised the subject at their meeting on 12th March, 1872 when it was estimated the cost of the telegraph, provision of new signal boxes and signals including installations at Wickham Market station and Wickham Market Junction, formerly known as Framlingham Junction, was £800. The improved arrangements would involve the additional wages cost to signalmen estimated at £8 per week or £400 per annum. The matter was, deferred, however, and not passed to the Board to sanction until 26th February, 1873.

During shunting operations at Marlesford on 9th May, 1872, station master George Hedges was thrown off a wagon and fell to the ground where the wheel of the moving vehicle passed over his right arm causing severe crushing. It was crucial to obtain the assistance of a doctor as quickly as possible and Doctor Cochrane of Wickham Market was summoned and set the arm to avoid amputation. At the end of the summer Hedges resumed duties and received a bill for £15 8s. 0d. from Doctor Cochrane for services rendered. As he was a member of the Provident Society the station master submitted the bill to the society for settlement, but was shocked to find that they would only agree to pay £3 on the grounds that the Provident Society doctor should have been called. This was not done because of the urgency of the case as the society doctor lived at Woodbridge, some 14 miles distant. Despite his pleas Hedges received no satisfaction from the Provident Society, who were adamant the maximum £3 payment was the most they would pay. In desperation the station master turned to his employers asking them to pay the balance. On 12th February, 1873 the company agreed to pay a donation of £10 to Hedges to help him settle the outstanding fee.

The Framlingham station master frequently complained of the limited accommodation provided in the station house and in the autumn of 1873 made application for an additional bedroom to be provided. The work was duly authorized on 19th November at a cost of £55. The following year the question of staff accommodation at Wickham Market was raised when the superintendent recommended the provision of four cottages. The matter was discussed on 11th March, 1874 and passed to the Chairman for a decision. On the same day it was reported the gas prices at Framlingham station were 7s. 6d. per 1,000 cubic feet with an annual expenditure of £26 5s. 0d.

On 22nd April, 1874 the superintendent reported that Garrett's warehouse, built on land originally sold by the ESR, at Wickham Market was being offered for sale before the 21 years lease agreed in 1860 had expired. The asking price was £350 and the officer was of the opinion the building might be of advantage to the railway company. The matter was passed to the General Manager for a decision. On investigation the offer was declined and Garrett advised of the decision on 20th May, 1874. In the meantime the superintendent continued to press for a decision on the provision of four cottages at Wickham Market and on 17th June, 1874 the Engineer was instructed to prepare plans and estimates, and seek tenders from contractors. By 15th July he shocked the Way & Works Committee when he advised that the cost was estimated at £750 and was told to re-estimate the scheme. On 5th August the cost was reduced to £650 and on 9th September Maitland, Chairman of the Committee, advised he would approach a local builder to construct the cottages. Later in the year on 2nd December the scheme for extending the platforms at the junction station was agreed at a cost of £113.

On 24th February, 1875 it was announced that the price of gas at Framlingham had been reduced to 6s. 8d. per 1,000 cubic feet. Along the line at Wickham Market the question of the four cottages was again raised at the Way and Works Committee meeting on 6th October, 1875 but was deferred to the next meeting. During the autumn of 1875 booking clerks had complained of the poor conditions experienced in the booking office on the down platform at Wickham Market, especially during cold or wet weather. After consulting with the local staff, the Engineer suggested a wooden screen be erected halfway across the ticket office and estimated the cost at £6. The Traffic Committee duly approved of the expenditure on 1st December, 1875, so that work could be completed before the worst of the winter weather.

The question of the four cottages at Wickham Market was again raised at the Way & Works Committee meeting on 4th April, 1876 when it was decided the location would be visited on the next tour of inspection and a decision made. A fortnight later it was agreed that a total of four cottages were required. At the beginning of October 1876 an odd request was made by the Reverend Archer asking for permission to walk along a mile of railway near Wickham Market station. The matter was discussed at the Way & Works Committee meeting on 31st October and passed to the General Manager who promptly declined the request on the grounds of safety.

Since the opening of the line passengers waiting at Wickham Market for trains in the up direction were forced to wait on the open platform, which in inclement weather was highly exposed to north and easterly winds. Various requests had been made for a waiting room and finally the Engineer was requested to prepare drawings and estimates. On 9th January, 1877 the matter was discussed at a Board meeting when the plans were approved and cost estimated at £200. The decision was deferred pending authority from Lord Claud Hamilton and, after he agreed the expenditure on 30th January, 1877, the Directors authorized the provision of a new waiting room on the up platform at Wickham Market. Then at a meeting on 11th July, 1877 the construction of four cottages, later known as Railway Terrace, was (at last) sanctioned at a cost of £950.

Poor signalling and inadequate track layout had for some years been the main factor in delays incurred by trains when approaching or departing from Wickham Market station. By carrying out track improvements and signalling alterations it was thought the problem would be eliminated, and at a Board meeting on 4th June, 1878 the proposed signalling alterations at Wickham Market were tabled for discussion. The Engineer estimated the new works would cost £505 and at the meeting on 19th June, 1878 authority was given for the work to proceed at the estimated cost. Then the station master complained of the lack of adequate water supply to both the station house and station, and alterations to the pump and well for domestic water supply were authorized on 27th August, 1878 at a cost of £16. During an inspection of their system on 1st and 2nd October, 1878, the GER Directors visited Saxmundham and the Snape branch, where they had a short meeting with Newson Garrett, before travelling across the branch to Framlingham.

The night of 21st/22nd July, 1879 was one of heavy and continuous rain and on the morning of 22nd a culvert between Marlesford and Parham was damaged by the rising floodwater. The branch traffic was immediately suspended and was not resumed until the culvert was repaired the following day. Single line working was also instituted on the main line as floodwater had damaged the infrastructure. The remedial work took longer than planned and on 12th August, 1879 it was announced the underpinning of the bridge abutment would be completed within 10 days when both up and down main lines would reopen.

As traffic increased on the East Suffolk main line there was concern that some stations still lacked the interlocking of points and signals. Included in those requiring attention was Wickham Market and on 3rd August, 1880 the Way & Works Committee duly rectified the omission by authorizing the interlocking work at a cost of £1,400. The contract was later awarded to Messrs Saxby &

Farmer Limited. Major General C.S. Hutchinson subsequently inspected the new works at Wickham Market on 10th August, 1881. He found the connections had been carried out satisfactorily and complied with the BoT regulations. The points and signals were now concentrated in a new signal box and were interlocked. Because of the sharply falling gradient towards Framlingham Junction, Hutchinson advised that runaway points should be placed on the up line about 300 yards on the north side of the up home signal. Interlocked safety points were also required for the siding joining the passenger line at the back of the up platform. Subject to the completion of these requirements the inspector sanctioned the use of the new equipment.

The lack of adequate siding space at Wickham Market was of continuing concern to local GER management as goods traffic from the Snape and Framlingham branches gradually increased. The need to sort wagons from both branches for working to forward destinations was paramount and often traffic was being delayed waiting siding space. To obviate the problem, expenditure of £60 was authorized on 6th February, 1882 for the provision of an additional siding. Later in the same year, on 31st August, as the empty branch train was being shunted at Wickham Market the stock derailed blocking the main lines. No injuries were reported and services were delayed until the offending vehicles were re-railed. The superintendent reported the particulars of the incident to the Traffic Committee with his recommendations on 5th September.

After many complaints from the incumbent station master on lack of space in the station house at Wickham Market, the Engineer was requested to prepare plans for the enlargement of the sitting room by taking over the former lamp room and the building of a new lamp room. These were presented for inspection on 20th February, 1883 when it was estimated the cost would be £50. On 6th March, 1883 authority was duly given for the alterations and work was completed by July.

By 1884 the East Suffolk main line was open continuously to handle the increasing number of goods and fish trains which ran during the night. When the timetabled service was running to schedule there were few problems but the late docking of fishing boats at Lowestoft or Yarmouth seriously affected the pathing of trains and last minute alterations were often made to get services away as quickly as possible. Here the GER local officers met difficulties for any rescheduling of trains had to be advised to intermediate signal boxes along the route and in most instances the 'speaking telegraph' instruments were located in station booking offices, which were closed for about 11 hours from early evening to early the following morning. During the hours of closure considerable delays occurred as signalmen had no idea what trains were coming and which should take priority. Having received considerable complaints from farmers and traders, the General Manager reported to the Way and Works Committee on 30th December, 1884 that the solution was the provision of a separate signal box telephone circuit between Ipswich and Beccles. The Signal & Telegraph Engineer estimated the cost of the circuit at £350 and due authority was given for the work to be completed as a matter of urgency.

As passenger trains on the East Suffolk increased in length so the short platforms originally installed at Wickham Market became totally inadequate to accommodate the coaching stock. Trains were required to stop and then pull up and stop for a second time to allow passengers to alight or join the train. Severe delays were incurred and local people also complained that the level crossing gates to the north of the station were blocked for an inordinate length of time. To obviate the problem it was agreed that the platforms should be lengthened and authority for the extension at a cost of £235 was given on 6th July, 1886. Having agreed the lengthening of the platform, associated signalling and permanent way alterations were also required and this work was belatedly sanctioned on 5th October, 1886, by which time the task was almost completed. Major General C.S. Hutchinson conducted the BoT inspection of the new works at Wickham Market on 29th October, 1886. He found the alterations included an extension to the siding connecting with the up main line and the lengthening of the up platform had been satisfactorily completed. The points and signals, which were correctly interlocked, were worked from the existing raised signal box now containing a 31-lever frame, with 27 working and four spare levers. Hutchinson noted that because of the falling gradient towards Yarmouth runaway points were located in the up line to the north of the station.

On 15th February, 1887 authority was given for the enlargement of the booking office at Wickham Market at a cost of £25. Then on 18th July, 1887 alterations to the station master's house at Marlesford were sanctioned at a cost of £28. Further improvements at Wickham Market were authorized on 5th February 1889 when the paving of the approach roadway was sanctioned at a cost of £32.

The Regulation of Railways Act 1889, amongst other things, enforced major railway companies to adopt block working on all single lines except where the Train Staff without Ticket and One Engine in Steam systems existed. As the Framlingham branch was worked on the Train Staff and Ticket method of operation it was thus evident that the branch would have to be fully upgraded. In accordance with procedures the company was required to confirm to the BoT within two years the method to be adopted for working the branch. The Act also required the interlocking of points and signals at Marlesford, Parham and Framlingham, which had yet to receive attention. On 3rd December, 1889 it was tentatively agreed that the Wickham Market to Framlingham branch was to be worked by Train Staff only with One Engine in Steam (thus avoiding the expenditure of upgrading). Subsequently on 21st April, 1891 the contract for the interlocking and improvements to signalling at Marlesford, Parham and Framlingham was awarded to Dutton & Company of Worcester, although the latter subsequently received a Saxby & Farmer 27-lever frame. Then on 29th September, 1891 the Way & Works Committee agreed to the installation of additional sidings at Wickham Market at a cost of £395 and for improvements to the down side waiting accommodation at the same station for an estimated £350. The contract for the work on the covered way, awning, waiting room and scullery was awarded to building contractor Dupont who tendered at £355.

On 3rd December, 1891 the GE authorities confirmed to the BoT the future working of the branch would be by One Engine in Steam using the existing Train Staff. At the same time the BoT was asked to extend the time permitted for the introduction of interlocking of points and signals from 18 months to three years. On 2nd February, 1892 a certificate was forwarded to the BoT showing the method of working adopted on the Framlingham branch from 25th January, the document also giving details of the operating of the neighbouring Snape goods branch line.

On 22nd March, 1892 Major General C.S. Hutchinson inspected the alterations at Framlingham station. He noted the changes included the rearrangement of siding connections and resignalling of the station. The points and signals were operated from a new raised signal box containing a 27-lever frame, with 20 working and seven spare levers. The inspector was satisfied with the works but required No. 1 and No. 20 levers to be interlocked, No. 22 lever to lock No. 19 lever in both positions and when No. 19 lever was pulled over it should lock No. 18 lever. The view of No. 27 distant signal from the signal box was to be improved or if that was not possible a repeater provided for it. Subject to the requirements being completed within one month, Hutchinson sanctioned the new works.

The following day Hutchinson visited Parham to view the alterations and noted these included the change in the position of the siding connection in the single line, a 200 ft extension of the goods yard siding, a short extension to the platform and remodelling of the signalling arrangements. The points and signals, which were correctly interlocked, were worked from a new raised signal box containing a 20-lever frame, with 15 working and five spare levers. Subject to the background of the down distant signal being improved and a repeater provided for it and the up distant signal, Hutchinson approved of the new works. The inspector then visited Marlesford where the signals and points were worked from a new raised signal box containing a 21-lever frame with 15 working and six spare levers. Later in the same day the inspector examined the alterations at Wickham Market, which included new siding connections with the loop line at the back of the up platform, used for the departure of trains to the Framlingham branch, a new siding to the south of the station, the extension of the down platform to the level crossing and the necessary changes to the signalling. The new connections were worked from the existing signal box containing a 31-lever frame, now with 30 working and one spare lever. The arrangements were satisfactory save that No. 16 and No. 27 levers required interlocking whilst No. 29 lever required to lock Nos. 20 and 24 levers in both positions, and Hutchinson required this work to be completed within two weeks.

On 3rd May, 1892 the General Manager advised the GER Board that the new works at Wickham Market, sanctioned by the Works Committee in 1891, had been completed and inspected. He also noted that the BoT inspector had viewed the up platform at the junction station, where works estimated at £1,620 had been requested, but the Traffic Committee stipulated that such expenditure be deferred until a future date. Then on 4th October, 1892 the installation of the block telegraph at Wickham Market Junction was authorized at cost of £46.

On 1st January, 1893 second class accommodation on passenger trains was abolished except in the London suburban area. For some time the poor condition of the canopy over the platform at Framlingham had been the subject of correspondence between the station master and the district officer at Ipswich. Rain was filtering through the tarpaulin and timber roof covering and many passengers had complained. At long last on 21st February, 1893 the replacement of the canopy at Framlingham was agreed at an estimated cost of £400 and the contract was duly awarded to Messrs Collins, Barber, who tendered at £335. However, on closer inspection it was found that the existing covered way could be repaired at the reduced cost of £220 and the same firm received the contract after re-tendering at £180. Work was completed in June of the same year. It was agreed on 5th September, 1893 to raise the height of the platform at Wickham Market at a cost of £60, but no such work was subsequently carried out and portable steps were provided in the latter years to help passengers to alight from and join trains.

At the end of 1895 a decision was made to transfer coaching stock equipped with gas lighting to various branches and cross-country routes to replace the oil-lit carriages. On 4th February, 1896 the General Manager announced that 10 sites were to receive gas storage holders, which were to be regularly re-filled from travelling gas wagons, so that coaching stock could be replenished as and when required. Framlingham was included in the proposal, which was costed at £1,200 for the complete scheme. By 28th July it was established that five new gas wagons were required at a cost of £1,200 and that the cost of fixing the static gas holders at stations with the necessary piping and one filling point was £200.

On 17th March, 1896, authority given to provide new toilets at Wickham Market at a cost of £36 and work was completed in September of the same year. Along the branch at Framlingham further improvements were authorized on 1st December, 1896 when an extension to the cramped booking office was sanctioned at cost of £52. In 1896 Framlingham station was recorded as issuing 18,349 tickets and dealt with 8,308 tons of coal and 25,809 tons of other freight traffic. The following year these had increased to 20,449 tickets sold, 20,263 parcels handled, 1,370 boxes of Framlingham produce and 28,637 tons of freight traffic.

Problems with shunting movements resulted in further signalling alterations being authorized at Wickham Market on 4th May, 1897. This minor amendment costing £45 involved a ground disc signal being locked to No. 24 points both ways and a trap point being provided on the back platform line protecting the horse dock siding. Two years later, on 21st March, 1899, sanction was given for the installation of cattle pens at Wickham Market at a cost of £73 after local farmers had complained of the lack of such facilities at the station. Work was completed in July.

Adverse weather affected the branch when a severe blizzard and driving winds on 14th February, 1900 caused snowdrifts to block the line in several places especially in shallow cuttings near Marlesford and on the approach to Framlingham. Although priority was given to clearing the main lines, the branch was cleared the following day after permanent way staff had worked through the night.

Despite the various minor improvements and modifications since the opening of the line, delays continued to be experienced at Wickham Market by most train services because of the relatively short platforms. On 3rd July, 1900 the General Manager reported to the Traffic Committee that down passenger trains, especially during the summer months, were again having to pull up twice and subsequently blocked the level crossing located north of the station. The crossing was busy and as the gates were often closed for excessively long periods, public complaints were on the increase. After investigation it was proposed to lengthen the down platform so that trains did not have to pull up more than once and at the same time replace the level crossing with an overline bridge. Parliamentary powers were required to close the crossing permanently. The elimination of gate boys would result in a saving of £1,000 per annum as the gates were released from the signal box, but hand-operated on a three-shift basis. The subject was first raised in 1897 and a resolution was passed by the Traffic Committee on 16th June, 1897 after the local authority had written saying they were prepared to support the scheme and contribute towards expenses when it was estimated the cost would be £2,693. The matter had lapsed and despite the cost increasing to £3,788, the Traffic Committee sanctioned the expenditure. There was, however, a delay in the tendering process and it was 15th January, 1901 before the contract for the provision of the new bridge at Wickham Market was awarded to J. Westwood & Company, who had tendered at £856 5s. 0d. In the meantime on 18th September, 1900 it was reported that the price of gas to Framlingham station had been increased by 2½d. per 1,000 cubic feet.

The branch railway was the centre point of the small community of Framlingham and the villages served by the intermediate stations. A number of men had enlisted to serve with British troops in the Boer War and departed their native Suffolk by train. Although the war had another 12 months to run, a great procession and associated festivities were held in May 1901 to welcome back volunteers arriving by train at Framlingham station. Others were not so fortunate and perished in the conflict.

On 15th April, 1902 a contract was awarded to Messrs A. Theobald to carry out repairs and repainting of Wickham Market station at a cost of £269, this to coincide with the extension of the platforms and the on-going work on the overbridge. These were completed in December 1902 at a reduced price of £3,676 against the estimated £3,788.

In early March 1903 Messrs Gooderham & Hayward applied for a siding to be provided at Marlesford. The siding was sanctioned on 17th of the month at a cost of £345 with the seed merchants paying 10 per cent of the cost as an annual rental.

Along the branch at Framlingham, the local firm of Hayward received the contract for repairs and painting of the station on 21st July, 1903 after tendering at £259. The new siding at Marlesford was completed in mid-October 1903 at a cost of £303 and was inspected by Lieutenant Colonel P.G. Von Donop on 19th November. He found that the connection facing down trains had been added in the single line with points and signals worked from the existing station signal box containing a 21-lever frame, with 20 working and one spare lever. The arrangements were satisfactory and the additional necessary interlocking correctly provided.

Yet another fatality occurred when the branch train collided with F.W. Welton on 9th January, 1905. At the subsequent inquiry the engine driver said that as the train travelled between Marlesford and Parham, the deceased had jumped out in front of the train. A verdict of suicide was recorded. Nine days later William Mann, a 25-year-old labourer received injuries to his right foot during shunting operations at Framlingham. Mann had gone to the Framlingham and District Agricultural Co-operative Stores, which adjoined the goods yard, to speak to one of two men who were unloading coal from a wagon in the adjacent siding. The

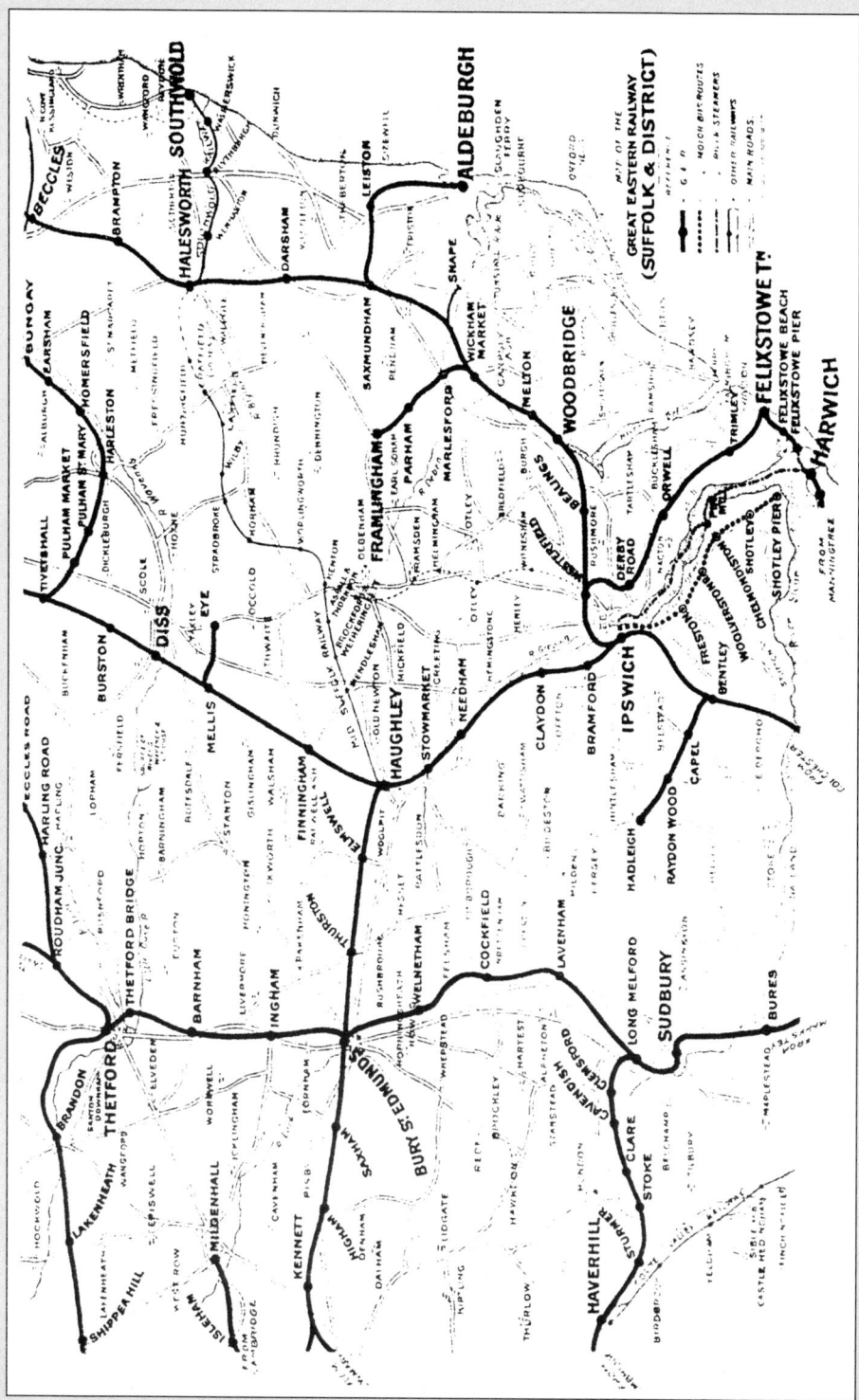

Map of Suffolk District railways from GER Public Timetable 1910.

door of the wagon was resting on an arranged opening in the sidewall of the Society's coal shed and whilst Mann was in conversation the coal wagon was moved in a shunting operation. As the door moved along the opening Mann's foot was crushed between the door and the shed wall. At the subsequent inquiry, porter guard H. Hunt, who was in charge of the shunting operations, was wholly blamed for the accident due to the non-observance of Rule 112a.

After much negotiating by local railway officers, the price of gas supplies to Framlingham station was reduced by 1½d. per thousand cubic feet on 7th May, 1905. Later, on 19th December, authority was given for the installation of an up main advanced starting signal at Wickham Market. This was provided to allow the main line train to draw ahead of the points to the back platform to allow a late running branch train access to the back platform and provide its booked connection. The dangers of not providing a footbridge between the down and up side platforms at Wickham Market station were again cruelly exposed on 22nd January, 1906 when a Mrs Woodhouse was killed as she crossed the railway by the foot crossing. As before there was the usual outcry from the local press for the provision of the bridge but, once again, the GER authorities took no action.

The *Framlingham Weekly News* for 31st October, 1908 reflected the period atmosphere of the branch railway under the headline, 'Exciting Scene Near Framlingham Station'. It reported:

A traction engine and a spirity horse were the leading characters in an exciting scene outside the Railway Station on Thursday afternoon. It seems the engine drawing two empty trucks, bound for Coddenham, was leaving the station yard and just at this time Mr Robert Berry drew up with several crates of chickens to put on the train for market. The horse, on sighting the traction engine, began to plunge about and overturn the cart, the occupants, Mr Berry and Mr George Abbot being, of course, thrown out and the crates containing the caviling and frightened chickens scattered all about the road. This was not the whole of what happened, for as soon as the cart was upturned, the horse, still panting with fright, made a dash for Station Road but failed to notice a cart driven by Mr D H Reeve, and both vehicles were overturned. In Mr Reeve's cart was a new root pulper, which was considerably damaged. Mr Berry's horse proceeded with the overturned vehicle down Station Road but was stopped near the Co-operative Stores by a man named Thrower, of Kettleburgh, and handed over to its owner little the worse for the escapade. Both men were much bruised and shaken but beyond the damage already mentioned, little damage was done.

Parham station goods yard road received remedial attention in December 1909 after repairs estimated at £65 were authorized. The work, completed the following spring, actually cost £52. Excessive rainfall across Suffolk on 8th and 9th December, 1910 caused severe flooding in many areas and the Framlingham branch was affected when water covered the permanent way to rail level at Marlesford. Unlike the neighbouring Snape branch and the Southwold Railway where traffic was suspended, the Framlingham branch service was only delayed as the Engineer authorized trains to pass over the affected track at walking pace. The water soon subsided and by 10th December traffic was back to normal.

On 18th April, 1911 the services were disrupted for a short time after the branch train killed a man trespassing on the railway between Wickham Market station and Wickham Market Junction. At the subsequent inquest the coroner recorded a verdict of suicide. Another fatality occurred at Framlingham on 10th

'T26' class 2-4-0 tender locomotive No. 476 has charge of the branch working in the early years of the 20th century as she departs Framlingham with her four-coach train. No. 476 was subsequently renumbered 7476 by the LNER. The locomotive was withdrawn from service in March 1937. *Author's Collection*

Wickham Market station looking north from the signal box steps in 1911. Overbridge No. 438 replaced an inconvenient level crossing in 1901, and the down platform was extended the following year. The granary and granary siding are to the right, whilst a van stands by the loading dock in dock road. Framlingham branch trains either departed from the down main platform or occasionally from the up back platform via the crossover to the south of the overbridge. *Hilton Collection*

February, 1912 when H. Woodward suffered fatal injuries during shunting operations at the terminus. Further flooding occurred on 26th August, 1912 after heavy rain. The branch was blocked between Marlesford and Parham by rising water as the River Ore overflowed its banks. Traffic was suspended and the line reopened to traffic the following day after the water subsided.

After Germany declared war on France and Belgium, Britain declared war on Germany on 4th August, 1914 and within two days 93 volunteers for the armed forces departed from Framlingham station, and by the end of September a further 91 had enlisted. The departures by train were proud but sad occasions and some did not return. On the outbreak of World War I, the GER with other British railway companies came under Government control. The Framlingham branch services initially continued to run to pre-war timetables. Goods traffic increased as additional produce from local farms was sent to towns and cities to make up for the loss of imported goods. During the war considerable hay and straw traffic was generated from the branch stations and sent to military stables. Some local railwaymen also quickly answered the call to arms and joined the colours in the first few months of hostilities.

By powers granted by the Great Eastern Railway Act 1915 (5 and 6 Geo. 5 cap. xvi) the company was authorized to divert the footpath leading from Abbey Mills to Campsea Ash near Wickham Market station. Despite the hostilities, improvements continued to be made on the railway, and on 8th April, 1915 the contract was awarded for the provision of four cottages in Mill Lane, Wickham Market to F. Baldry at a cost of £900. The regular programme of repairs and painting of stations also continued and, on 1st June, 1916, the contract for work on the branch stations was awarded to Messrs W. Staines who tendered £760 for Framlingham, £98 for Parham, £93 for Marlesford and £298 for Wickham Market. The GER, serving a mainly rural community was ever keen to promote ideas which would increase revenue. One such innovation was an exhibition train on egg and poultry farming which visited many locations in East Anglia in 1916. During its tour Mr E.G. Warren of Framlingham was one of the experts who accompanied the train.

By December 1916 the strain of the war effort was taxing the resources of all British railways to such an extent that the Railway Executive issued an ultimatum that they could only continue if drastic reductions were made to ordinary and non-essential services. The Lloyd George Coalition government agreed to the reduction in passenger services from 1st January, 1917, but with these economic measures the Framlingham branch lost only one train in each direction as many services operated as mixed trains conveying goods.

A feature of the wartime GER was the War Relief Fund to assist servicemen and collections were made at all stations throughout the system. Donations from the Framlingham branch stations showed a marked lack of benevolence as takings from Framlingham alone for the three months ending 31st December, 1917 only amounted to 5s. 0d. In comparison takings on the Downham and Stoke Ferry branch for the same period totalled £2 16s. 6d. Sadly Albert William Elgie, the 34-year-old former goods foreman at Framlingham, died from wounds received on 10th October, 1918. He had entered service with the GER in May 1903 and enlisted with the Royal Army Medical Corps on 22nd August, 1914.

Marlesford level crossing from a rather deserted road *c.*1910, looking north and showing the rear of the signal box and in the background the distinct double chimney of the station building. The down starting signal protects the level crossing and to the left beyond the gates is the road bridge, which replaced the ford over the River Ore. The entrance to the goods yard is between the signal box and the semi-detached cottages. The deserted road is now the A12 trunk route to Great Yarmouth.   *Author's Collection*

Marlesford station, 86 miles 23 chains from Liverpool Street and 1 mile 60 chains from Wickham Market, was the first station on the branch. The 195 ft-long platform on the up or north side of the line was host to a two-storey ornate building, including station master's house, booking office, waiting rooms and staff rooms. This was fronted by a modest canopy, which gave some protection for waiting passengers in inclement weather. The goods yard on the down side of the line was initially served by a 410 ft-long loop siding with entry points facing trains in both up and down directions. Later headshunts were provided at each end of the loop. Points and signals were controlled from Marlesford signal box, on the right, equipped with a 21-lever Dutton frame with 15 working and six spare levers, and after 1903 20 working and one spare. This view taken looking towards Wickham Market *c.*1910 shows the station master and staff on the platform and in the distance the up starting and down home signals. A fine show of geraniums are growing in pots on the signal box walkway.   *Author's Collection*

The general feeling of elation felt by the cessation of hostilities was shattered by a railway strike which halted services on the branch from 26th September to 5th October, 1919. This action undermined the patronage enjoyed by the railway as prospective passengers sought alternative modes of transport. Serious inroads were being made into the monopoly enjoyed by the GER as the Eastern Counties Road Car Company had commenced services along the main London Road (later A12) to and from Ipswich and thus removing much of the local Marlesford traffic.

This industrial unrest began the slow decline in the freight services. Farmers and growers realised for the first time that with improving roads, goods could be conveyed by lorry, using in some cases vehicles purchased second-hand from the military. Thus short haul journeys to Ipswich and other local markets were possible at rates cheaper than charged by the GER. The door-to-door services were more convenient than the double handling into and out of railway wagons. The primitive road vehicles of the day were not, however, capable of continuous long hauls, and middle and long distance traffic remained safely in the hands of the railway company. Then in March 1921 Messrs Potter's announced a regular motor coach service to Ipswich from Framlingham and by July had persuaded the local Mothers' Union and Methodist Sunday School to travel to the seaside by coach. No Whitsun bank holiday special trains were operated as 'every available motor coach' was 'mobilised for the Whitsuntide holidays'.

Parham Station.

Parham station 88 miles 51 chains from Liverpool Street and 4 miles 08 chains from Wickham Market c.1910 viewed from the main Wickham Market to Framlingham road. In the foreground is the infant River Ore, which the branch followed for a considerable distance. A bridge over the stream has superseded the ford and in the background is the level crossing carrying the lane to North Green and Cransford across the railway. Next the crossing is Parham signal box containing a 20-lever Dutton frame with 15 working and five spare levers. The up starting signal stands sentinel protecting the crossing whilst the much taller down home signal can be seen towering above the roof of the cottage on the right. To the left is the station building, similar to those at Marlesford and Snape, with the ornate chimney with a central arch. The station offices, waiting room and staff rooms and toilets were situated on the ground floor of the building and the station master's accommodation on the first floor. *Author's Collection*

With a view to counteracting the bus competition and working the Framlingham branch with the utmost economy, the conductor-guard method of working was proposed by the GER, with the guard issuing tickets on the train. Subsequently the booking offices at Marlesford and Parham were closed. To facilitate the new method of operation, the branch was allocated a six-wheel brake third and six-wheel first/third composite with a six-wheel full third as standby, each vehicle having a centre gangway and end drop plates to enable the guard to walk through the vehicles to collect the fares and check tickets. A new halt was to be provided at Hacheston, with a simple rail level platform so the brake third was provided with retractable steps, which were operated by the guard to enable passengers to join and detrain at the halt. Suitable instructions were subsequently published in the timetable that tickets from Marlesford, Hacheston Halt and Parham were issued on the train. In addition passengers wishing to use Hacheston Halt were required to travel in the brake/third vehicle with access to the steps. The alterations on the Framlingham branch were agreed on 16th June, 1922 with estimated annual savings of £150 and services commenced in November. To assist passengers joining and alighting at Hacheston Halt notices were provided inside the vehicles stating that 'Passengers for Hacheston Halt must not attempt to alight until the steps have been fixed and the guard has opened the door'. The brake third was also labelled externally with the notice, 'This car for Hacheston Halt'. Further economies were made in the final month of 1922 when station master A. Green at Marlesford gained promotion, for the post was withdrawn and the station placed under the control of the station master at Wickham Market. At the same time Parham was placed under the supervision of the station master at Framlingham. In the dying days of the GER it was hoped enough had been done to sustain the continuing prosperity of the branch.

The approach to Framlingham station from Station Street with Victoria Mill Road on the right *c*.1910. The aptly named Station Hotel serving Cobbold's Fine Ales, always popular with the local railwaymen and travellers, stands guardian on the corner of the two roads. The station building has a small canopy over the frontage and entrance door to the booking hall, with two gas lamps for night time illumination. The gated entrance to the goods yard is between the station and the hotel.   *Author's Collection*

Chapter Three

The LNER Years

As a result of the 1921 Railways Act, from 1st January, 1923 the GER was amalgamated with the Great Northern, Great Central, North Eastern and North British and several smaller railways to form the London & North Eastern Railway. In this rural outback of Suffolk the new ownership continued the rationalisation programme begun by the GER by planned reduction of signalling and the abolition of the signal boxes at Marlesford and Parham. A revised method of operation was also introduced, with trainmen opening and closing some of the intermediate level crossing gates, enabling staff numbers to be reduced. The work was completed in April 1923 when a 3-lever ground frame released by the key on the single line Train Staff was provided at the south end of Marlesford station to operate the points to the goods yard. At the same time the points from the main single line to the down side siding were removed so the yard could only be shunted by up trains using the trailing points and a 2-lever ground frame was provided alongside the level crossing gates to work the gate distant signals. At Parham a 2-lever ground frame released by the key on the Train Staff was provided opposite the north end of the platform to operate the points to the goods yard and the former facing connection for up trains was removed. A 2-lever ground frame was provided by the level crossing gates to work the gate distant signals. At Framlingham a King Lever was provided in the signal box, interlocked with the key on the Train Staff to enable the points to continue to be operated from the signal box by the porter/signalman. All signals were removed except for the down 'fixed' distant.

As the months passed so the identity on the locomotives and rolling stock working the branch services gradually changed. However, before all items of rolling stock received the LNER livery, industrial action affected affairs and a seven day rail strike from 20th January, 1924 brought a further decline in traffic. The deteriorating relationship between trades unions and the railway company only served to encourage competition and gradually bus services offering almost door-to-door services appeared on local roads.

On 22nd July, 1924 Major G.L. Hall of the Ministry of Transport (MoT) belatedly inspected Hacheston Halt, located between Marlesford and Parham. He found the halt had a 30 ft-long platform erected at rail level with a sleeper revetment at a distance from the rail corresponding with the coping edge of a normal platform. The inspector noted that in accordance with a letter dated 27th August, 1923 from the LNER management, the coaching stock employed on the branch was fitted with a whistle, which was blown in the guard's compartment during the whole time the folding steps giving access to the low platforms were in use. The Major was satisfied with the arrangements. On the same day Hall also inspected the altered working arrangements for the branch. He noted that at Framlingham all signals had been abolished except for the down distant, which had been retained and fixed in the warning position. The points and connections at the terminus continued to be worked from the signal box, to which had been added a 'King Lever', which was interlocked with the key on the single line Train Staff. At Marlesford and Parham the signal boxes had been abolished and all signals removed except for the up and down distant signals at both locations which were retained as 'gate distants', and interlocked with the level crossing gates. The point connections at both Marlesford and Parham were operated from a ground frame released and locked by the key on the Train Staff. In consequence of the abolition of the signal boxes at Marlesford and Parham and conversion of Framlingham box to the status of a ground frame, certain modifications had been made to the three public level crossings on the line. At Marlesford and Parham the level crossing gate bolts and distant signals were worked from the adjacent ground frame operated by station staff, and Hall noted that arrangements had been made for the men concerned or their wives always to be on duty during traffic hours to open and close the gates. At Cornish level crossing (also known as Lime House), between Marlesford and Hacheston Halt, the gates were fitted with a special lock and key similar to that equipped at level crossings on the Hadleigh branch. The inspector was informed that the LNER company had not applied for an order from the Ministry under section 47 of the Railway Clauses Act 1845 but with the method adopted, Hall recommended the company apply for such an order. This order required the level crossing gates to be normally secured across the railway and open to the public road and for the fitting of special locks to secure the gates either across the road or across the railway. Although Broadwater level crossing had not been included in the altered method of operation, the Major recommended that the company consider the erection of distant signals for each direction as the view for enginemen approaching the crossing was not good. These were subsequently provided and worked from a 2-lever ground frame. A new up branch outer home signal had been erected on the approach to Wickham Market Junction and worked from that signal box which had a 15-lever frame, with 13 working and two spare levers. Hall found the interlocking was correct. In connection with the outer home signal, a 'train waiting' rail contact operating bell had been provided in the signal box, but the inspector wondered if the company might consider the provision of an earlier warning either by an additional rail contact or track circuits as heavy trains had difficulty starting away if detained at the outer home signal because of the sharp curve and rising gradient. 'If longer notice is given of the arrival of a train the signalman will be in a position to set the junction at once and this stopping might be avoided.' The programme of painting and repair of stations continued under the new regime and on 31st July, 1924 A. Bagnall & Sons were awarded the contract for cleaning and painting Wickham Market station after tendering at £240 1s. 0d.

After complaints were received from farmers, traders, local councils, the National Farmers Union and other interested bodies regarding the lack of accommodation and facilities for dealing with sugar beet traffic, the Chief General Manager announced on 29th April, 1926 a proposal to provide additional sidings at certain stations. Amongst those to benefit was Wickham Market where the lack of siding space seriously impeded the interchange of traffic from the Snape and Framlingham branches. As a result of site surveys the cost of providing the new sidings was estimated at £4,284 including £50 for the acquisition of additional land. The expenditure was authorized and it was readily agreed that the additional sidings would be provided in time for the 1926/27 beet-harvesting season. The work not only involved the installation of the new sidings but also incurred improvements to the track layout and signalling at the station.

The affairs of the branch were again disrupted by the General Strike in early May 1926. Railway union members withdrew their labour in support of the miners and subsequently train services could not be guaranteed. On several days the Framlingham services were suspended. Fortunately within a week regular railwaymen returned to duty and services resumed. The impact of the continuing miners strike meant reduced coal stocks available to the railway companies and the LNER authorities decided on the only course of action available to conserve stocks by reducing train services. Thus from 31st May, 1926 a much-reduced service of three trains each way, Tuesdays excepted, and four on Tuesdays only was operated until the situation improved a few weeks later.

Lieutenant Colonel G.L. Hall inspected the alterations at Wickham Market on 10th May, 1927. He found a new trailing crossover had been laid in the up main line from the up siding and at the same time a through crossing from the down sidings to the up main line had been moved further south. To protect this through crossing, the down home signal had been moved further south to a point 428 yards from the signal box and the up advance starting signal 788 yards from the signal box. The new trailing connection from the up siding was worked from the signal box and was equipped with a 'shunter asking lever', a mechanical device, operated by means of a run of wire to an indicator in the signal box. (The lever was pulled when the shunter required the points to be altered by the signalman.) The through crossing from the down side was worked by a 2-lever ground frame electrically released from the signal box. Hall noted similar arrangements were in operation at Tottenham on the Liverpool Street to Cambridge main line. He noted the control lever was normally free but it was necessary for this to be reversed before the point lever could be interlocked electrically by the movement of the control lever in the signal box. The latter having been pulled was back locked so long as the control lever in the ground frame was reversed, and this in turn was back locked by the lever working the points. New track circuits were installed in both up and down roads, on the down line for 200 yards in the rear of the down home signal controlling the block working to the signal box in the rear and on the up line from the up starting signal to the up advance starting signal controlling a lock on the lever working the former. Hall was of the opinion there was a certain drawback to the mechanical type of shunter-asking indicator and opined that a telephone instrument and telephone code be provided.

The last few days of 1927 brought the first serious wintry weather to affect the Framlingham branch for some years. The blizzard came at a most inconvenient time as local railwaymen settled down with their families on the evening of Christmas Day. The wind rose and snow fell so that by Boxing Day morning the branch was blocked in several places by snowdrifts. Train services were abandoned until the Ipswich snowplough, which had initially been used to keep the main lines clear, could concentrate on clearing the East Suffolk line branches. It was 27th December before services were resumed from Framlingham despite permanent way staff assisting with clearance of snow by hand.

The problems encountered during the early years of Grouping saw the branch passenger and parcel receipts reduce dramatically as the figures below show.

	Passengers	Passenger Receipts	Parcel Receipts	Season Ticket Receipts	Total
1923		£	£	£	£
Marlesford					
Hacheston	6,910	281	317	–	598
Parham					
Framlingham	15,227	2,565	1,606	135	4,306
Total	*22,137*	*2,846*	*1,923*	*135*	*4,904*
1924					
Marlesford					
Hacheston	5,939	208	403	–	611
Parham					
Framlingham	12,078	2,167	1,692	147	4,006
Total	*18,017*	*2,375*	*2,095*	*147*	*4,617*
1925					
Marlesford					
Hacheston	5,443	198	523	2	723
Parham					
Framlingham	10,494	1,891	1,714	60	3,665
Total	*15,937*	*2,089*	*2,237*	*62*	*4,388*
1926					
Marlesford	3,865	110	172	–	282
Hacheston	75	2	–	–	2
Parham	239	31	195	1	227
Framlingham	8,150	1,498	1,474	37	3,009
Total	*12,329*	*1,641*	*1,841*	*38*	*3,520*
1927					
Marlesford					
Hacheston	4,250	138	684	–	822
Parham					
Framlingham	8,076	1,484	1,427	37	2,948
Total	*12,326*	*1,622*	*2,111*	*37*	*3,770*
1928					
Marlesford					
Hacheston	6,156	157	958	–	1,115
Parham					
Framlingham	8,314	1,336	1,064	34	2,434
Total	*14,470*	*1,493*	*2,022*	*34*	*3,549*

In 1923 an average of 71 passengers were booking daily from the branch stations with receipts of £9 2s. 6d. but by 1926 this had reduced to 39 and £5 5s. 0d. respectively. By 1928 there was a slight improvement in passengers to 46 per day but receipts had further reduced to £4 15s. 7d. From the individual station figures released for 1926, Marlesford was by far the busiest of the intermediate stations with an average of 12 passengers per day, whilst Parham could only muster a passenger every alternate day and Hacheston Halt just over one passenger a week!

In 1929 major army manoeuvres were held with units based in and around Framlingham and the railway dealt with several special trains conveying men and equipment, both before and after the event. Then on 13th November, 1929 the Divisional General Manager (Southern Area) reported that it was planned to hold the 1930 Suffolk Agricultural Show at Framlingham. It was fully expected that much of the equipment and livestock would be conveyed by rail but operators envisaged difficulties as the single branch was operated by 'One Engine in Steam' using the Train Staff only and the only signal at the terminal was a down fixed distant. After consultation with the show organisers and his local officers, to establish the estimated amounts of traffic, it was proposed to provide a down home and up starting signal with separate locking bars to the points in the single line to ease operations. The additional signalling costing £242 was also expected to be advantageous under normal circumstances and help yard shunting especially during harvest time in the autumn and sugar beet traffic around Christmas. The Traffic Committee discussed the matter at their meeting on 28th November, 1929 and the £242 expenditure was agreed. A special service of trains running at regular intervals ran during the duration of the show and single fares for the return journey were offered from many stations in East Anglia. For the duration of the show Train Staff & Ticket working was reinstated, whilst the signals were retained until the signal box was abolished on 9th February, 1958. In November 1929 the LNER entered into an agreement with the Eastern Counties Road Car Company for the inter-availablity of road and rail tickets on bus and train services between Ipswich, Wickham Market and Framlingham.

The LNER at this period was suffering traffic losses, which deemed it necessary for the management at Marylebone and Liverpool Street to seek economies. Various branch lines in East Anglia were investigated as to their viability in the future passenger network and the Framlingham branch came under close scrutiny for, despite the operational economies made in 1922 and 1923, the branch receipts continued to decline. Thus, despite the withdrawal of passenger services from the Somersham to Ramsey East and Downham to Stoke Ferry branches on 22nd September, 1930, and Ely to St Ives and Mellis to Eye branches on 2nd February, 1931, the Framlingham branch earning some £3,500 per annum on passenger and parcels traffic, and not much more than the above lines, was allowed to continue. It had been a close call but factors in favour of retaining the service included the holding of the Suffolk Agricultural Show, the regular traffic to and from Framlingham College and the working of the lucrative freight traffic by the passenger services downrated to run as mixed trains if necessary.

On 12th January, 1933 passenger guard E.W. Howard sustained a broken collarbone in a shunting operation at Framlingham. Part of Howard's duties included the working of the branch goods train and at 1.45 pm on the day in question he was in charge of a movement to draw two wagons out of the goods shed. The first of these vehicles was projecting slightly through the shed doorway at the end nearest the points and Howard used his shunting pole to couple the two wagons in the shed to those being set back by the engine, without the vehicles coming to a stand. He managed to throw the link over the hook as the buffers met, but before he could withdraw the pole the butt end came into contact with the shed door. Unfortunately the guard was unable to get out of the way and

'F3' class 2-4-2 tank locomotive No. 7150 stands on the down loop road at Wickham Market with the Framlingham branch train waiting for the down main line service to connect. The train is formed of a two-coach ex-GER bogie conductor-guard set, comprising a brake/third and a composite, together with a former Great Central six-wheel goods brake van. Behind the train is the goods shed capable of storing 75 quarters of grain. *Author's Collection*

An earlier derailment resulted in 'D16/3' 4-4-0 tender locomotive No. 8855 being allocated as the Framlingham branch locomotive in August 1936. Here she stands with a Framlingham to Wickham Market train at Cornish level crossing, also known as Marlesford Lime House, waiting for the fireman to open the gates. With a view to making economies, from 1923 train crews were required to open and close these level crossing gates located between Marlesford and Hacheston and trains were allowed an extra three minutes running time for the purpose. The coaching stock is formed of the usual six-wheel conductor-guard formation of a composite, a third and a brake third. *The late Dr Ian C. Allen*

sustained his injuries through being carried into a narrow space and twisted round by the moving wagons. At the subsequent enquiry the inspecting officer J.L.M. Moore found that the clearance between the shed doorway and the nearest rail on the main line side was only 2 ft 9 in. The door swung outward and when opened to its full extent hung practically flush with the door post and parallel with the track. Consequently the limited clearance in which Howard was working extended for nearly six feet. Moore concluded that the accident was primarily due to the grave and unnecessary risk taken by Howard in attempting to use the shunting pole in the confined space whilst the wagons were in motion. He concluded the lack of clearance 'is a feature which should not be lost sight of in the event of any reconstruction of the goods shed taking place'.

Later in the same year on 8th August, locomotive fireman J.A. Turner received injuries to the back of his head at Wickham Market Junction, whilst on the locomotive working the 10.20 am down passenger train from Wickham Market to Framlingham. After speed had been reduced at the Junction signal box to pick up the single line Train Staff, the brakes on the train appeared to be slow in releasing. Turner leant out of the cab to try and discover the cause when the back of his head came into contact with the ladder of the branch up home signal. Again J.L.M. Moore investigated on behalf of the MoT and established that although the signal post was sufficient distance from the track, the foot of the offending ladder was only 3 ft 6 in. from the nearest rail owing to the signal being set at an angle because of the curvature of the track. The accident was wholly caused by the lack of clearance of the signal ladder and by the time of the inquiry the LNER signal engineer had rectified the situation by repositioning the offending ladder.

For several years collections were made at East Suffolk stations for the East Suffolk and Ipswich Hospital Contributory Fund to help further medical services. The donations made by passengers and staff at the branch stations in 1934 were Wickham Market £7 17s. 3d., Marlesford 13s. 0d., Parham 19s. 6d. and Framlingham £4 17s. 6d.

Wickham Market station again received the attention of painters and decorators in 1938 when A. Bolton received the contract at a cost of £646 17s. 6d. which also included work at Bealings, Woodbridge and Melton stations. The next year, following many hours of continuous rain, the River Ore burst its banks in several places and the Framlingham branch train services were suspended entirely on 26th January, 1939, only to resume at caution the next day. During this period Ipswich was inundated and the East Suffolk line between Melton and Wickham Market blocked when the River Deben burst its banks. Other casualties were the Mid Suffolk line from Haughley to Laxfield, where services were suspended from 26th to 27th January and the Waveney Valley line, which was breached each side of Bungay. Here services were not resumed until 31st January. On a brighter note Wickham Market station was awarded first class certificates in both the 1938 and 1939 Best Kept Station Competitions.

Just prior to the outbreak of World War II the LNER with all other railway companies came under the control of the Railway Executive Committee. Within weeks of the commencement of hostilities local bus services were reduced and some removed from the road by petrol rationing. In May 1940 some improvements were made when the six-wheel coaches, which had formed the branch train for almost

'F3' class 2-4-2 tank locomotive No. 8068 standing outside Framlingham engine shed on 29th March, 1937. *The late W.A. Camwell*

By the end of World War II the 'F3' class 2-4-2 tank locomotives were showing their age and with little serious maintenance during hostilities, failures were above average. They soldiered on, however, until replaced by the 'F6' class in 1949. Here 'F3' class No. 7140 sporting an ugly stovepipe chimney passes Wickham Market Junction with a down branch train in August 1946. The leading coach carries a destination board on the side of the vehicle immediately behind the engine. *The late Dr Ian C. Allen*

two decades, were withdrawn from service and replaced by ex-GER corridor bogie coaches. Then in 1941 first class facilities were withdrawn from the branch trains and remained so until after hostilities whilst cheap day tickets were also withdrawn. In order to safeguard against air raids, especially at night when station lamps remained dimmed, staff utilised shielded hand lamps to attend to train or shunting duties. As a precaution against enemy attacks the station nameboards were initially removed and stored in lamp rooms or signal boxes but were later reinstated. The agricultural nature of the freight handled on the branch was of utmost importance as vital provisions of home grown food, grain and vegetables were dispatched and conveyed to markets at Ipswich, Norwich and London. In addition to the outflow of traffic the war years brought an influx of tinned foods and dried milk for distribution in the area under the auspices of the Ministry of Food.

As the branch was not far from the Suffolk coast in an area considered vulnerable to enemy attack, coastal defence armoured trains patrolled to Framlingham as well as working across the Aldeburgh and Snape branches between June 1940 and July 1943. The line was covered intially by train 'D' and then train 'C' which made its last recorded run across the branch on the afternoon of 26th March, 1943, although it was not officially disbanded until June. After returning from patrols in Cornwall train 'D', now based at Mistley, resumed its activities on Essex and Suffolk branches until disbanded in July 1943.

Framlingham airfield was used by the United States Air Force 95th Bomber Group flying 'B17' 'Flying Fortresses' during May and June 1943. From July, the 390th Bomber Group (402 Air Bombardment Division) flying 'B17F' aircraft superseded the 95th until August 1945, when the base was closed down. Air raids on the branch were sporadic for the area was littered with various wartime airfields, which provided some insurance against air attacks. Despite this reassurance the driver of a down branch service had the presence of mind to halt his train in woodland between Wickham Market Junction and Marlesford when he noticed Luftwaffe fighters wheeling round to attack. Fortunately the aircraft

'F3' class 2-4-2 tank locomotive No. 8081 at Framlingham with, *from left to right*, ganger Cecil Salter, fireman Jack Dale, ganger Bill Fordham and driver Ted Manthorpe.

The late Dr Ian C. Allen

passed over without firing any shots. The only other serious attack came at about 7.10 pm on the evening of 14th November, 1944 when a 'V1' Flying Bomb fell near Marlesford station shattering some windows in the station building. There were no trains in the area at the time and the formation of the railway was undamaged. At the end of December 1944 a United States Air Force 'Flying Fortress' bomber, struggling to get airborne from Framlingham airfield with a full bomb load on an icy morning, lost height and careered into the centre of Parham, destroying the Methodist Chapel. All the crew perished in the resultant explosion, which damaged every house in the village but fortunately the inhabitants sustained only minor injuries. The station was damaged and debris was deposited on the track but there was no delay to train services. Hacheston Halt was used extensively by air force personnel as there was a short cut across the fields to Parham airfield. To the Americans, the branch service was nicknamed 'The Framlingham Flyer'.

It was on a Saturday evening during the hostilities that Framlingham station master Thomas Simpson received an urgent message from railway Control at Shenfield stating that a military special would be working down to Framlingham early the next morning. As the last down train had arrived at the terminus and staff had left for home Simpson realised the single line Train Staff, safely locked away in the signal box, would be required at Wickham Market Junction signal box to allow the special train on to the branch. Simpson had been invited to enjoy a drink at the local hostelry with the station foreman, who was celebrating his birthday with several of the station staff, and had received the message just as he was about to leave. By the time he arrived the beer was flowing freely and he mentioned to the foreman the impending special train and the predicament regarding the Train Staff. Without further prompting, the foreman volunteered to cycle with the Train Staff the seven or so miles to Wickham Market Junction signal box in the blackout and there wait for the special so that he could cadge a lift back on the train. The offer was made subject to the quaffing of a few more pints of ale, which were duly provided at the expense of his work colleagues, whilst the station master went to get the Train Staff. What Simpson did not know when the foreman set off to the cheers of his colleagues was that instead of following the winding road to get to his destination the intrepid cyclist was following the railway and cycling in the 'cess' beside the track. This method was far from comfortable and by the time the foreman was approaching Parham, the combination of alcohol and the heavy brass Train Staff weighing some seven and a half pounds, and the addition of some soft clinker ballast resulted in the rider losing control of his machine. As the bike fell one way and the rider the other the Train Staff flew into the air and down into the adjacent stream.

Picking himself up, the foreman waded into the stream but in the pitch darkness could not locate the item. Within minutes an equally inebriated local reveller on hearing his oaths had joined in the search, but as luck would have it a detachment of the Woodbridge Home Guard, covering for the Framlingham-based battalion, came marching along the road adjacent to the railway. On hearing the broad Suffolk dialects emanating from the darkness, the commanding officer thought the pair were German spies and promptly arrested them. They were immediately transported to GHQ at Colchester under armed escort for questioning. On arrival the foreman had sobered up sufficiently to persuade the authorities the true nature of his mission and the gravity of the situation was then realised. Without further ado the crestfallen duo were returned with a detachment of troops in six armoured cars to assist in the search for the missing Train Staff. The latter was ultimately recovered but in the meantime the military special was standing at Wickham Market Junction home signal, whilst the signalman was explaining on the phone to the authorities at Ipswich that the Train Staff had not arrived from Framlingham and was apparently lost somewhere between the two points. As tempers frayed the signalman was aghast to see six armoured cars appearing down the approach road and in the darkness thought he was under attack by Germans. He decided surrender was the only way out and walked on to the signal box steps with his hand raised above his head. As the truth dawned and British soldiers appeared with the foreman and the missing Train Staff, we can only surmise the signalman must have been the most relieved man in Britain at that moment. Without further delay the military special was signalled on to the branch but there was an awful lot of explaining yet to be done.

Framlingham goods yard was utilised for offloading supplies for the local military airfield, including bombs and armaments. The ammunition trains usually ran at night and the dangerous cargo was quickly transferred into waiting road vehicles for onward transit to the airfield. The trains ran regularly whilst the base was operational from May 1943 until VE Day on 8th May, 1945. The final

'D16/2' class 4-4-0 tender locomotive No. 2590 leaves the Framlingham branch at Wickham Market Junction and swings over to the up East Suffolk main line with an excursion to Felixstowe in July 1947. This was the last survivor of the 'Super Clauds' to come into BR ownership and was finally withdrawn in January 1952. The signs of an earlier buffer beam impact is evident on the nearside footplate.   *The late Dr Ian C. Allen*

review of the USAF 390th Bomber Group was three weeks later; flying duties continued, however, for a further month as part of the emergency supply of food for those starving in the newly-occupied countries in Europe. Food supplies were initially brought to Framlingham by train for road transfer to the airfield. The last aircraft left the base on 26th June, leaving ground staff to clear the base and a special train took away some of this equipment on 5th August, 1945.

After the war the railways resumed peacetime activities with run-down and life-expired rolling stock and equipment and infrastructure in need of maintenance. Questions were raised in Parliament regarding the deteriorating services offered by the LNER and the Framlingham branch was no exception.

The severe weather early in 1947 brought problems, initially with drifting snow blocking the shallow cuttings along the line and then the rapidly thawing snow causing minor flooding on sections of the branch. Damage was so severe that permanent way staff had to replace waterlogged sleepers and replace the clinker ballast washed away by the excess water. Mother nature was not the only problem for as petrol rationing eased so the Eastern Counties Omnibus Company improved the frequency of its services in East Suffolk. The resultant decline in passenger traffic finances was cause for concern to local railway management and with the imminent Nationalisation of the railways the future outlook for the Framlingham branch appeared decidedly bleak.

In the latter years the 'F3' class 2-4-2 tank locomotives showed a decided lack of attention to cleaning as shown by No. 7150 still bearing the legend LNER on the side tanks as she approaches Wickham Market Junction with a mixed train in July 1948. Note the up branch home signal with co-acting arms to enable easier signal sighting on the curved approach to the junction. No. 7150 was condemned without receiving a BR number in October 1949.

The late Dr Ian C. Allen

Chapter Four

Nationalisation and Closure

The Nationalisation of the railways from 1st January, 1948 brought few changes to the Framlingham branch, which retained its GER/LNER atmosphere until the withdrawal of steam traction from the line. Most stocks of LNER tickets remained in use until the branch closed for passenger traffic. Tickets in constant demand were soon replaced by those bearing the legend 'Railway Executive' or 'British Railways'. Locomotives working the line soon lost the 'NE' or 'LNER' on the side tanks or tenders, although varnished teak or brown paint remained on the branch coaching stock until the withdrawal of passenger traffic.

British Railways (BR) made few alterations to the timetable in which trains were inconveniently timed for people wishing to travel to Ipswich to work or to London. Even market day numbers were a shadow of pre-war totals, and takings at stations and by the conductor guard were minimal. Needless to say, the finances of the passenger service on the branch came in for serious investigation by the new management at Liverpool Street. Freight traffic also showed a decline as fuel rationing ended and farmers and traders increasingly preferred to dispatch their produce and goods by motor lorry. Livestock traffic also declined as cattle and sheep destined for markets in the surrounding area were sent by road, a method obviating the double handling of animals at both forwarding and receiving stations. The only good news was that Wickham Market station received certificates for third class awards in the Best Kept Station competition in 1949 and 1950, whilst Framlingham station was awarded a third class certificate in 1950.

The cost conscious Railway Executive had directed the railway Regions to investigate unremunerative lines and by the autumn of 1951 it became all too clear that services on the neighbouring Mid Suffolk Light Railway from Haughley to Laxfield were totally unviable in the new national railway network. The rumours of impending closure were confirmed in November when railway management officially informed members of staff and NUR and ASLEF trade unions that proposals were actively in hand. The public was informed in December and the Eastern Area Transport Users' Consultative Committee (TUCC) meeting was held in February to consider the arguments for retaining the passenger and goods services. All was to no avail, for complete closure of the line was advocated on and from 28th July, 1952, but as no Sunday services operated the last trains ran on Saturday 26th July. The publicity associated with the closure of the 'Middy' completely overshadowed the announcement of the intention of withdrawing passenger services from the Framlingham branch. The same procedure followed, the local staff and trades unions were advised, followed by the public announcements. Once again representations were made against closure to the TUCC and after due consideration the announcement was made that, subject to adequate alternative bus services being provided, no case could be found for the retention of

Super power for the branch train on a cold miserable December day in 1949. 'J15' class No. 65467 pilots sister engine No. 65459 as the pair await to depart from Framlingham with the formation consisting of former Great Central Railway goods brake van, a two-coach branch conductor-guard set and another vehicle. No. 65459, the allocated branch engine, had become a partial failure and required attention at Ipswich so No. 65467 was sent down to relieve. No. 65467 took over the branch diagram after arrival at Wickham Market, allowing the ailing 65459 to return to home depot. *The late Dr Ian C. Allen*

'F6' class 2-4-2 tank locomotive No. 67230 departing from Framlingham with the branch train in July 1952. Vans occupy the dock road behind the platform. *The late H.C. Casserley*

Wickham Market station facing south from the overbridge with a special train propelled by 'B12' class No. 61572 conveying judges for the 'Best Kept Station' competition, standing in the down platform. The judges can be seen behind the fence railings. The down platform 500 ft in length contained the main station buildings, whilst to the left is the 150 ft dock road serving the up side loading dock, the granary and beyond that the signal box and up side island platform, 430 ft in length.   *The late Dr Ian C. Allen*

passenger trains, which carried on average seven passengers a day! British Railways, Eastern Region (BR, ER) duly advised that passenger services would be withdrawn on and from Monday 3rd November, 1952, and in the absence of Sunday services the last trains actually ran on the previous Saturday, 1st November. Freight services were to continue serving the branch goods yards with parcels traffic conveyed in a passenger brake van attached to one of the goods trains serving the line.

In the meantime on 31st July, 1952 two small pieces of land totalling an area of 30 square yards, adjacent to Marlesford level crossing were conveyed to the Ministry of Transport at a cost of £20 to permit the widening of the A12 main road. BR civil engineering staff subsequently carried out the work on the crossing at the expense of the Ministry.

The last day of passenger operation, Saturday 1st November, 1952, was tinged with sadness as many local people and some railway enthusiasts travelled on the various services throughout the day. The last up train, the 6.52 pm from Framlingham and the 8.00 pm return from Wickham Market was worked by 'F6' class 2-4-2 tank locomotive No. 67239 carrying a laurel wreath and in charge of driver John Turner. The trains were formed of seven coaches, including both the branch two-coach conductor guard sets, augmented by two ex-GER corridor thirds and an ex-London Midland & Scottish Railway (LMS) corridor open third. Crowds gathered at the stations and by the lineside in the

'J15' class 0-6-0 tender locomotive No. 65454 rouses the echoes with a heavy mixed train on a cold winter's morning. The train is approaching Framlingham and crossing River Ore underbridge No. 1105. *The late Dr Ian C. Allen*

An up branch mixed train hauled by 'F6' class 2-4-2T No. 67239 accelerates away from Framlingham near Hoggate Hill in July 1952. The engine is working 'wrong way round' for the Framlingham branch with the boiler towards Wickham Market. It was usual for the engine to work chimney first towards Framlingham to facilitate coaling and water at Framlingham shed but No. 67239 had deputised for a failure the previous day. *The late Dr Ian C. Allen*

The 1.40 pm Wickham Market to Framlingham train hauled by 'F6' class 2-4-2 tank locomotive No. 67230 passing Parham up distant signal (upper arm) and Brick Lane level crossing down gate distant (lower arm) and sharing the same post on 23rd August, 1952. The signal post is surmounted by an ornate finial. In true branch line malpractice the locomotive carries no headlamp to denote the class of train. *G.R. Mortimer*

'F6' class 2-4-2 tank locomotive No. 67239 waits in the down side reception siding at Wickham Market with the two-coach Framlingham branch train in August 1952. The up and down main lines are in the foreground. *D. Trevor Rowe*

During the last few days of regular passenger services, local people and enthusiasts made an effort to ride the branch train for the last time. Not the least was Mrs Murphy, the head teacher of Hacheston Primary School who arranged for her pupils to take advantage of a return trip to Framlingham. 'F6' class 2-4-2 tank locomotive No. 67239 draws to a halt at Hacheston Halt to allow pupils to join the train. The formation has been strengthened by the addition of an ex-LMS corridor third.   *The late Dr Ian C. Allen*

Last handshakes on the last day of passenger services on the branch, 1st November, 1952. In the cab of 'F6' class 2-4-2T No. 67239 are *from left to right* driver Harry Double, fireman A. Chittock and driver Jack Turner.   *Author's Collection*

darkness to watch the train pass. Because of the heavyweight train carrying some 450 to 500 people, four minutes were lost on the last up journey to Wickham Market, whilst the last down train was 10 minutes late departing. As the train departed those on the platform and on the train sang 'Pack Up Your Troubles' and exploding detonators resounded in the night air as the locomotive struggled to get the train underway. Further detonators were exploded at Wickham Market Junction as the train swung on to the branch for the last time. Crowds greeted the cavalcade at Marlesford and Parham, the latter decorated with fairy lights and streamers, although there were no passengers in the darkness at Hacheston Halt. At each of the intermediate crossings, where the locomotive whistle was sounded, small groups gathered with torches and at some children let off fireworks or held sparklers. Further delay was incurred after an unknown person pulled the communication cord as the engine approached the platform end at Framlingham but the taps were quickly reset and No. 67239 pulled into the platform to the staccato of exploding detonators and to the singing of 'Auld Lang Syne'. The Reverend M. Bulstrode, Rector of Framlingham, dressed in Edwardian attire greeted the train on arrival. It was an especially sad moment for Edgar Gladwell, the booking clerk at Framlingham, as he had witnessed and been displaced by the closure of the former Mid Suffolk Light Railway only four months earlier. After arriving at Framlingham the locomotive was released from the train and later, to an almost deserted station, set off light engine to Ipswich shed, leaving the coaching stock to be worked away on the following Monday. On the Monday following the closure the *Daily Telegraph* gave its readers under the headline 'The Flier Lets Off Steam For The Last Time' a graphic account of the final journey:

> Carrying passengers dressed in Victorian and Edwardian style, to whom hot punch was served, the 'Framlingham Flyer' ended on Saturday evening its 93 years of service over the seven miles of rail between Wickham Market and Framlingham, Suffolk. With a laurel wreath over its funnel and carrying more passengers than it usually does in a month, the 'Flier' was cheered by hundreds of people along the track. Villagers set off fireworks as the train passed by.

The report also quoted a claim that in the previous six months there was an average of only seven passengers daily. According to the *Daily Telegraph* most of the travellers on the train were guests of Lord and Lady Alastair Graham and their family who lived in the locality, most in Edwardian attire, His Lordship sporting long side whiskers had placed a laurel wreath bearing the letters R.I.P. on the front of the locomotive for the last run, and commented, 'the end was inevitable, the old order changeth and we must accept the new'. Not to be outsmarted Sir Peter Greenwell 'clad in a smock and flowing white beard blew blasts on his hunting horn' to start the train away from Wickham Market and then every time the engine whistle was sounded.

After the withdrawal of the passenger service the future of the branch was again questioned, but heavy grain loadings at Framlingham appeared to ensure a short- term continuation to which some additional traffic had been taken as a result of the closure of the former Mid Suffolk Light Railway from Haughley to Laxfield.

Super power for the annual weedkilling train in May 1955 as 'B12/3' class No. 61577 propels the train over River Ore underbridge No. 1105 between Parham and Framlingham, whilst working back to Wickham Market. The train is formed of a 'Toad D' brake van leading, two ex-Southern Railway 4-wheel utility vans, six tank wagons holding the chemical and another 'Toad D' brake van. The leading utility van has the weedkiller spraying on the track.   *The late Dr Ian C. Allen*

'J15' class 65435 accelerates away from Framlingham near Hoggate Hill with the branch goods train in 1958, the formation including several bulk grain wagons. The Framlingham to Kettleburgh road runs parallel to the railway to the left.   *The late Dr Ian C. Allen*

On 3rd May, 1958 'J15' class 0-6-0 No. 65389 shunts Marlesford yard whilst working the 'bonus' goods from Ipswich to Ipswich via Framlingham and Snape. The locomotive has left the wagons brought from Framlingham on the main single line as it goes to collect wagons from Marlesford siding. The point connection to the siding was operated from the three-lever ground frame on the right. The trap points under the locomotive originally led to a headshunt siding.

The late Dr Ian C. Allen

In the latter years of branch operation trainmen were required to open and close the level crossing gates on the branch for the passage of a train. 'J15' class No. 65389 waits for the guard to open the gates at Marlesford Ford level crossing No. 4 in 1958. *The late Dr Ian C. Allen*

Having partially repaired the hole in the tender water tank (*see page 67*), the fire was re-lit in 'J15' class 0-6-0 No. 65454 on 19th May, 1959. She was coupled ahead of sister locomotive No. 65478 to work the branch freight train back to Ipswich. The pair are seen negotiating the crossover at Wickham Market Junction with a train consisting of a six-plank open wagon and a former Southern Railway brake van. No. 65454 later ran light engine to her home depot of Stratford where she was immediately withdrawn for scrapping.   *The late Dr Ian C. Allen*

Steam brake-only 'J15' class 0-6-0 No. 65389 stands in the shed road at Framlingham after taking water. In order to save time No. 65389 has dragged the completed branch goods train into the siding and once replenished the train was reversed on to the main single line to set off for Wickham Market. Even in the dying days of steam traction the Framlingham branch freight could muster a train of seven vans and three open wagons in addition to the brake van.
                                                                                    The late Dr Ian C. Allen

'J15' class 0-6-0 No. 65478 trundles the branch freight train along the branch near near Brick Lane crossing in 1959. *The late Dr Ian C. Allen*

During its sojourn in the Ipswich area, Stratford based 'J15' class No. 65454 was often used to work the branch 'bonus' goods. Here she is approaching Broadwater level crossing with a down train conveying bulk grain wagons. The notice regarding the level crossing on the near side of the line advised enginemen of the approach to Brick Lane crossing. *The late Dr Ian C. Allen*

On the night of 1st/2nd May, 1956 the Royal Train conveying HRH The Duke of Edinburgh on a visit to various destinations in East Anglia was taken on to the Framlingham branch and stabled between Wickham Market and Marlesford, so that the Duke could enjoy an undisturbed night's sleep. An immaculately turned out 'B1' class 4-6-0 tender locomotive No. 61253 was coupled to the Wickham Market end of the train to provide steam heating for the comfort of the passengers. On the morning of 2nd May No. 61253 is shown hauling the train off the branch and on to the down main line where it was uncoupled. Immaculate sister locomotive No. 61399, is waiting clear of the junction ready to haul the train forward to Lowestoft. Similar arrangements were made the previous night when the train was stabled on the Hadleigh branch between Bentley and Capel. *The late Dr Ian C. Allen*

'B1' class 4-6-0 No. 61399 backs on to the Royal Train conveying HRH The Duke of Edinburgh at Wickham Market Junction on 2nd May, 1956, before hauling the train forward to Lowestoft. Sister locomotive No. 61253 has already been detached from the formation. The signalman has cleared the signal for the down main despite the train being well forward of the signal post. The Duke leaning out of the window of the carriage indignantly asked Doctor Ian Allen why he was standing so close to the train and possibly providing a security risk? Prince Philip was satisfied to hear that all he was doing was 'taking photographs of the special, with the unofficial permission of local railwaymen'. *The late Dr Ian C. Allen*

At about 10 am on 26th July, 1955, a minor accident occurred during shunting operations at Wickham Market station. T.A. Sharp, a 21-year-old labourer in the employ of a local coal merchant, was assisting the driver of a motor lorry to unload coke when he suffered severe bruising to the right foot, which necessitated him being off work for five weeks. The MoT inquiry into the incident was conducted by Mr C.H. Hewison who established that the coke wagon being unloaded stood on the extension of the shed road, through the goods shed and some 30 yards beyond the building. Having set the rear of a road trailer against the wagon, Sharp and the lorry driver lowered the wagon side door on to the end of the trailer. After about 20 minutes transferring coke the two were surprised when a shunt was made into the siding, which moved the wagon. Sharp's right foot was trapped between the wagon door and the trailer side and severely bruised. Hewison also learned that when the two men arrived at the station at about 9 am, porter A.V. Smith was engaged marshalling the morning freight train to Framlingham and they were warned not to work until shunting was completed. After an interval they moved the road trailer up to the wagon in readiness to start unloading, when they happened to see porter P. Cox, accompanied by guard A. Ball who was rostered to work the freight train. The motor driver asked them both if it was yet convenient to commence unloading. Both men admitted to Hewison they gave permission for the men to commence unloading. The shunting movement concerned was conducted by Smith from a position close to the entrance to the shed road, from where the trailer was not readily visible because wagons were obstructing his view through the goods shed. The inspector absolved Smith from any blame and placed full responsibility for the accident on porter Cox and guard Ball. Neither had anything to do with the shunt movement and had no authority to tell the coal merchant's men to start work unloading the coal wagon. Cox, who later assisted Smith by operating the shed road hand points for the movement concerned failed to advise him that the men might be engaged unloading a wagon. His excuse was that, in his opinion, the movement would not reach the coke wagon was unacceptable and he took the principal responsibility for the accident, which fortunately did not have more severe consequences. Hewison noted both men had admitted their mistake and would be more careful in future.

In its declining years the Framlingham branch was privileged to receive a visit by the Royal Train. On the night of 1st/2nd May, 1956 the train, conveying HRH the Duke of Edinburgh on a visit to East Anglia, was taken on to the branch and stabled between Wickham Market Junction and Marlesford so that the Duke could enjoy an undisturbed night's sleep. 'B1' class 4-6-0 tender locomotive No. 61253 was coupled to the Wickham Market end of the train to provide steam heating for the comfort of passengers. On the morning of 2nd No. 61253 hauled the train off the branch, and on to the down main line, where it was uncoupled and 'B1' class No. 61399, which had been waiting clear of the junction points, backed on and hauled the train forward to Lowestoft.

On 4th May, 1957 a wedding special train of first class stock from Liverpool Street to Framlingham for the Pryor family was worked from Ipswich by 'B12/3' class 4-6-0 No. 61571. After the ceremony the engine hauled the train back to Ipswich tender-first.

'B12/3' class No. 61571 is in unblemished condition and is displaying express train headcode as she departs from Framlingham with a special train, returning guests of the Pryor family to London after a wedding on 4th May, 1957. The stock is formed of a mixture of Gresley LNER vehicles and BR Mark I coaches. *The late Dr Ian C. Allen*

A motley collection of coaching stock, including two Thompson suburban coaches form a special end of term train for students of Framlingham College approaching Wickham Market Junction behind 'B12/3' class No. 61564 in 1954. The locomotive is displaying the express train headcode. The coaches were coupled to a normal service train at Ipswich for onward conveyance to Liverpool Street. *The late Dr Ian C. Allen*

Approaching Kettleburgh Road level crossing No. 17, railway and road converged for a short distance and here 'J15' class 0-6-0 No. 65459 hauls empty stock for a Framlingham College end of term special. The vehicles are a motley collection of ex-GER, LNER Thompson and LNER Gresley corridor stock. *The late Dr Ian C. Allen*

'J15' class 0-6-0 tender locomotive No. 65459 working down to Framlingham with a College special train at the beginning of the May 1955 term. The train is approaching Broadwater level crossing where the road from Wickham Market to Framlingham converged with the branch line for a short distance. The train is formed of ex-LNER Thompson suburban coaching stock. *The late Dr Ian C. Allen*

'J15' class 0-6-0 No. 65454 standing on the yard loop road with stock ready for the special morning exercise held at Framlingham on Sunday 10th May, 1959 when the local emergency services were expected to deal with a simulated railway accident. *The late Dr Ian C. Allen*

Before the emergency exercise on Sunday 10th May, 1959, 'J15' class 0-6-0 No. 65454 and the two condemned suburban coaches were stabled in the dock road behind the platform building at Framlingham. *The late Dr Ian C. Allen*

After the withdrawal of the branch passenger services, British Railways entered into an arrangement with the authorities at Framlingham College to run a through train to and from Liverpool Street at the beginning and end of each term. Gerald Leedham, a Framlingham resident and one time General Manager of the Cheshire Lines Committee, had made the initial approach when petrol was still rationed. Through tickets for Framlingham were issued at Liverpool Street to any members of the public who wished to travel on these trains. The initial service ran in 1954 and from then onwards it was usual for a 'B12' class 4-6-0 tender locomotive to work tender first with the empty coaching stock from Ipswich to Framlingham. On arrival at the terminus the engine ran round the coaches ready to haul the train to London. Ample time was allowed to load trunks and cases on board before departure and, as the long train exceeded the length of the platform, passengers had to board in the rear three coaches and walk through to reach the front coaches. Similarly, when the through train from London arrived at Framlingham there was always a scramble as students pushed their way to the front coaches to alight. The last up special train ran in April 1958, when, in the absence of anything larger, 'J15' class 0-6-0 No. 65459 was provided to haul the coaches to Wickham Market to be coupled to a through Yarmouth to Liverpool Street service. The locomotive was in such poor condition that on arrival at Framlingham with the empty coaching stock it had almost run out of steam. An hour was spent as the footplate crew cleaned the fire and raised steam and the train subsequently missed the connecting service! The last down run on 2nd May, 1958 was formed of three coaches attached to the 3.33 pm train from Liverpool Street, which then formed a special from Ipswich departing at 5.09 pm; the three coaches would normally have formed the 5.20 pm Ipswich to Felixstowe which was cancelled on that day. The train was hauled by 'B12/3' class 4-6-0 tender locomotive No. 61561 and after a brief halt at Wickham Market arrived at Framlingham nine minutes early at 5.53 pm. The cessation of these special workings was welcomed by the carriage and wagon maintenance staff at Ipswich for when the coaching stock returned from the school runs the vehicles had suffered from vandalism, with leather window straps missing and the netting of the luggage racks broken. After one such trip the Ipswich station master wrote to the Bursar of Framlingham College complaining of the 'wanton damage - expecting better of public schoolboys'.

On the morning of Sunday 10th May, 1959 an exercise was held at Framlingham station for the Suffolk county rescue services to test their reactions to emergency calls. The exercise include a simulated train crash using two condemned coaches headed by 'J15' class 0-6-0 tender locomotive No. 65454, with casualties provided by members of St John's Ambulance Brigade. The arrangements were extremely lifelike and the exercise was considered a success. At the end of the day No. 65454 shunted the stock clear of the main line in readiness for the branch freight train the next morning, before the fire was dropped and the engine stabled on the goods shed road. The engine was not required for any other duties and was left at Framlingham but when an Ipswich crew went to collect her on 19th May, the tender was found to be completely empty as the water had drained away through a hole in the tank. After temporary repairs the engine was shunted by 'J15' No. 65478 working the

The annual weedkilling train working down the branch near Marlesford in May 1959 hauled by 'J15' class No. 65467. By now the train was operated by the Chipman Chemical Co. and was formed of a converted brake van for spraying, four tank wagons for the chemicals, a van and a 'Toad D' goods brake van at the rear.   *The late Dr Ian C. Allen*

The annual weedkilling train waiting to leave Framlingham behind 'J15' class No. 65447.
                                                                        The late Dr Ian C. Allen

branch freight train, to the water column and the tanks replenished. She then piloted the freight train back to Ipswich. Later the same day No. 65464 ran light engine to Stratford for scrapping.

In the late 1950s further rationalization was achieved when trainmen were required to open and close the level crossing gates at Marlesford station, Cornish, Ford, Parham station, Brick Lane, Broadwater and Kettleburgh Road level crossings. Self-locking padlocks were placed on all gates and a key attached to the single line Train Staff. Instructions were issued that after the engine or train was stopped well clear of the gates, the fireman (or guard in the case of a train or engine single-manned) would open the barriers for the passage of the engine or train over the crossing. Once the engine or train was clear of the crossing, the guard (or fireman in the case of a light engine), was required to close the gates across the line and re-lock them. The driver before proceeding was also required to ensure he had received the 'all right' signal from the guard before proceeding on the journey.

The Framlingham branch received the benefit of British Railways modernisation programme from 1959 when diesel-electric locomotives built by BTH/Paxman (later BR class '15'), North British type '2' (later BR class '21'), BR/Sulzer type '2' (later BR class '24' and '25') and Brush type '2' (later BR class '31') took over the working of the freight services. The last occasion when passengers were conveyed across the branch was on Good Friday 12th April, 1963 when a buffet car excursion for ramblers was worked through from Liverpool Street to Framlingham by Brush type '2' (later class '31') diesel-electric locomotive No. D5595. It was also the only time that a diesel locomotive worked a passenger train across the branch.

The North British Locomotive Co.'s 1,160 hp Bo-Bo diesel-electric locomotive, later BR class '21', were introduced in 1958 but were not successful in East Anglia and were soon transferred to the Scottish Region to be nearer the manufacturer, so that remedial repairs could be more easily effected. Their use on the Framlingham branch was short-lived and here No. D6117 trundles along the branch shortly after leaving Framlingham near Hoggate Hill with a brake van in tow. Later the same day the locomotive failed at Haughley hauling an Ipswich to Whitemoor freight train. *The late Dr Ian C. Allen*

The Eastern Region General Manager's inspection train visited the Framlingham branch in April 1961. Here the two-coach formation is being propelled in the down direction near Marlesford by 'J15' class 0-6-0 No. 65469 immaculately turned out by Norwich shed staff led by shed master D.W. Harvey. This was the last occasion a steam locomotive worked across the Framlingham branch. *The late Dr Ian C. Allen*

'J15' class 0-6-0 tender locomotive No. 65469 sporting a stovepipe chimney and express train headcode approaching Wickham Market Junction with the Eastern Region General Manager's inspection train in April 1961. After inspecting the line in the down direction lunch was taken on board the train at Parham. *The late Dr Ian C. Allen*

British Railways commenced the disposal of surplus assets in January 1960 when the Kettleburgh level crossing cottage near Framlingham was sold to J. King at a cost of £600, to be followed on 12th August by Broadwater level crossing cottage and an area of 1 rood 13 perches of land to E.J. Shepherd for £800. The following year on 27th April, Brick Lane crossing cottage together with 0.143 acres of land was sold to F.A. Davies at a cost of £275.

In 1963 the infamous Beeching Report was published and whilst referring specifically to passenger traffic, the map included with the report also showed average freight tonnages and receipts. Stations on the branch provided poor results, Marlesford and Parham showing only 0 to 5,000 tons per annum and Framlingham 5,000 to 25,000 tons per annum. Even Wickham Market goods yard only registered 0 to 5,000 tons per annum. Road transport had by now removed all but coal traffic from Wickham Market, Marlesford and Parham, whilst Framlingham still generated receipts from dwindling grain and fertilizer exports and imports. The continuing ailing receipts finally forced British Railways' Eastern Region authorities to effect economies and freight facilities were withdrawn from Wickham Market, Marlesford and Parham on and from 13th July, 1964.

Freight trains continued to serve Framlingham for another nine months but early in March 1965 it was announced that freight facilities would be withdrawn from the terminus on and from Monday 19th April, 1965. As this was Easter Bank Holiday Monday the last through freight train ran on Maundy Thursday 15th April, hauled by BR/Sulzer class '24' Bo-Bo diesel electric locomotive No. D5047. The locomotive cleared the branch of wagons except for one cripple vehicle, and two others, which had to be left at Marlesford until repairs could be completed. A week later on 22nd April these final wagons were collected, when the up freight train from Leiston to Ipswich propelled down the branch from Wickham Market Junction to Marlesford.

The track from Wickham Market Junction to Framlingham remained *in situ* for some weeks, gathering an increasing carpet of weeds and brambles, before a contract was awarded for the removal of the permanent way and other assets. Once negotiations were concluded, the demolition contractor commenced work at the end of June 1965 cutting up the rails into convenient lengths and removed sleepers working from the junction towards Framlingham. The task was completed by early August.

On 11th September, 1964 Ford Crossing cottage and an area of approximately 700 square yards of land had been sold to G.E. Bailey for £925. The former station house, buildings and land comprising an area of 2,057 square yards at Parham were sold to Lynton Vale Properties for £1,700 on 28th December, 1966, whilst sections of the former trackbed on both sides of the Marlesford Road at Marlesford, 111 square yards at Peasenhall Road at Parham and 32 square yards on either side of Brick Lane at Framlingham were passed to East Suffolk County Council for road improvements. Sections of the former trackbed were then sold including 1,210 square yards at Marlesford for £80 in December 1966, and five acres 1,936 square yards at Marlesford on 6th March, 1967. Disposals then continued in earnest:

The loss of freight traffic from Framlingham can be gauged by the short goods train consisting of two open wagons, a van and brake van that BR/Sulzer type '2' diesel-electric locomotive No. D5036 is about to haul back to Wickham Market from the terminus on a wintry January day in 1963. The carriage dock siding is to the centre and the cattle dock siding to the left.

The late Dr Ian C. Allen

For a short period after the withdrawal of steam traction, BR/Sulzer type '2' 1,160 hp Bo-Bo diesel-electric locomotives were used on the goods train serving the Framlingham branch. No. D5041 is shown shunting a brake van and a 16-ton all-steel mineral wagon at the terminus. The granary siding serving the granary is to the right.

The late Dr Ian C. Allen

The branch freight train has been formed at Framlingham and is ready to depart behind BR/Sulzer type '2' diesel electric locomotive No. D5042. Note the undergrowth is beginning to encroach on the platform whilst the canopy has been cut back almost level with the concourse canopy. *The late Dr Ian C. Allen*

Freight traffic was withdrawn from the Framlingham branch on and from Monday 19th April, 1965, but as this was Easter Bank Holiday Monday, the last train ran on Maundy Thursday 15th April. Here BR/Sulzer type '2' 1,160 hp diesel electric locomotive, later BR class '24', No. D5047 hauls the last train consisting of five open wagons and a 'Toad D' brake van past St Mary's Church, Parham on 15th April. *The late Dr Ian C. Allen*

After the passing of the last freight train on Maundy Thursday 15th April, 1965, a crippled wagon and two others were left at Marlesford pending attention by the local carriage and wagon examiner from Ipswich. Once remedial repairs were completed arrangements were made for the wagons to be collected and on 22nd April, 1965 Brush type '2' diesel-electric locomotive No. D5576 propelled the Leiston to Ipswich goods train down the branch from Wickham Market Junction to collect the wagons. Here D5576 stands on the main line to detach from the wagons whilst the guard waits to operate the ground frame lever to allow the locomotive to set back into the yard to collect the vehicles. *The late Dr Ian C. Allen*

The last ever goods train from the Framlingham branch, hauled by Brush type '2', diesel-electric locomotive No. D5576 waits at the Wickham Market Junction branch up home signal for clearance to the main line on 22nd April, 1965. *The late Dr Ian C. Allen*

10th April, 1967	Framlingham	3,460 square yards	£2,500
24th May, 1967	Parham	3,436 square yards	£400
12th June, 1967	Framlingham	2,420 square yards	£150
30th June, 1967	Framlingham	1 acre 2,420 sq. yards	£1,500

On 18th September two further plots of land adjacent to Kettleburgh road crossing were released to East Suffolk County Council, again for road improvements whilst on 22nd January, 1968 the sale of Framlingham station, including station offices, station master's house, goods shed and 2 acres 774 square yards of land was made to A.J. O'Connell Limited for £6,000. On 19th April the 402 square yards of the station forecourt was sold to East Suffolk County Council for £10. Along the former trackbed disposals continued,

23rd May, 1968	Parham	1,210 sq. yards	£80
31st May, 1968	Parham	5 acres 1,028 sq. yards	£350
23rd June, 1968	Parham	6 acres 1,936 sq. yards	£520
6th August, 1968	Parham	1 acre 3,001 sq. yards	£325
14th November, 1968	Parham	2 acres 580 sq. yards	£150
3rd December, 1968	Framlingham	2 acres 919 sq. yards	£165
14th February, 1969	Marlesford	2 acres 3,727 sq. yards	£195
27th February, 1969	Framlingham	3 acres 4,598 sq. yards	£395
27th February, 1970	Framlingham	1 acre 3,775 sq. yards	£300
17th August, 1973	Marlesford	1,500 square yards	£490

Wickham Market station facing north with the 12.48 pm Ipswich to Lowestoft train formed of Craven diesel-multiple-units at the platform on 7th September, 1974. Since closure of the Framlingham branch much rationalization has taken place. The signal box and sidings on the up side have been removed, as has the canopy over the down platform. In subsequent years the line was singled with all trains using the down platform, whilst the overbridge was renewed in 2005/2006. *G.R. Mortimer*

Framlingham goods shed in use as a store in 1998. *Author*

Finally, under an order made at Woodbridge Magistrates Court on 30th July, 1970 under Section S 108 of the 1959 Highways Act, authority was given to close for public use Blackstock Level Crossing on the main line, located at 85 miles 33 chains. The level crossing was, however, to be retained as an occupational crossing for the benefit of the adjoining landowners and their tenants. Attendance was subsequently withdrawn on 24th March, 1971 after the installation of wicket gates and attendant phones and the handing over of keys to the users. On the same date Wickham Market Junction signal box was abolished.

The station building, platform and carriage body at Marlesford are now in private hands. Upon closure of the line there was no electricity supply to the house whilst at the back a well supplied drinking water which was pumped daily and which was close to the cesspool. Along the line at Parham the station is greatly altered and is a private house.

The large goods shed at Framlingham has a preservation order on it to ensure its survival whilst the station became a vintage motor-cycle showroom and offices.

View of Framlingham station frontage in 1998. *Author*

Chapter Five

The Route Described

Wickham Market station, 84 miles 43 chains from Liverpool Street, was the junction station for the Framlingham branch. The station was not situated in Wickham Market but in the parish of Campsea Ash, the village bearing the station name being over two miles distant with the hamlet of Loudham in between. The double track East Suffolk main line was served by staggered platforms at Wickham Market, the down side originally 260 ft in length had the main station buildings including station master's house, booking office, booking hall, waiting rooms and staff rooms. The booking hall had two steps up to platform level, whilst the glazed waiting room had a wooden front and in the floor was a trapdoor covering the hand pump, a two-wheeled machine by which the porter filled the storage tank in the station house. A similar pump was used in the Union Workhouse. The awning was extended to include this waiting room. Next to the waiting room was the porters' room with the chimney and then W.H. Smith's timber bookshop.

The up side platform was an island originally 280 ft in length with the back platform served by the 520 ft up loop line, the normal arrival and departure point for Framlingham branch trains in the early years. Later the branch trains usually departed from the down main platform. Both platform faces were of a substandard height and steps were provided for the elderly and infirm passengers to join and alight from trains. No footbridge was provided at the station and a sleeper crossing connected the platforms. This was a dangerous place to cross especially when a train occupied the down platform and often the signalman in the adjacent box warned passengers of any danger. Despite this several people were killed on the crossing over the years. The abolition of the Campsea Ash road level crossing to the north of the station and its replacement with an overbridge in 1901 permitted the down platform to be extended to 500 ft to accommodate longer trains and avoid trains pulling up twice. Similarly on the up side the island platform was extended to a length of 430 ft, whilst the up loop line was lengthened to 930 ft. In the latter years both up and down platforms and up back platform could accommodate trains of seven 63 ft 6 in. bogie coaches. It was possible to run-round a train of nine bogie coaches in the down siding and 13 coaches in the up siding, by using the crossovers at each end of the station. In the event of longer trains requiring reversal the engine could run round the stock by using the crossover at Wickham Market Junction.

The goods yard was located on the down side of the main line south of the down platform and was served by two sidings, the 470 ft loop road and the 450 ft shed road serving the goods shed. At the north-east end of the layout the 140 ft-long dock road served the cattle dock and cattle pens at the back of the down platform. On the up side a 200 ft siding served the granary, whilst a trailing connection from the up main line served the 150 ft up dock road. As alterations were made to the platforms and loop lines so the goods yard siding layout was revised and roads extended. On the down side the loop road was extended to

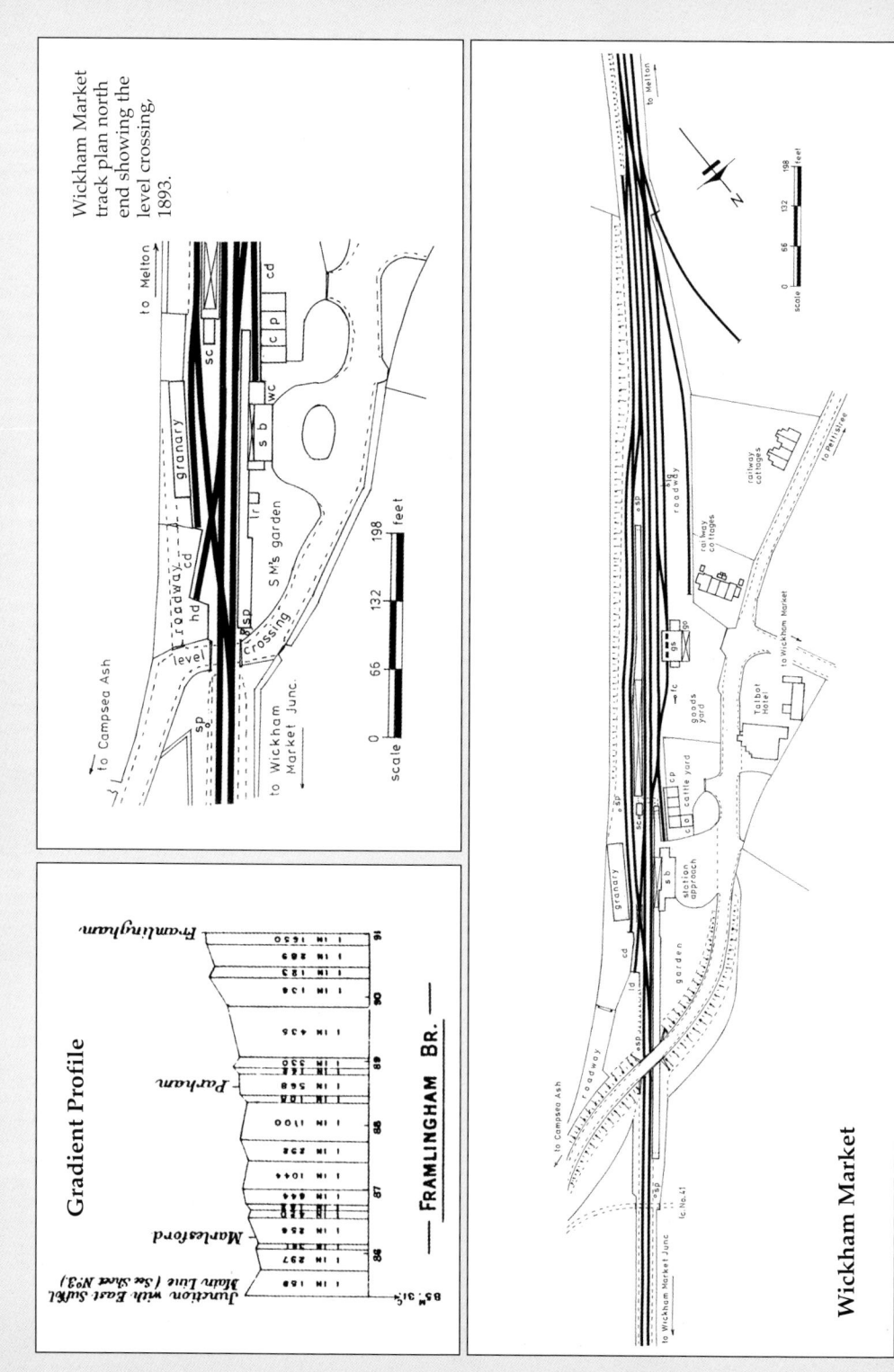

Wickham Market track plan north end showing the level crossing, 1893.

Gradient Profile

FRAMLINGHAM BR.

Framlingham

1 IN 1650
1 IN 289
1 IN 183
1 IN 136
1 IN 435
1 IN 330
1 IN 144
1 IN 568
1 IN 104
1 IN 1100
1 IN 234
1 IN 1044
1 IN 464
1 IN 256
1 IN 297
1 IN 159

Parham

Marlesford

Junction with East Suffolk Main Line (See Sheet No 3)

85° 31'½

feet
0   66   132   198
scale

to Melton

to Campsea Ash

granary

roadway

cd

level crossing

sp

S M's garden

Tr

s b

wc

sc

c p

cd

to Wickham Market Junc.

Wickham Market

to Melton

N

feet
0   66   132   198
scale

railway cottages

big roadway

railway cottages

to Pettistree

goods yard

Talbot Hotel

to Wickham Market

cattle yard

s b

station approach

garden

granary

cd

roadway

to Campsea Ash

to Wickham Market Junc.

lc No.41

The station approach to Wickham Market with the usual railway offices and staff accommodation on the ground floor and the station master's accommodation on the first floor. W.H. Smith's bookstall to the north of the station building is prominently advertised.

Author's Collection

Wickham Market station down side platform looking north viewed from the up platform with the signal box to the right and the infamous timber crossing in the foreground. Despite several deaths caused as passengers or staff crossed in front of approaching trains, the GER, LNER and later BR (ER) ignored demands for the provision of a footbridge. A cattle van is berthed in the carriage dock siding whilst the main station building incorporating booking hall, booking office and waiting and staff rooms is fronted by a canopy to afford waiting passenger some comfort from the elements. The down platform was extended in stages to accommodate increasingly lengthy main line trains and full extent to 500 ft was achieved in 1902 after the level crossing to the north of the station carrying the Wickham Market to Campsea Ash road was replaced by overbridge No. 438 the previous year. Note that the nameboard on the platform quotes the name as Campsea Ashe. *The late Dr Ian C. Allen*

Wickham Market station facing south in 1952. The crossover enabling Framlingham branch trains to depart the up side back platform and gain access to the down main line is in the foreground. The granary and attendant house is to the left served by granary road, which terminated in a loading dock. A second dock and dock siding is in the foreground. The signal box controlling all signals and points at the station is to the centre of the picture with the up side island platform beyond. The 500 ft-long down side main line platform, also used by the Framlingham branch train is to the right.   *The late Dr Ian C. Allen*

Wickham Market station facing towards Ipswich from the back of the up side loading dock. To the right is the down main platform with station buildings fronted by an ornate canopy whilst beyond the platform is the down side goods yard dominated by the goods shed. Some rationalization has already taken place in this view taken in 1965. One siding has already been removed from the up yard and the crossover points from the dock road are truncated to form a trap point to prevent vehicles running away on to the up main line by way of the trailing points near the signal box.   *The late Dr Ian C. Allen*

Wickham Market for Campsea Ash station, 84 miles 43 chains from Liverpool Street on the East Suffolk main line was the junction for the Framlingham branch. This view facing north from the up island towards Yarmouth and Lowestoft, dating from the 1930s, shows the down platform to the left, which was host to the main station buildings including the station master's house and station offices and staff rooms. To the left the points lead to the down side goods yard, whilst at the back of the down platform is the cattle dock siding serving the dock and cattle pens. The up side island platform, originally 280 ft in length and later extended to 430 ft, was relatively narrow and the awning was cut back on the up main platform. Framlingham branch trains usually terminated in the up back platform before the engine ran round the train to return along the branch. On occasions the branch train instead of starting from the up bay departed from the up main platform or after reversing over the crossover departed from the down main platform. The up side goods yard is to the right.   *Stations UK*

Wickham Market station looking north in 1948, with the up island platform to the right and the down platform beyond the goods wagon standing on the dock road. Wickham Market signal box, which controlled all points and signals at the station stands guardian at the north end of the island platform.   *Hilton Collection*

'B17' class 4-6-0 tender locomotive No. 61666 *Nottingham Forest* passing Wickham Market with a down parcels and milk empty train. This view from the overbridge north of the station shows the loading dock and granary to the left with Wickham Market signal box and the up yard beyond. The up and down platforms were staggered and the up island platform is hidden by the signal box. *The late Dr Ian C. Allen*

Wickham Market station facing towards Ipswich viewed from the over bridge north of the station. 'B12' class 4-6-0 No. 61577 hauling the annual weedkilling train is crossing from the back platform road to the down main line. On the right is the down main line platform and in the centre the signal box and up island platform. To the left of the picture is the loading dock served by the 150 ft dock road. *The late Dr Ian C. Allen*

600 ft, with 180 ft headshunt at the south end, whilst the shed road was extended to 550 ft and a crossover road installed between the two. The dock road at the north end was unaltered. On the up side an additional loop siding, 600 ft in length, was provided on the outside of the platform loop line and this had a 400 ft headshunt at the south end. The granary road at the north end of the loop was extended to a length of 300 ft whilst the rearrangement of track reduced the up dock siding to a length of 90 ft. Wickham Market station became an unstaffed halt in March 1967, with the introduction of pay-trains on the East Suffolk line. The main line was singled using the down road and only a simple glass shelter was provided on the down side platform.

Wickham Market signal box, dating from 1881, had a 31-lever Saxby & Farmer frame and controlled the points and signals at the station. It was located on the up side of the line at the north end of the up side island platform and opposite the south end of the down platform.

Leaving Wickham Market the Framlingham branch trains usually departed from the down main platform or crossed from the up loop to the down main lines via the crossover and followed the down main on a 1 in 104 falling gradient. Until 1901 the main lines bisected the level crossing, which carried the road linking Campsea Ash with Tunstall across the railway, but in that year the crossing was replaced by an overbridge constructed on the skew, No. 438 at 84 miles 49 chains. After construction of the bridge the down platform was extended under the structure to accommodate longer main line trains. Initially the up home signal stood protecting the level crossing gates, but when in 1901 the crossing was replaced by the overbridge the signal remained in the same position and drivers were obliged to read the signal over the bridge or a repeater through the arch. The down starting signal also protected the crossing but was moved further away from the signal box after the building of the bridge and stood at the end of the extended down platform. Later it was again moved further north so that the Wickham Market Junction down distant signal could be incorporated on the same post.

Away from Wickham Market the Framlingham branch train followed the double track East Suffolk main line on the 1 in 104 falling gradient in a north-easterly direction on a slight right-hand curve to pass over Buck's Head bridge No. 439 at 84 miles 78 chains. The line then negotiated two cuttings before bisecting Blackstock level crossing No. 44 at 85 miles 33 chains, where the road from Wickham Market to Blaxhall crossed the railway. Just before the level crossing was Wickham Market Junction down home signal with the left-hand arm denoting the Framlingham branch and the right hand the main line. The level crossing and junction with the Framlingham branch was controlled by the adjacent Wickham Market Junction signal box, equipped with a 15-lever McKenzie & Holland frame, originally with all levers working and later with 13 working and 2 spare levers. The structure was located on the down side of the line, immediately north of the level crossing, 85 miles 34 chains from Liverpool Street.

At this point the branch negotiated an 18 chains radius left-hand curve away from the East Suffolk main line and descended at 1 in 159 through a short cutting passing the up branch home signal on the up side of the line, with Blackstock Wood to the north of the railway, and where a 15 mph, later 20 mph,

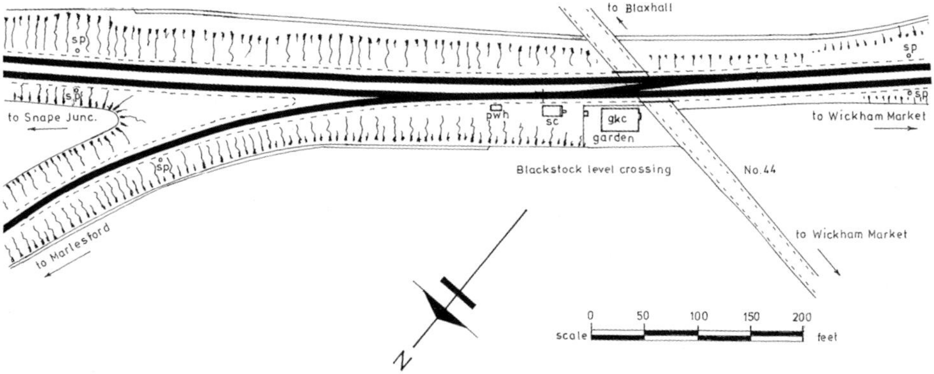

to Blaxhall

to Snape Junc.

pwh
sc
gkc
garden

Blackstock level crossing

No. 44

to Wickham Market

to Wickham Market

to Marlesford

scale

| 0 | 50 | 100 | 150 | 200 |

feet

N

Wickham Market Junction

'J15' class 0-6-0 tender locomotive No. 65447 sweeps left on to the Framlingham branch at Wickham Market Junction with the down 'bonus' goods train from Ipswich.

The late Dr Ian C. Allen

With the branch up home signal 'off', 'B12/3' class 4-6-0 No. 61561 eases round the curve at Wickham Market Junction with a through Sunday excursion from Framlingham to Liverpool Street in 1954. Further portions from either Norwich or Bury St Edmunds were connected to the Framlingham portion at Ipswich. The Wickham Market Junction up main line home signal stands guardian to the right of the picture. *The late Dr Ian C. Allen*

The signalman at Wickham Market Junction waits to collect the single line Train Staff from the fireman of 'J15' class 0-6-0 No. 65459 as she sweeps round the curve off the Framlingham branch with the daily goods train in 1958. The Train Staff weighing some 7½ lb., was round in shape and coloured green. *The late Dr Ian C. Allen*

'B1' class 4-6-0 tender locomotive No. 61223 speeds past Wickham Market Junction with an up express from Lowestoft and Yarmouth to Liverpool Street. Awaiting on the Framlingham branch at the branch up home signal and in the shelter of Blackstock Wood is an unidentified 'J15' class 0-6-0 tender locomotive with the up branch goods train. Because of the embankment the upper arm of the branch home co-acting signal is set at an angle to enable drivers to view for some distance on the approach to the junction. *The late Dr Ian C. Allen*

A down Liverpool Street to Yarmouth South Town express speeds past Wickham Market Junction in 1949 behind 'B1' class 4-6-0 tender locomotive No. 61056. The Framlingham branch swings away to the right. *The late Dr Ian C. Allen*

James Holden's 'C32' class 2-4-2 tank locomotives, with 5 ft 8 in. diameter driving wheels were built between 1893 and 1902 at Stratford works. A total of 50 locomotives were introduced into traffic, principally for use on longer distance semi-fast services from Liverpool Street to Southend and Bishop's Stortford. Soon after the turn of the century many were displaced and sent to GER country depots. At one time Framlingham shed had two of the class outbased from Ipswich but this was later reduced to one engine. The 'C32s' were later reclassified to 'F3' by the LNER and remained the mainstay motive power on the branch for many years. The engines based at Ipswich also worked the Felixstowe, Aldeburgh, Brightlingsea and Hadleigh branches. 'F3' class No. 67127 pulls on to the Framlingham branch at Wickham Market Junction with her two-coach train in June 1949. The locomotive was withdrawn from traffic in April 1953.

The late Dr Ian C. Allen

'F6' class 2-4-2 tank locomotive No. 67239 swings left from the East Suffolk main line at Wickham Market junction and makes for Framlingham with the branch train. In the background can be seen the gates of Blackstock level crossing. The signalman has yet to place the branch home signal back to danger. *The late Dr Ian C. Allen*

Marlesford

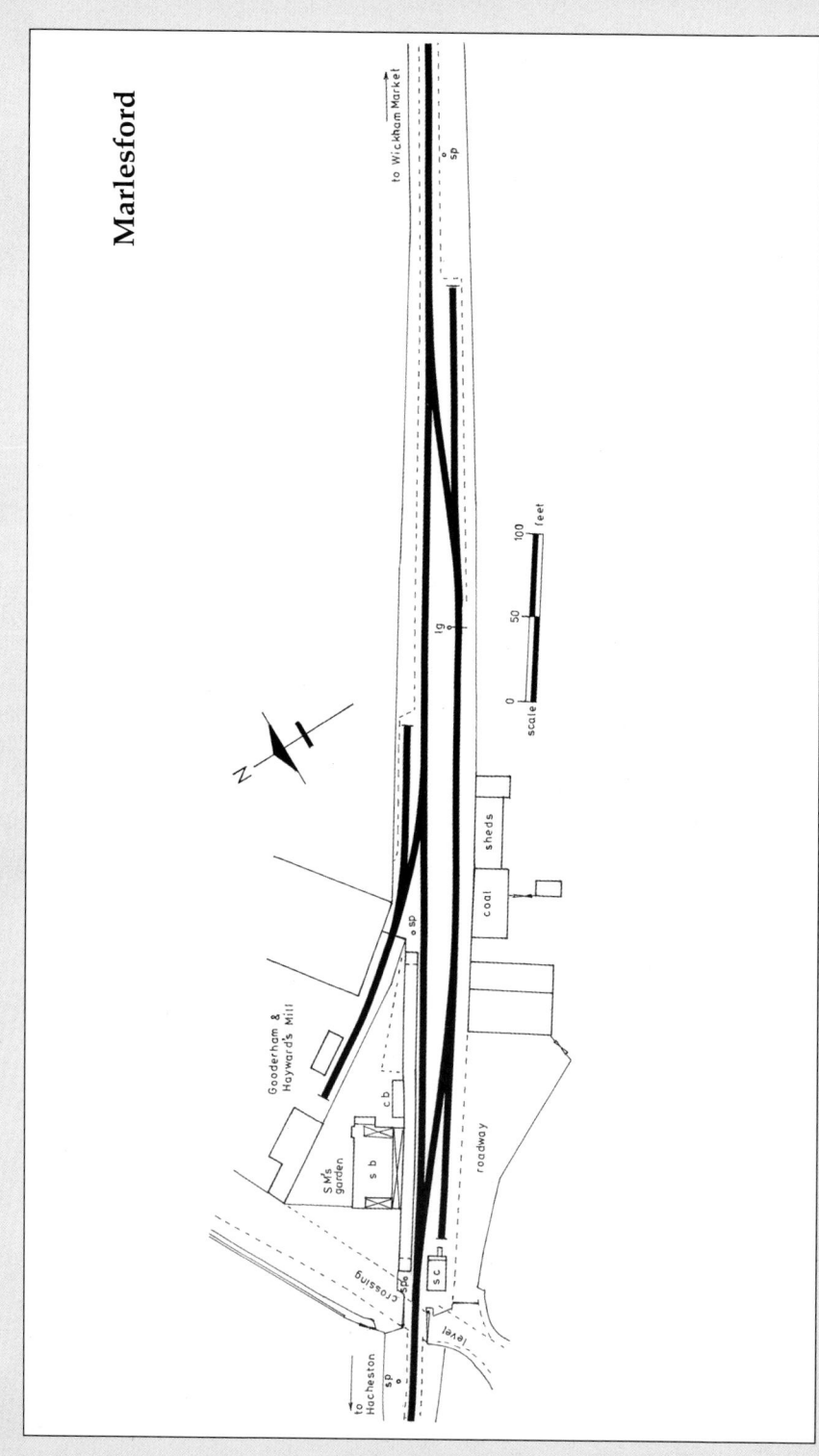

to Wickham Market

to Hacheston

Gooderham & Hayward's Mill

S M's garden

coal sheds

roadway

level crossing

sp

lg

c b

s b

s c

N

scale

0   50   100   feet

speed restriction was enforced in LNER days. The curve continued as the line emerged from the wood passing Wickham Market Junction up branch distant signal on the down side of the branch. This originally had a Coligny Welch lamp housing whilst the ladder was in front of the post. Wickham Market Junction up home signal was also unique in that it had co-acting arms, the higher arm at normal angle to the track whilst the lower arm was at an angle convenient for viewing from locomotive cab level. The line straightened out across arable land, with the River Ore close on the right-hand or up side of the railway, and then started to climb at 1 in 297 passing Marlesford down distant signal on the down side, before curving slightly to the right through a short tract of woodland known as Alder Carr where the 86 milepost was on the down side of the railway. Emerging from the wood the line dipped slightly at 1 in 381 over Alder Carr footpath crossing No. 1 at 86 miles 09 chains before climbing at 1 in 256 on the right-hand curve passing Marlesford down home signal on the down side of the line. Immediately beyond the signal the branch passed the entry points to the goods yard on the down side of the main single line and then entered Marlesford station, 86 miles 23 chains from Liverpool Street and 1 mile and 60 chains from Wickham Market. The 195 ft-long single platform, which could accommodate three 63 ft 6 in. bogie coaches, was located on the up or northern side of the line, with the up starting signal located immediately at the eastern end of the platform. Here were the ornate two-storey station buildings, including station master's house, booking office, waiting rooms and staff rooms. This was fronted by a modest canopy, which gave some protection for waiting passengers in inclement weather. Alongside the building was a coach body, which served initially as a waiting room and then as an oil and material store. The coach body was provided in 1902 and was formerly a suburban brake third No. 297 built to diagram 501 at Stratford at a cost of about £260. It was one of 72 constructed between 1871 and 1876 for the Enfield and Chingford suburban services and was withdrawn in December 1901.

The goods yard on the down side of the line was initially served by a 410 ft-long loop siding with entry points facing trains in both up and down directions. Later at each end of the layout headshunts were provided, the west end being 200 ft-long and the east end 110 ft in length. In 1923 the west end points of the loop siding were removed and only up trains could serve the yard. In 1903 a short 210 ft-long siding was installed on the up side of the line east of the platform to serve Gooderham and Hayward's mill at a cost of £303. This siding remained rail-served until goods traffic was withdrawn from Marlesford on and from 13th July, 1964.

Points and signals were controlled from Marlesford signal box located on the down side of the line opposite the station platform and adjacent to the level crossing. This was equipped with 21-lever Dutton frame with 15 working and 6 spare levers, later 20 working levers and 1 spare. As part of the rationalisation of branch working, the signal box was abolished in April 1923 and replaced by a 3-lever ground frame which controlled the points, the frame being released by Annett's key on the single line Train Staff. A 2-lever ground frame was also provided by the level crossing to operate the gate distant signals in conjunction with the level crossing gates.

Marlesford station facing towards Framlingham on 12th December, 1964 with the facing points to the goods siding on the down side of the line in the foreground. By this time a catch point had replaced the headshunt and the points from the main single line were operated from the three-lever ground frame. The station and level crossing gates are in the background.   *John Watling*

Marlesford station and goods yard siding on 12th December, 1964. The 210 ft-long siding to the right leading from the main single line served Gooderham and Hayward's Mill and was installed in 1903.   *John Watling*

The ornate station building at Marlesford with arched chimneys and ornate canopy over the platform. The station master's accommodation was on the first floor. The back wall of the platform is decorated with an array of advertisements as the porter-signalman and lad booking clerk pose for the photograph.   *Author's Collection*

The rear view of the ornate station building at Marlesford viewed from the A12 road on 12th December, 1964. The gate in the fence leads to the station master's garden and the front door to his premises, which mostly occupied the first floor.   *John Watling*

Marlesford station, 1 mile 60 chains from Wickham Market facing towards Framlingham with the signal box and entry points to the goods loop siding on the left. The gates protecting the London to Yarmouth main road, later A12 trunk road, are beside the signal box, themselves protected by the down starting signal at the end of the platform and beyond the level crossing the up home signal, with the spectacle located at a lower level on the post than the arm. The station building with station master's accommodation on the first floor has a central arch under the chimneys similar to buildings at Parham and Snape. A canopy fronts the usual ground floor station offices and rooms, whilst the coach body on the 195 ft-long platform was provided in 1902 for additional storage accommodation. The coach was formerly a suburban brake/third No. 297 built to diagram 501 at Stratford at a cost of about £260 and withdrawn in 1901.

Author's Collection

Marlesford station view facing towards Framlingham in November 1952 with the main A12 trunk road level crossing beyond the end of the platform. The points at the Framlingham end of the station leading to the single goods yard siding have already been removed so that access was only obtained at the east end of the layout. *The late Dr Ian C. Allen*

Marlesford station from the main road with level crossing gates in the foreground, viewed facing towards Wickham Market with the main entrance to the booking hall and office to the left. The curved building in the background is Gooderham and Haywood's Mill, which from 1903 was served by a siding off the main single line. The two-lever ground frame used to lock and unlock the level crossing gates and operate the associated gate distant signals can be seen just above the fence. *Author's Collection*

A view of Marlesford station and level crossing through the rear spectacle plate of approaching 'F6' class 2-4-2 tank locomotive No. 67230. *A. Forsyth*

Marlesford station 86 miles 23 chains from Liverpool Street and 1 mile 60 chains from Wickham Market with 'J15' class 0-6-0 tender locomotive No. 65389 running through the platform with the 'bonus' goods on 3rd May, 1958. The single siding on the down side of the line has now had the points removed from the west end and so No. 65389 will shunt the yard from the east end. Beyond the level crossing gates on the A12 can be seen in the distance the cottage at Lime House crossing, which was not railway owned.   *The late Dr Ian C. Allen*

A panoramic view across the shallow valley of the River Ore with St Andrew's church, Marlesford to the right and Marlesford Hall in the trees to the left. In the left foreground are the gates of Marlesford Ford level crossing No. 4, at 86 miles 55 chains from Liverpool Street.

Author's Collection

Away from Marlesford station the branch passed the down starting signal on the up side of the line before bisecting the main London to Yarmouth road, later A12, by level crossing No. 2 at 86 miles 25 chains and then passed the up home signal also on the up side protecting the crossing, and which had the arm at a greater height than the spectacle and lamp. The branch continued climbing at 1 in 256 as the line curved gradually across meadowland beside a footpath and over a culvert to Marlesford Lime House, also known as Cornish, crossing No. 3 at 86 miles 37 chains. No crossing cottage was provided adjacent to the railway and in GER days a crossing keeper operated the gates working from a lineside hut. After Grouping the LNER authorities quickly abolished the post to save costs and required trainmen to open and close the gates for the passage of trains and which were allowed extra running time on the journey across the branch. At Cornish crossing the branch line bisected the lane linking the minor road to Hacheston with Lime House. The gradient altered from 1 in 256 rising to 1 in 420 falling as the line entered a short shallow cutting to emerge on to a straight section climbing at 1 in 162 and bisecting Marlesford Ford level crossing No. 4 at 86 miles 55 chains from Liverpool Street, where the railway crossed a minor road leading to Marlesford village. The crossing keeper's cottage on the down side of the line west of the crossing was occupied by a permanent way ganger whose wife acted as gatekeeper. A concrete pillbox was erected adjacent to the level crossing in World War II and during air raids the family of the level crossing keeper would take shelter therein, usually joined by some people from the village. The gradient eased to 1 in 644 rising as the railway continued its relatively straight course passing Marlesford up distant signal on the down side with a view of St Andrew's Church, Marlesford away on the up side of the railway and on the banks of the winding River Ore. A footpath ran parallel on the up side of the line as the branch continued across a shallow embankment before bisecting Decoy footpath crossing No. 5 at 86 miles 77 chains and River Ore (Hacheston Culvert) underbridge No. 1102 (also at 86 miles 77 chains) in quick succession.

The single track railway then continued its relatively straight course climbing at 1 in 644 with the meandering River Ore and adjacent main road to Framlingham on the down side of the line. Soon after passing the 87 mile post the local road called Pound Lane approached the railway and ran parallel on the up side to Red Barn. The branch then descended at 1 in 1044 passing All Saints' Church, Hacheston away on the down side of the line. At the 87¼ mile post the formation followed a right-hand curve over a culvert where the Ore momentarily passed under the line to the up side. The railway then crossed Hacheston River underbridge No. 1103 at 87 miles 42 chains as the Ore again passed under the line to flow on the down side, and with the hamlet of Hacheston to the south-east of the railway. The line then climbed at 1 in 292 and at 87 miles 58 chains bisected a minor road from the village by Hacheston level crossing No. 6. Immediately beyond the crossing was Hacheston Halt also at 87 miles 58 chains from Liverpool Street and 3 miles 15 chains from Wickham Market, opened by the GER in 1922. The ground level platform 30 ft in length formed of ashes and clinker with timber revetment facing the track was located on the down side of the line. The basic facilities included a nameboard and a platform oil lamp for illumination during the hours of darkness.

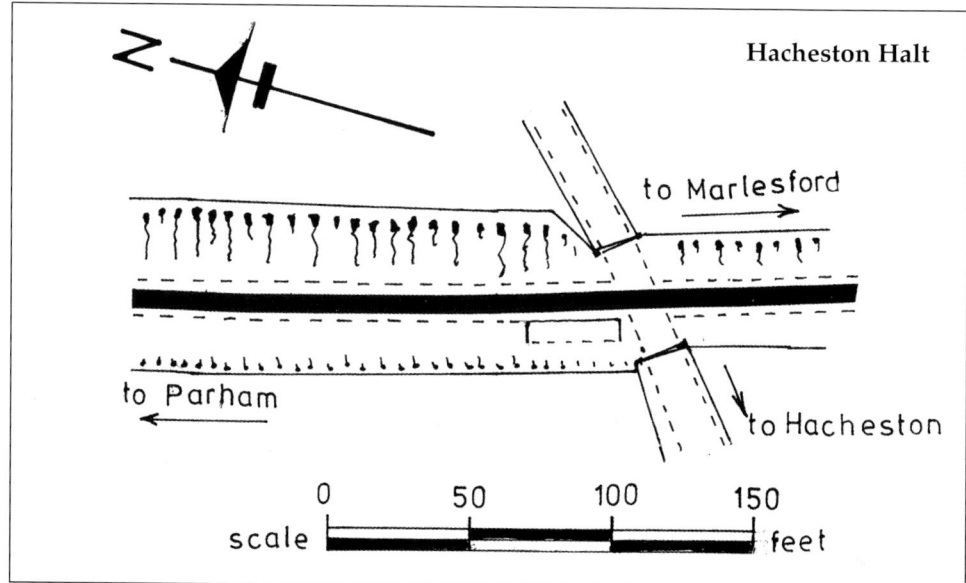

'D16/3' class 4-4-0 tender locomotive No. 62552 stops at Hacheston Halt whilst working a Framlingham to Liverpool Street Sunday excursion train in May 1952. As the main line stock was devoid of power-operated steps fitted to the branch stock, the Framlingham station master's household steps were carried in the brake van to allow the four adults and little girl to join the train, ably assisted by the guard.
The late Dr Ian C. Allen

Hacheston Halt, 87 miles 58 chains from Liverpool Street and 3 miles 15 chains from Wickham Market, was provided in the dying days of 1922 by the GER to counteract competition from local bus services. Located on the down side of the branch the halt had a 30 ft-long ground level platform with a sleeper revetment at a distance from the rail corresponding with the coping edge of a normal platform. A single oil lamp, lit and extinguished by the guard, a notice board and low level station nameboard completed the amenities. 'D16/3' class No. 62526 passes with a train of four Gresley corridor coaches forming a Framlingham to Liverpool Street excursion in 1952. *The late Dr Ian C. Allen*

A Sunday excursion from Framlingham to Liverpool Street pauses at Hacheston Halt, behind 'J15' class 0-6-0 No. 65447. A lady passenger is being assisted up the steps by the guard. Care had to be taken returning at night to ensure the brake van was located adjacent to the raised clinker of the halt platform. *The late Dr Ian C. Allen*

Parham

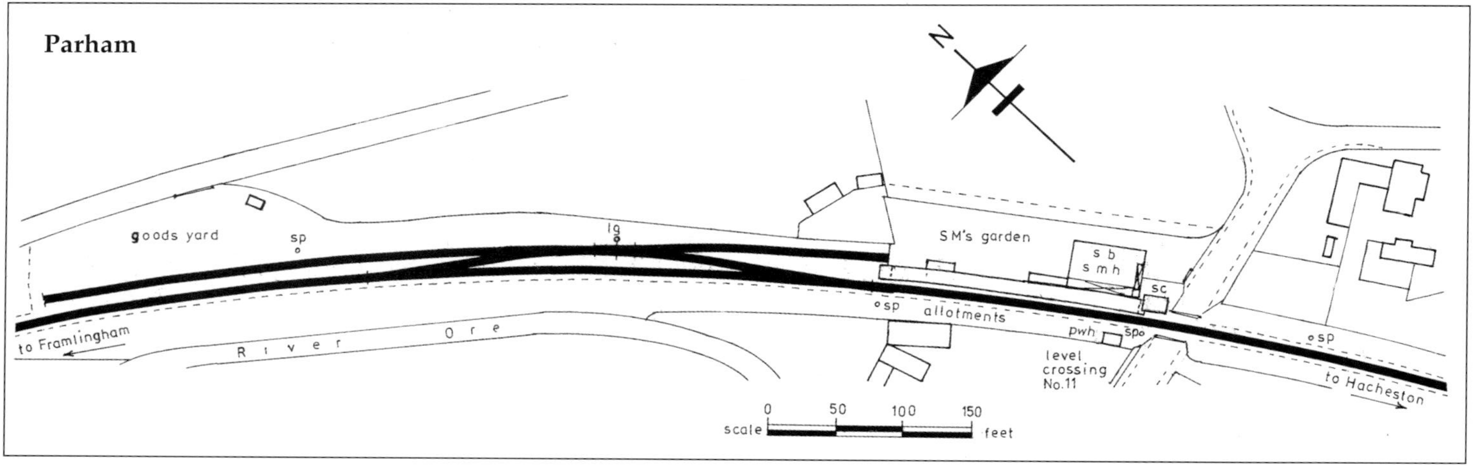

N

0	50	100	150

feet

scale

to Framlingham

to Hacheston

River Ore

goods yard

sp o

SM's garden

sp o allotments

s b

s m h

sc

Pwh

Spo

level crossing No.11

Left: For the last day of passenger working the branch train was strengthened to five coaches, formed of two, 2-coach ex-GER conductor-guard bogie coaches and a former LMS corridor coach. The formation is seen running into Parham station on 1st November, 1952 hauled by 'F6' class 2-4-2 tank locomotive No. 67239. In true branch line style the locomotive is devoid of a headlamp to denote the class of train. For the final up and down runs two additional ex-GER vehicles were added to the formation to cater for the 450-500 passengers who travelled.   *The late B.D.J. Walsh*

Beyond the halt the gradient fell at 1 in 1100 as the railway continued on a gentle right-hand curve and entered a cutting to emerge near the 88 mile post, with the River Ore meandering on the down side and a sand pit on the up side of the branch. Two occupation crossings, Nos. 8 and 9, were negotiated on this section but they were closed with the agreement of the owner in March 1917. The branch then followed a straight course and entered another short shallow cutting with Parham down distant signal located on the up side of the line. Here the moated Parham Hall was close by on the up, or north-east, side of the line. After a short straight section the line climbed at 1 in 108, with the River Ore closing in on the down side, and swung on a long left-hand 40 chain radius curve over Church crossing No. 10 at 88 miles 40 chains, where the footpath connecting the main road to St Mary's church, Parham, crossed the railway. There was a magnificent view of the flint building in the Perpendicular style on the up side of the line, whilst the river ran on the down side of the railway before meandering away. A short straight section of line on a 1 in 568 rising gradient brought the railway past Parham down home signal on the up side of the line to level crossing No. 11 at 88 miles 49 chains, where the lane from the main road to North Green and Cransford bisected the route. Immediately beyond the crossing the branch passed the up starting signal on the down side of the line and entered Parham station, 88 miles 51 chains from Liverpool Street and 4 miles 08 chains from Wickham Market, with its 200 ft-long platform located on the up side of the railway. The station, centrally located for the village and close to the main road had buildings of the ornate style, with hipped roof associated with the ESR, containing station master's accommodation, booking office, station master's office and waiting rooms. A projecting platform canopy afforded a covered area for waiting passengers.

Beyond the end of the platform, which could accommodate two 63 ft 6 in. bogie coaches, was the goods yard located on the up side of the line served originally by a 470 ft-long loop siding with a 220 ft headshunt at the south end serving a loading dock. A separate connection from the main line and facing down trains was also provided. Later the connection at the Framlingham end of the loop was removed and a 600 ft-long single siding installed served by facing and trailing points from the main single line with the north end 380 ft in length and south end 200 ft in length. The points and signals at Parham were controlled from the signal box, located on the up side of the line, immediately north of the level crossing. The signal box contained a 20-lever Dutton frame with 15 working and five spare levers. After the signal box was abolished in April 1923 the points were worked from a two-lever ground frame and all signals were abolished except the distant signals, which were retained as 'gate' distants and worked from a 2-lever ground frame located by the level crossing. The points leading to the goods yard at the Framlingham end of the station were also abolished.

Away from Parham the branch passed the down starting signal, located on the down side of the line and the up home signal located at the back of the goods yard loop before it continued climbing at 1 in 568 on a left-hand curve past the down advanced starting signal with the river again close on the down

Parham station 4 miles 08 chains from Wickham Market, was central to the small village. This view *c.*1910 shows the 200 ft-long platform on the up side of the line and the ornate station building, which had the usual station offices waiting rooms and staff rooms on the ground floor and the station master's accommodation on the first floor. Beyond the platform adjacent to the level crossing gates is the signal box, which contained a 20-lever frame with 15 working and five spare levers. The up starting signal, located on the down side of the line, and the tall down home signal in the background on the up side of the branch, protected the gates. The porter/signalman appears to be taking a close interest in the photographer. *Suffolk Record Office*

Detail of the station building and canopy at Parham on 16th May, 1965. There is evidence of settlement in the back wall to the platform. *John Watling*

Parham station showing the ornate station buildings and 200 ft-long platform on the up side of the railway. The gates of Parham crossing No. 11 are across the line. In the latter years of passenger train working Parham was reduced in status to a halt and the level crossing gates were opened by trainmen but closed by a member of station staff who acted as gatekeeper. The two-lever ground frame in the foreground worked the points which gave access to the small goods yard. View facing towards Wickham Market in 1952.   *The late B.D.J. Walsh*

Parham station and level crossing gates, view facing towards Wickham Market on 16th May, 1965. The former station master's garden was behind the fence.   *John Watling*

Parham station facing towards Framlingham in 1952; the small canopy provided for passenger protection in adverse weather fronts the station building. Beyond the platform points lead to the small goods yard, also located on the up side of the railway. *The late B.D.J. Walsh*

The lamp room by the level crossing at Parham station on 22nd January, 1966. *John Watling*

side. The branch then followed a straight course across arable fields before entering a cutting on the edge of a copse and bisecting a footpath at Parham Wood No. 1, crossing No. 12 at 88 miles 79 chains, where the gradient altered to a short 1 in 142 rising followed by 1 in 330 falling. Just after the 89 mile post, the branch emerged from the cutting and climbed at 1 in 435 for almost a mile, initially crossing Parham Wood footpath No. 2, level crossing No. 13, at 89 miles 06 chains before running across a shallow embankment where Parham up fixed distant signal and Brick Lane/Broadwater crossing down distant signal shared the same post on the up side of the line. At the end of the straight section the line again curved to run alongside and then cross the infant River Ore by Parham River bridge No. 1104 at 89 miles 27 chains. The left-hand curve continued as the railway then crossed the minor road to Parham House and Coles Green at Brick Lane crossing No. 14 at 89 miles 35 chains, also known locally as Sot's Hole, with the crossing keeper's cottage on the up side of the line and west of the road.

The branch continued its left-hand arc to run parallel to the Wickham Market to Framlingham road, where the gradient altered to 1 in 136 rising. The line then negotiated a long 40 chains radius right-hand curve with Broadwater Farm prominent on the down side of the line. The railway soon crossed the main road at Broadwater crossing No. 15 at 89 miles 73 chains with the crossing keeper's cottage on the down side of the line and west of the road. Just beyond the crossing the branch passed the 90 milepost and continued on its right-hand curve along a shallow embankment passing the local rifle range on the down side of the line, before again crossing the meandering River Ore and an occupational road by River Ore No. 1 underbridge No. 1105 at 90 miles 18 chains. Beyond the bridge the embankment gave way to a relatively deep cutting as the railway cut through Hoggate Hill on a falling gradient of 1 in 123. Framlingham down fixed distant and Broadwater crossing up distant signals sharing the same post were perched high on the bank on the down side of the line. In later years the down distant was relocated near the entrance to the cutting and further from Framlingham but before 1923 Framlingham's operating distant signal was located nearer to the terminus. Emerging from the cutting the line climbed again at 1 in 289 and bisected Hoggate Hill footpath No. 16 at 90 miles 32 chains and then ran across a shallow embankment and over the River Ore for the last time on River Ore No. 2 underbridge No. 1106 at 90 miles 45 chains. The branch then followed a straight course through the outskirts of Framlingham passing over Kettleburgh level crossing No. 17 at 90 miles 55 chains where the road from Brandeston and Kettleburgh bisected the railway and with the crossing keeper's cottage on the down side of the line north of the crossing. The line then continued its straight course on a 1 in 1650 rising gradient passing the rear of houses in Station Road, passing Framlingham down home and up advanced starting signals and then past the engine shed, granary, goods shed and associated sidings to terminate in Framlingham station, 91 miles 00 chains from Liverpool Street and 6 miles 37 chains from Wickham Market, although the buffer stops were actually 91 miles and 02 chains from Liverpool Street. The up starting signal was located at the immediate end of the platform.

A morning mixed train approaching Brick Lane crossing between Parham and Framlingham hauled by 'D16/2' class 4-4-0 No. 62590 deputising for the usual 'F6' class tank engine.

The late Dr Ian C. Allen

'F3' class 2-4-2 tank locomotive No. 7143 leaving Framlingham and approaching Hoggate Hill crossing with a mixed train in 1946. The two-coach conductor-guard set at the head of the formation consisted of a composite to diagram 227-1 and brake/third to diagram 527 followed by three covered vans, five open wagons and a goods brake van.   *The late Dr Ian C. Allen*

View facing towards Parham along the single main line at Framlingham with the Kettleburgh Road level crossing gates located in the distance beyond the down home signal. To the left are the back road and the goods loop road converging by points into the main single line. To the right is the 55 ft by 20 ft Framlingham engine shed just large enough to accommodate a single locomotive and in front ot the entrance a locomotive coal wagon. 'J15' class 0-6-0 tender locomotive No. 65467 is the allocated branch engine standing at the coaling dock and by the water tower supplied by Richard Garrett of Leiston in 1859.   *The late Dr Ian C. Allen*

'D16/3' class 4-4-0 tender locomotive No. 62552 trundles along the goods loop line in order to run-round its train at Framlingham in May 1952 prior to working a through Sunday excursion to Liverpool Street formed of BR Mark I and LNER corridor coaching stock. As it is the Sabbath the branch locomotive 'F6' class 2-4-2 tank locomotive No. 67239 stands out of steam on the adjacent shed road.   *The late Dr Ian C. Allen*

Framlingham

scale

40 0 40 80 120 160 feet

Left: View facing towards Framlingham station from the main single line showing the goods yard track layout on 16th May, 1965 just before the track was lifted. To the left is the shed road serving the locomotive shed, whilst to the right are the yard loop road, goods shed road and granary road. On the right is back road serving an assortment of traders' premises. *John Watling*

During shunting duties at Framlingham 'J15' class 0-6-0 tender locomotive No. 65445 is propelling an empty wagon and goods brake along the main single line and past the locomotive water tower alongside the shed road. A bulk grain wagon stands in the granary siding.

The late Dr Ian C. Allen

'J15' class 0-6-0 tender locomotive No. 65389 is working the 'bonus' goods trip from Ipswich to Saxmundham and return via Framlingham and Snape on 3rd May, 1958. Here she is shunting wagons along the goods loop line in readiness to form her train for the onward journey. The points leading to the goods shed road are in the foreground, whilst Framlingham signal box, bathed in sunlight, is to the left. The buffer stops of the granary road are to the right.   *The late Dr Ian C. Allen*

'B12/3' class 4-6-0 locomotive No. 61561 shunting round a train at Framlingham. The locomotive stands on the main single line almost at the extent of station limits. The shed road now devoid of the engine shed is on the right, flanked by the water tower and water crane. To the left is the goods yard run-round loop and back road. Note the home signal had also been removed by this time. *The late Dr Ian C. Allen*

A scene at Framlingham on 14th August, 1965 after the removal of the track. Sleepers litter the area whilst grain sacks are stored adjacent to the wall of the granary. In the background is the goods shed. Both buildings had capacity for the storage of 400 quarters of grain, which in the heyday of the railway reflected the large amount of traffic handled. *John Watling*

'B12/3' class 4-6-0 tender locomotive No. 61561 prepares to run-round the stock of a College special at Framlingham after having hauled the train from Ipswich. The goods shed is to the left and H.A. Walne Ltd's granary in the centre of the picture at the rear of the goods yard. Framlingham signal box can be seen through the trees alongside the train.   *The late Dr Ian C. Allen*

A close-up of the goods shed at Framlingham, which appears to be deputising as an engine shed to 'J15' class 0-6-0 No. 65454. However the truth is stranger than fiction. On Sunday 10th May, 1959 a morning exercise was arranged at Framlingham for the county rescue services, involving a simulated rail crash. St John's Ambulance Brigade provided the casualties and they were positioned in a most realistic manner in the two condemned coaches, seen in the loading dock siding by the station. No. 65454 borrowed from Stratford shed was positioned at the head of the train and worked to and fro within the station limits. At the end of the exercise the locomotive was positioned by the goods shed to await return to Stratford but when a crew were sent to collect her it was found the tender was devoid of water which had leaked through a small hole. It was 19th May before the tender was partially repaired and refilled and No. 65454 then piloted sister locomotive No. 65478 on the daily goods train to Ipswich. Later that day No. 65454 ran light engine to Stratford for scrapping.   *The late Dr Ian C. Allen*

A general view of the south end of the goods shed at Framlingham with the station beyond on 16th May, 1965. The shed road runs through the shed to terminate in the up side dock road whilst next to the shed is the goods loop line. The crossover leads to the main single line, the carriage dock siding and the cattle dock road. The buffer stops to the right are on the granary road.   *John Watling*

View taken on 14th August, 1965 after the contractors had removed the track at Framlingham, looking towards the station with the goods shed and associated goods office nearest the camera. Sleepers are heaped at various locations whilst weeds are beginning to encroach.   *John Watling*

Close up of the large goods shed at Framlingham from the yard access road showing the four doors available for loading and unloading carts, waggons and lorries from the shed platform. Note the canopy over two of the doors and the weeds beginning to encroach on the building; 14th August, 1965. *John Watling*

Framlingham possessed three fixed cranes. The 5 ton capacity crane was located in the goods yard, whilst the remaining two, each of 1 ton 10 cwt capacity were located on the loading platform in the goods shed. They are shown here with No. 40F nearest the camera. Note the beam roofing of the building. *John Watling*

A view facing towards Wickham Market from the end of the platform at Framlingham on 16th May, 1965 with the goods shed and associated goods office in the foreground. To the right the points from the main single line lead to the dock road and cattle dock road. Domestic coal is heaped beside the shed road to the left.   *John Watling*

Framlingham goods shed from the access road showing the four doors used for loading and offloading goods into and out of road vehicles, two of the entrances are protected by a short canopy. The goods office is nearest the camera, whilst back road is in the left foreground, 16th May, 1965.   *John Watling*

Framlingham station from the buffer stops in September 1953. Although 10 months have elapsed since the withdrawal of the passenger train service, the ornate canopy still protects the single platform but platform seats have been removed. The up starting signal stands at the end of the platform and beyond that is the goods shed. A rake of covered vans occupy the dock road behind the platform.
Stations UK

A view from the buffer stops at Framlingham station on 16th May, 1965 just before contractors removed the permanent way. The canopy over the platform has gone and only a stark wall gives evidence of the former station rooms. The goods shed is beyond the end of the platform and the carriage dock siding is to the right.
John Watling

Steam brake-only 'J15' class No. 65389 pulls wagons clear of the cattle dock siding at Framlingham on 3rd May, 1958. The engine was working the 'bonus' goods from Ipswich and after travelling to Framlingham returned to Wickham Market, where the wagons from the branch were deposited before continuing on to Saxmundham and the Snape branch. The train then returned to Wickham Market to collect the deposited wagons and continued on to Ipswich. After the initial departure from Ipswich no intermediate times were quoted in the working timetable for the 'bonus' goods and the train ran as expeditiously as possible to serve the intermediate stations. One way of achieving a quick turnround was by using a steam brake-only locomotive where no brake pipes had to be attached, hence No. 65389 and other unfitted 'J15s' with three-link couplings became firm favourites for the job. In the event of a brake fitted 'J15' locomotive with screw coupling being allocated to the diagram, invariably the brake pipes were never coupled. *The late Dr Ian C. Allen*

Framlingham station facing the buffer stops on 31st July, 1961 showing the full length canopy over the single platform, carriage dock road and cattle dock siding. *John Watling*

Framlingham station, facing the buffer stops, which were 91 miles 02 chains from Liverpool Street. This 1930s view shows a six-wheel coach berthed by the buffer stops and a rake of cattle wagons in the carriage dock road. Period advertisements for Hudson Super Soap, Wincarnis and Sunlight Soap adorn the wall backing on to the platform. A passenger waits in the sunshine on the platform seat for the next arriving train.   *Stations UK*

Framlingham station looking towards the buffer stops, with the dock siding and loading dock to the left on 16th May, 1965. By now the canopy over the platform had been cut back almost level with the concourse canopy. The carriage dock is to the left.   *John Watling*

Framlingham station, terminus of the branch on a wet day in 1952 showing the platform and coaching stock berthed in the down side dock road. The iron post and tubular rail fencing at the back of the platform is host to various shrubs, whilst the wooden post of the up starting signal is located to the right. The crossover in the foreground leads to the cattle dock road. In the background a number of covered vans stand on back road siding.   *The late B.D.J. Walsh*

Framlingham station, facing towards the buffer stops with the single platform on the up or northern side of the single line. A two-coach bogie set of coaches stands in the dock road. The difference in platform construction denotes where the extensions was made in 1930. The canopy in this view fronts the complete length of the station buildings but was later cut back.

The late Dr Ian C. Allen

The calm of an East Anglian branch line terminus. Framlingham station on 19th July, 1952 with 'F6' class 2-4-2 tank locomotive No. 67230 waiting to depart with the branch train to Wickham Market. The formation consists of former Great Central Railway fitted goods brake van No. E509451 and the branch two-coach conductor-guard set consisting of former GER corridor composite E63612E and corridor brake/third No. E62386E. A three plank open wagon and another brake/third coach occupy the carriage dock road. The cattle dock siding is to the left.

John H. Meredith

Close-up of the station buildings by the buffer stops at Framlingham, with the shortened canopy over the platform on 16th May, 1965.

John Watling

Framlingham station showing the goods yard access road and station buildings on 16th May, 1965, a month after closure. The additional buildings along the platform were added in 1893, the same date as the canopy was renewed and extended.   *John Watling*

The platform on the up side of the railway was 350 ft in length, having been extended by some 125 ft in 1930 for the Suffolk Show, and had a canopy for the protection of waiting passengers at the north end. The platform could accommodate four 63 ft 6 in.-long bogie coaches The main station buildings including station master's house, booking office, waiting rooms, lamp rooms and toilets were at the north end of the complex and the station entrance and exit faced on to the road junction of Station Road and Victoria Mill Road. On the corner of these roads was the Station Hotel.

On the down side of the line at the south end was the 55 ft by 20 ft engine shed with its associated water tank served by the 400 ft engine shed road, whilst at the north end and opposite the platform was the 250 ft carriage dock road and 130 ft headshunt, with the 270 ft cattle dock road running parallel to and at the back of the loading dock road. The goods yard was to the south of the station on the up side of the line and here the 105 ft by 30 ft goods shed was served by the 410 ft-long shed road off the down side goods loop line. Another connection off this loop was the 440 ft granary road and an extension from the loop was the 280 ft loading dock road, which served the dock at the back of the station platform. A connection from the goods loop served the 450 ft-long back road on the east of the yard together with the 180 ft headshunt, whilst a 510 ft-long extension to the back road served the various premises backing on the railway. It was possible to accommodate an eight-coach set of 63 ft 6 in. vehicles and locomotive between the pair of crossovers leading to and from the main single line off the goods loop line. The points and signals at Framlingham were controlled from Framlingham signal box, which contained a 27-lever Saxby & Farmer frame originally with 20 working and seven spare levers, then 18 working and nine spares, but later with reduced working levers after rationalisation of signalling on the branch in April 1923 when all working signals were removed. As a result of the Suffolk Show coming to the town in 1930 two signals were reinstated, including a down home on the up side of the line opposite the engine shed and up starter at the end of the platform together with the existing down fixed distant. The signal box and operating signals were abolished on 9th February, 1958.

The speed limit of Framlingham branch trains was restricted to 10 mph when passing over the points at Wickham Market Junction, later raised to 15 mph and then 20 mph by the LNER. On the branch the speed limit was 30 mph, later raised to 40 mph, although this was often exceeded. After the withdrawal of passenger services the speed limit was reduced to 25 mph. Mileposts were generally located on the down side of the line and gradients posts on the up side.

In GER days station staff rang a platform bell at Framlingham five minutes before the starting time of the train and again at starting time to warn passengers of the imminent departure.

(*Note*: The mileages shown are from GER, LNER and early BR documents - later surveys by BR showed differences of up to + 8½ chains.)

The ornate road frontage to Framlingham station in a semi-derelict condition on 16th May, 1965, a month after the withdrawal of the freight services and complete closure of the branch to all traffic. The station master's accommodation was on the first floor of the building and the booking hall, booking office, station master's office, waiting rooms and toilets were situated on the ground floor.   *John Watling*

'B12/3' class 4-6-0 tender locomotive No. 61533, working tender first, has just hauled the annual weedkilling train off the Framlingham branch and on to the up main line at Wickham Market Junction. The signal box and Blackstock level crossing can be seen by the rear brake van of the train.   *The late Dr Ian C. Allen*

The permanent way is formed of bullhead rails with the sleepers laid on a ballast of ashes and clinker. The annual visit by the permanent way weedkilling train to the Framlingham branch finds 'J15' class 0-6-0 tender locomotive No. 65478 easing round the curve away from Wickham Market Junction with her train consisting of a 'Toad D' goods brake van, two former Southern Railway utility vans, six tank wagons holding the chemicals, and another 'Toad D' brake van bring up the rear. The spray can be seen gushing on to the track from the leading utility van.

The late Dr Ian C. Allen

Chapter Six

Permanent Way, Signalling and Staff

Permanent Way

The initial permanent way of the Framlingham branch was formed of bridge rails weighing 60 lb. per yard fastened by means of dog spikes to sleepers laid on average 2 ft 4 in. apart. Ballast was a mixture of gravel and sand. The GER Engineer soon found the track to be unsuitable and in the late 1860s some sections were relaid with 75 lb. per yard bullhead rails. By the late 1870s the whole branch had been relaid with 80 lb. per yard bullhead rails in 24 ft lengths laid in chairs weighing 38 lb., fastened by iron spikes and wooden trenails to creosoted sleepers measuring 8 ft 6 in. by 10 in. by 5 in. Fishplates weighing 40 lb. per pair connected the rails.

Around the turn of the century bullhead rails weighing 85 and 90 lb. per yard gradually replaced the lighter track and these sufficed with the replacement of worn-out rails until just before the Grouping. From 1923 the LNER commenced replacing the 24 ft lengths with 30 ft and 45 ft rails, initially weighing 85 to 87 lb. per yard, but just before World War II 90 lb. per yard rails were introduced. Much of the track on the branch was second-hand after use on the main line. Bullhead track remained in use until closure of the branch and latterly some lengths of 95 lb. per yard rails were introduced.

The original ballast formed of a mixture of sand and gravel was soon found inadequate for it rotted the sleepers and was unsuitable for supporting the fairly light weight of the rolling stock used at that period. As tonnages increased the GER introduced ashes and clinker, having found that ashes were adequate for ballasting secondary and branch lines, and that supplies were readily available from the motive power depots on the system. When supplies were not available from locomotive sheds, wagon loads were obtained from Tate and Lyle's sugar refinery at Silvertown and, after the mid-1920s, from the British Sugar Corporation factories at Ipswich, Bury St Edmunds and Cantley.

George Summers was registered as a platelayer on the branch in 1859 but was later transferred to Halesworth and then served on the Snape branch. George Luck was a platelayer in the early years. Gangers employed on the branch in 1914 included William Bugg, who lived at Ford crossing cottage, Charles Barham at Brick Lane, James Winwright at Broadwater crossing and Arthur Henry Catchpole at Kettleburgh. All lived rent free in the crossing cottages in return for the employee and his wife opening and closing the gates for the passage of trains. By 1924 Henry Self was at Ford crossing, D. Fordham at Brick Lane, Robert Darnell at Broadwater whilst Arthur Catchpole was still at Kettleburgh. In later years Cecil Salter and his wife were at Broadwater crossing, Frank Ling at Marlesford, with Bill Fordham and Tom Nash, the latter from Campsea Ash. In the early years Charles King, who was gatekeeper at Broadwater crossing, was severely admonished on two occasions for failing to open the gates for the passage of a train. On the first occasion he admitted oversleeping and on the second for oversleeping 'at a religious meeting'. He was said to be 'of good report' but in a third unrelated incident one evening he was 'sitting on the railway arch near the target ground, waiting for his wife to return from shopping', when he fell asleep and dropped over the side of the structure into the River Ore. Shocked by his 24 ft fall and wet through he extracated himself from the water only to collapse unconscious on the adjacent occupational road track where he was discovered by his wife the following morning. Another malingering crossing keeper was John Pooley who was in charge of Sot's Hole or Brick Lane crossing. The gates were regularly smashed as Pooley 'could not hear the train approaching through the cutting in the fog', was 'hoeing his crops' or 'forgot the timetable'. In his defence it was stated the crossing cottage was not connected to the bell circuit system, which could have advised of approaching trains. Another crossing not connected to the bell system at one time was Marlesford Ford crossing where on one occasion the resident ganger had left his wife in charge. 'She in the meantime had developed toothache [as the *Framlingham Weekly News* reported] and in the arms of Morpheus took an Ariel flight into dreamland'. The 'shrill whistle of an engine failed to bring her mind back to sublunary matters' and the driver unable to stop the train was 'compelled to smash the gates'.

Two gangs were responsible for the maintenance of the permanent way, each gang comprising a ganger and four lengthmen. The Framlingham gang covered from Framlingham to Marlesford exclusive and the Wickham Market gang from Marlesford to Wickham Market Junction and the main line thence to Wickham Market. The permanent way staff allocated to the branch included Charlie Poacher, Jimmy Ling and Ganger Harry Taylor, whose wife Florrie was crossing keeper at Marlesford Ford level crossing in the 1930s where they lived rent free in return for her duties.

George Benham, a platelayer at Wickham Market retired on 13th May, 1927. On 4th February, 1927 H. Gray, who was employed as an underman at Wickham Market retired. A. Salisbury, a ganger based at Wickham Market retired on 26th December, 1930, whilst W.J. Haselup, a subganger for many years, died on 1st March, 1932 and ganger D. Edwards retired on 13th June, 1936. William Bugg a retired ganger from Marlesford died on 2nd September, 1932. Another long-serving member of staff at Marlesford was underman B. Knight who died in retirement on 19th May, 1935. W. Gibson, a lengthman retired on 14th August, 1948 after serving 41 years with the Wickham Market gang. W. Clow was also recorded as a platelayer on the Marlesford to Wickham Market Junction section of line. Other permanent way staff in the latter years were George Finch, Bill Fordham, Louis Ruffles, Jack Bennett and George Marjoram.

As well as attending to the day to day track maintenance, the permanent way gangs on the Framlingham branch were responsible for cleaning the toilets at stations where no mains sewerage existed and on hot summer days, especially during harvest time, they acted as beaters to extinguish any small fires caused by stray sparks emitted by passing locomotives. They also cut the grass on the side of the embankments and cuttings and this was used as fodder for railway horses, or in World War I sent to London and other East Anglia towns for feeding military horses.

The Framlingham branch always came under the control of the district engineer based at Ipswich, which in GER days was No. 6 District, later district civil engineer at Ipswich.

Signalling

The original signalling on the line was formed of semaphore signals with coloured aspect glasses rotating by the action of a connecting rod attached to bell crank levers and operated from station platforms. Each station and Wickham Market Junction had a stop signal for each direction of travel mounted on the same post on the platform and auxiliary or distant signals located 800 yards in rear of the stop signal.

As a result of the Regulation of Railways Act 1889, the GER authorities were required to renew most of the signalling equipment on the branch and by 1892 the old style semaphore signals were replaced by lower quadrant home and distant signals with pitch pine posts, cedar arms and cast- and wrought-iron fittings. The Act also required the interlocking of points and signals and new signals were provided to GER design. In common with GER practice, each signal arm was stamped on the reverse with the name of the controlling signal box. Around the turn of the century modifications were made to the operating distant signals on the branch. At that time the GER distant arms were painted the same red as stop signals and showed the same red and green aspects to drivers at night. To avoid confusion with home and starting signals, the distant signals were fitted with Coligny-Welch lamps which displayed an additional white > at night beside the signal aspect.

Wickham Market was provided with distant, home, starting and later advanced starting signals in the down direction and distant, home and starting signals on the up road. In addition starting signals were provided in each direction for the back platform loop road. Wickham Market Junction was provided with distant, home and starting signals for the down main line and a down home for the branch, the latter being on a bracket signal south of Blackstock level crossing, the left-hand arm denoting the branch and the right-hand arm denoting the main line. In the up direction distant, outer home, inner home and starting signals were provided on the up main line and a distant and home signal on the branch protecting the junction. The branch up home signal was difficult for drivers of approaching trains to view because of a shallow cutting so co-acting arms were mounted on a tall post, the upper arm at a different angle than the lower arm. An up outer home signal was provided on the branch for a short while from 1923 but this was later removed, as were the up and down starting signals on the main line. Marlesford and Parham stations were provided with distant, home and starting signals for each direction of travel with Parham having an additional down advanced starting signal, whilst Framlingham was provided with distant and home signals in the down direction and a starter and advanced starter for up road departures. After April 1923 Brick Lane and Broadwater crossings were provided with combined 'gate' distant signals for each direction of travel, the down distant signal on the approach to Brick Lane sharing the same post as Parham up distant signal, whilst the up distant for Broadwater shared the same post as Framlingham down fixed distant. The 'gate' distant signals were operated from a 2-lever ground frame by the Broadwater crossing keeper and the signals could not be cleared unless both crossings were clear for the passage of a train. After withdrawal of passenger services all remaining distant signals were fixed; the

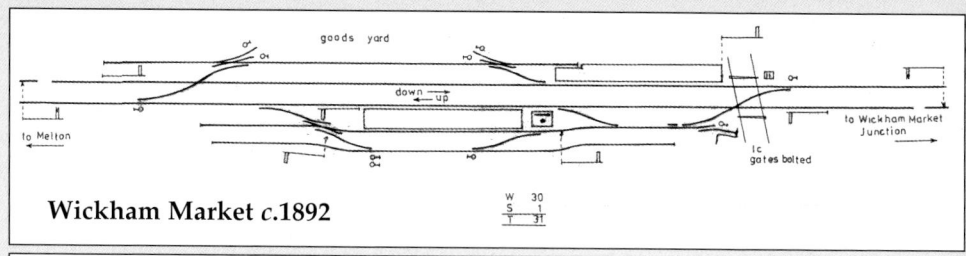

Wickham Market _c._1892

goods yard

down → up

to Melton

to Wickham Market Junction

lc gates bolted

W	30
S	1
T	31

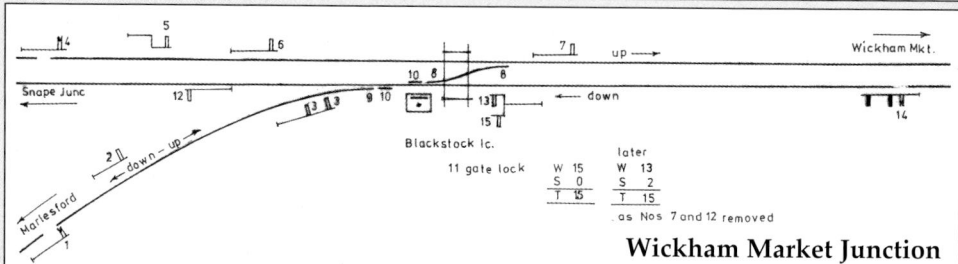

Wickham Market Junction

Snape Junc

← down

up →

Wickham Mkt.

Marlesford

down – up

Blackstock lc.

11 gate lock

W	15
S	0
T	15

later

W	13
S	2
T	15

as Nos 7 and 12 removed

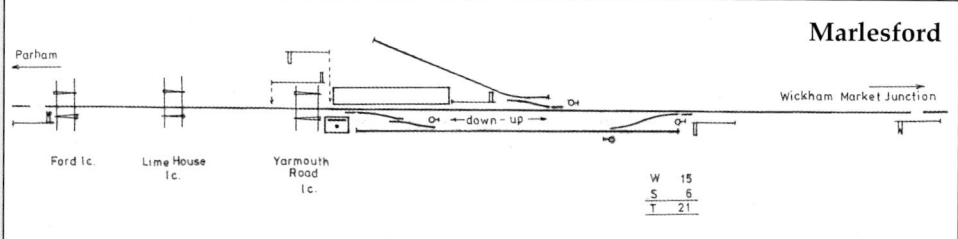

Marlesford

Parham

down – up

Wickham Market Junction

Ford lc.

Lime House lc.

Yarmouth Road lc.

W	15
S	6
T	21

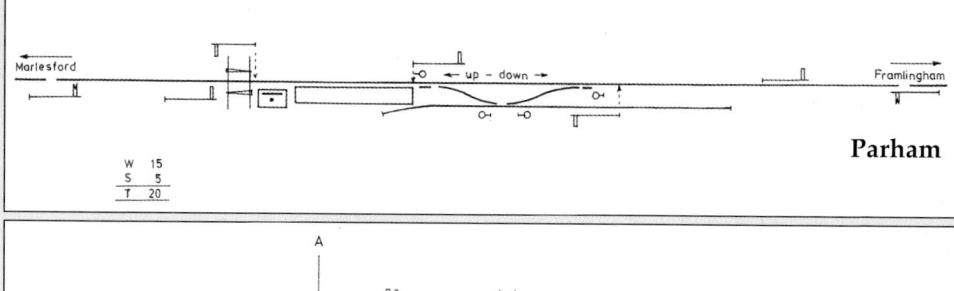

Parham

Marlesford

← up – down →

Framlingham

W	15
S	5
T	20

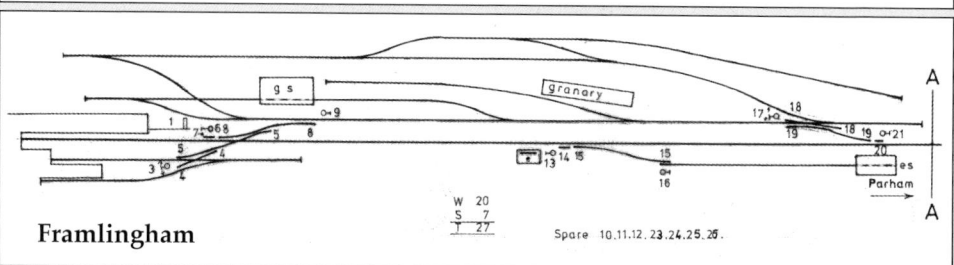

A

Parham

later fixed

Kettleburgh lc.

A

g s

granary

es Parham

A

Framlingham

W	20
S	7
T	27

Spare 10.11.12. 23.24.25.26.

A

Above: The fireman of the 'F3' class locomotive working an up branch service in 1937 hands the single line staff to the signalman at Wickham Market Junction. The gates of Blackstock level crossing No. 44 are in the foreground. *The late H.P. Lehmann*

Left: Framlingham down fixed distant signal located at an angle on the down side of the line. It was originally sited at the top of the cutting in the background. *Author's Collection*

An unusual view of the branch up home signal at Wickham Market Junction in June 1965 showing the lower arm angled to the post for sighting purposes. The upper arm behind the photographer was square to the post The lightly laid bullhead track with clinker and ash ballast forms a backdrop. *G.R. Mortimer*

Wickham Market signal box and up island platform viewed from the down platform facing towards Ipswich. The 'F6' class locomotive is shunting a goods brake van through the crossover from the up main line to the down main line after depositing the two-coach Framlingham branch train in the back platform. Note the low platform height of the island platform. The signal box contained a 31-lever Saxby and Farmer frame, initially with 27 working and four spare levers later with 30 working levers and one spare and from 1921 with all levers working. The signal box was abolished on 19th July, 1965. *The late Dr Ian C. Allen*

Wickham Market Junction signal box controlling the junction with the Framlingham branch was equipped with a 15-lever McKenzie & Holland frame, originally with all levers working but later with 13 working and two spare levers. Down branch trains gained access to the branch from the down main East Suffolk line whilst up branch trains entered the down main line before using the crossover to gain the up main line. The signalman also controlled the gates at the adjacent Blackstock level crossing. The signal box was abolished on 24th March, 1971. *Author*

Framlingham down distant being repositioned further from the station and in rear of the cutting which was its previous position, whilst Wickham Market Junction up fixed distant was located just beyond station limits at Marlesford.

With the advent of the LNER, the distant signals were gradually repainted the familiar yellow with black > and the Coligny-Welch lamps removed or modified to serve as ordinary lamps. As a result of the 1923 rationalisation programme the 'gate' distant signals at Marlesford and Parham were operated by lever on a ground frame at each station but this luxury was dispensed with after the withdrawal of passenger traffic in 1952 and all the distant signal arms were 'fixed' as non-operational. Gradually most of the crossing 'gate' distant signals were also removed. After World War II some of the remaining signal posts were found to be rotten and were replaced by those of tubular steel. Lower quadrant arms were replaced by LNER or BR upper quadrant arms on the same posts, including Wickham Market Junction up branch home and the down home and up starting signals at Framlingham, although the latter were removed on 9th February, 1958.

The Framlingham branch was initially worked on the One Engine in Steam or two or more coupled together principle utilising the Train Staff only. The Staff stations were Wickham Market Junction and Framlingham and the Train Staff was round in shape and coloured green and lettered 'Wickham Market and Framlingham'. By Special Order No. 1223 of 1st October, 1866 the working was converted to Train Staff and Ticket using the same Train Staff whilst the paper tickets were also green in colour. The Regulation of Railways Act 1889 amongst other things made block working mandatory on all lines, except those worked on the One Engine in Steam or Train Staff without Tickets principles. The GER commenced a programme of installation of block instruments but after investigation it was decided the volume of traffic on the Framlingham branch was insufficient to warrant the outlay on such equipment. To save costs and yet comply with the terms of the Act, One Engine in Steam or Two or more engines coupled together using the Train Staff only replaced the Train Staff and Ticket method of working. Block working using Tyer's single line instruments was, however, maintained between Wickham Market Junction signal box and Marlesford signal box to fully protect the junction with the main line until rationalisation of the branch working in 1923.

Wickham Market Station signal box of timber construction, measuring 24 ft by 11 ft with the operating floor 11 ft above rail level, and controlling block sections on the East Suffolk main line to Wickham Market Junction to the north and Melton station to the south, was initially equipped with a 28-lever Saxby & Farmer rocker and gridiron frame with 5 inch centres, with 27 working and one spare lever. In 1886 the frame was enlarged to 31 levers with 27 working and four spares but by 1892 this was altered to 30 working and one spare. By 1921 all 31 levers were in use. Wickham Market Junction signal box with stone lower section and timber upper section, and measuring 17 ft by 10 ft with operating floor 7 ft above rail level controlling access to the Framlingham branch, had block sections to Marlesford and also Snape Junction on the main line. It was equipped with a 15-lever McKenzie & Holland tappet frame with 6 inch centres, with 15 working levers, later 13 working levers and 2 spare levers. Both Wickham Market Station and Wickham Market Junction signal boxes were equipped with block switches. Marlesford signal box, built of timber and measuring 20 ft in length by 11 ft 6 in.

On an extremely wet Saturday 1st November, 1952, 'F6' class 2-4-2 tank locomotive No. 67239 hauling a branch train on the last day of passenger services swings over the junction points at Wickham Market Junction as the signalman waits to collect the single line Train Staff from the fireman. The leading coach of the train is a former LMS corridor vehicle, which was added to the formation to cater for the expected influx of extra passengers. *The late B.D.J. Walsh*

Steam brake-only 'J15' class 0-6-0 tender locomotive No. 65433 pulls off the Framlingham branch and on to the down East Suffolk main line past Wickham Market Junction signal box with the branch goods train. The fireman is handing the single line Train Staff to the signalman. The train would continue via the facing crossover onto the up main line to continue its journey to Wickham Market and Ipswich. *The late Dr Ian C. Allen*

wide with the operating floor 6 ft above rail level, had a 21-lever Dutton frame with 4½ inch centres, with 15 working and 6 spare levers and later 20 working and 1 spare. Parham signal box, also built of timber, measured 20 feet in length by 11 ft 6 in. in width with the operating floor 8 ft above rail level, had a 20-lever Dutton frame with 4½ inch centres with 15 working and five spare levers. In contrast the timber signal box at Framlingham measuring 23 ft in length by 11 ft 6 in. width with the operating floor 7 ft above rail level was equipped with a 27-lever Saxby & Farmer frame with 5 inch centres with 20 working and 7 spare levers, later 18 working and 9 spares. The working levers were much reduced after the 1923 rationalisation programme when all signals except the down distant were removed and a 'King Lever' installed, interlocked with the key on the Train Staff to enable the points and connections to continue to be worked from the signal box. During alterations LNER staff carried out the relocking of the frame. Four working levers were reinstated in 1930 to operate the down home and up starting signals and associated locking bars to ease movements of traffic for that year's Suffolk Agricultural Show traffic.

By 1897 Wickham Market Station signal box and Wickham Market Junction signal box were open continuously whilst Marlesford, Parham and Framlingham signal boxes were closed at night and on Sundays. In 1910 Wickham Market Junction signal box was open continuously, whilst the signal boxes on the branch were closed at night and on Sundays. During the summer months when a Sunday service was operated the branch boxes were open for the running of any booked trains but closed between the running of these services. Marlesford and Parham signal boxes were abolished in April 1923 as part of the branch rationalisation programme.

In 1926 Wickham Market Station signal box was open from 4.30 am until 8.30 pm on weekdays and from 8.00 am until 10.10 am and from 6.20 pm until 'Train Out of Section' was received for the last down or up evening passenger train on Sundays. Wickham Market Junction signal box was open from 6.00 am until 10.00 pm every day, whilst Framlingham signal box had to be manned for the running of trains shown in the working timetable and for trains specially advised. By 1940 Wickham Market signal box was open from 7.00 am to 10.00 pm on weekdays only, whilst Wickham Market Junction signal box was open on weekdays from 8.30 am until 7.40 pm and for Framlingham branch trains specially advised and on Sundays for Framlingham branch trains specially advised. The signal box at Framlingham was to be manned on weekdays and Sundays for the running of trains shown in the working timetable and for branch trains specially advised. By 1945 the only alteration was at Wickham Market Junction signal box, which was open on weekdays from 6.00 am until 10.00 pm.

In 1952 Wickham Market Station signal box was open from 7.00 am until 9.40 pm on Mondays to Saturdays whilst on Sundays it was open from 9.40 am until 'Train Out of Section' was received for the 9.10 am train ex-Yarmouth South Town and then from 6.45 pm until 'Train Out of Section' was received for the 7.10 pm train from Yarmouth South Town. Wickham Market Junction signal box was open from 8.20 am until 9.50 pm Mondays & Saturdays excepted and from 7.20 am until 9.50 pm Mondays & Saturdays only, whilst Framlingham signal box was open on weekdays for the running of trains shown in the working timetable and for trains specially advised and on Sundays by special

'F6' class 2-4-2 tank locomotive No. 67239 rolls the branch train past Framlingham signal box and into the terminus in August 1952. *D. Trevor Rowe*

Framlingham signal box located on the down side of the branch opposite the goods yard originally contained a 27 lever Saxby & Farmer frame with 20 working and seven spare levers and later 18 working and nine spares. After rationalisation of infrastructure and the installation of a 'King Lever' in April 1923, the number of working levers was much reduced but in 1930 for the Suffolk Show the number was increased to cater for the operation of new down home and up starting signals. The signal box was abolished on 9th February, 1958.

The late Dr Ian C. Allen

arrangement for branch trains specially advised. Framlingham signal box was abolished on 9th February, 1958 when the remaining signal arms were removed from the posts and all points converted to hand operation.

In 1961 Wickham Market Station signal box was open weekdays only during the winter months from 7.00 am until 'Train Out of Section' for the 6.08 am Ipswich to Leiston train and then from 10.20 am until 'Train Out of Section' for the Framlingham goods trip. It was then reopened from 12.45 pm until 'Train Out of Section' for the 12.00 noon ex-Framlingham. In summer the timings were slightly adjusted and the signal box was open weekdays only from 7.00 am until 'Train Out of Section' for the 6.10 am ex-Ipswich, from 10.00 am until 'Train Out of Section' for the Framlingham goods trip and finally from 12.45 pm until 'Train Out of Section' for the 12.45 pm ex-Framlingham. Wickham Market Junction signal box was open in the winter months from 7.20 am until 10.00 pm on Tuesdays and Wednesdays excepted and from 8.20 am until 10.00 pm on Tuesdays and Wednesdays only. In summer months the signal box was open on weekdays from 7.20 am (Tuesdays excepted) and 8.20 am (Tuesdays only) until 10.00 pm. Wickham Market Station signal box was abolished on 19th July, 1965 and Wickham Market Junction signal box was closed on 24th March, 1971.

As the only block telegraph on the Framlingham branch was between Wickham Market Junction signal box and Marlesford, no shunting was permitted at Marlesford, Parham or Framlingham unless the branch engine was at the station and performing the shunting. During adverse weather conditions including fog or falling snow it was not considered necessary to 'fog signal' at the intermediate stations but at Framlingham the signalman on duty was responsible for placing two detonators on the arrival line 200 yards in rear of the signal box. At Wickham Market Junction the junction signals on the branch were to be fog signalled as well as those on the main line. If it was necessary during fog or falling snow for stock or vehicles to cross the railway at Marlesford or Parham stations, two detonators were to be placed on the rail 200 yards from the level crossing in the direction whence the next train was due. After the abolition of the intermediate signal boxes at Marlesford and Parham in 1923, and in the absence of block telegraph working, no shunting was allowed on the branch single line unless the single line Train Staff was at the station.

In LNER and BR days it was permissible to shunt a main line train on to the Framlingham branch at Wickham Market Junction to enable more important trains to pass. In all cases the single line had to be cleared in sufficient time to avoid delaying the branch train. When shunting a train on to the branch single line, the Wickham Market signalman had to promptly advise the station master, or in his absence the person-in-charge, at Framlingham and carry out the same procedure once the branch single line was clear. If the single line at Wickham Market Junction was occupied by a main line train when the branch train was ready to leave Framlingham, the station master or person-in-charge had to advise the driver and guard of the branch train, instructing them to proceed cautiously and keep a sharp look out when approaching the signals protecting Wickham Market Junction. After the branch train had departed from Framlingham, a main line train was not to be shunted on to the branch single line at Wickham Market Junction. The branch single line could be used for shunting main line trains after the branch had closed for the night, but if the line was occupied when the line opened for traffic in the morning, the Wickham Market signalman had to advise Framlingham before the first train departed the terminus to enable the driver and guard to be cautioned. In foggy weather or during falling snow no main line train was to be shunted on to the branch unless fogsignalmen were stationed at the branch distant and outer home later home signals. The maintenance of the signalling and telegraph equipment on the Framlingham branch was always the responsibility of the signal fitting staff based at Ipswich

It is not always remembered that the railways first brought standard time throughout the country. Before the coming, each town or village varied in time from minutes to hours. The standard scheme finally adopted by the GER before the advent of the telegraph and radio was, like other companies, of giving a 10 am time signal via the single needle telegraph to each station and signal box on the system. By the time the headquarters at Liverpool Street had telegraphed down the line and the message had been manually passed on, it was three minutes past the hour before the stations and signal boxes on the Framlingham branch had received their time check. The gap in time was generally accepted and adjustments made, as this was a far better system of ensuring a standard time throughout the land than was possible by any other system. Once standard time was set, clocks and watches in the villages and town served by the line were invariably aligned with the station time.

Station Masters

Mr Brown was the initial station master at Framlingham but was dimissed in January 1860 to be replaced by Edward Whitehead who retired through ill health in November 1861. In November 1861 Frederick Peter Ketcher was appointed station master at Framlingham whilst Robert Saunders was in charge at Marlesford. Both were still there in 1868 when William Baldrey was station master at Parham and Frederick Short at Wickham Market. In 1872 Frederick Short replaced Ketcher at Framlingham whilst John Emms took charge at Parham as replacement for Baldrey and George Robert Hedges was at Marlesford. William James was appointed to the junction station in place of Short in 1889. He stayed at Wickham Market for 11 years before being replaced in 1900 by Alexander Dorling Gibbs. Gibbs was still at Wickham Market in 1914 when he was paying £22 0s. 0d. annual rent for the station master's accommodation, a rent that was raised to £24 0s. 0d. from 1st July, 1915.

By 1904 Emms was replaced by Francis H. Wadley at Parham, whilst along the branch at Marlesford Arthur Beeden had, in October 1901, taken charge in place of Hedges. In 1914 Beeden was paying annual rent of £14 11s. 8d. for the station house, which was increased to £15 0s. 0d. per annum from 1st June. After a stay of 19 years as station master Frederick Short retired from Framlingham and was replaced by Charles Murfitt in 1905. In 1912 Henry Jackson was appointed station master at Parham in succession to Wadley. Wadley had commenced his railway career in June 1881 and after Parham he served at Barnham on the Bury St Edmunds to Thetford line then Battlesbridge and finally Melton from where he retired on 31st May, 1930. Unfortunately within a month he had passed away. Jackson was paying £14 0s. 0d. annual rent in 1914 for the station house at Parham, which was increased to £15 0s. 0d. from 1st July, 1915. In complete contrast to Wadley, Henry Jackson who left Parham when control of the station passed to Framlingham enjoyed a long retirement and died on 26th March, 1948. Murfitt's incumbency at Framlingham was short for he retired on 31st January, 1914 and had a relatively short retirement for he died on 5th May, 1917. William James Gowen was the new station master at Framlingham and he remained at the terminus until October 1926. Murfitt had paid £20 3s. 4d. annual rental for the station house, but when Gowen moved in the rent was increased to £22 from 1st July, 1915 and then reduced to £21 by 1924. Gowen subsequently enjoyed nine years of retirement and died on 16th May, 1935. In July 1917 after a stay of almost 16 years at Marlesford Arthur Beeden transferred on promotion to Mellis where he served until 1930. In return Frederick John Stowe, who had been in charge at Mellis and prior to that at Wickford and Burnham Market, transferred to take charge at Wickham Market.

In the last month of 1922 station master A. Green of Marlesford gained promotion to Burnham Market, and the Marlesford post was then withdrawn, the station coming under the control of the station master at Wickham Market. At the same time the control of Parham station was transferred to Framlingham. Frederick John Stowe the station master at the junction, where he paid an annual rent of £23 for the station house in 1924, retired on 31st January, 1928 and lived until 29th April, 1940. He was succeeded by H.W. Holland, a relief clerk from Norwich Thorpe, but his stay was relatively short for he moved on to Halesworth in September 1930. The new incumbent at Wickham Market, including the charge of Marlesford was a local man, A.J. Morgan, who had previously been station master at Leiston. On 30th April, 1933, Charles Edward Reeve Banyard retired from the post of station master at Framlingham after 6½ years and in June it was announced that Thomas Walter Simpson, who had been chief clerk at the terminus, had been appointed to the vacant position to succeed him. After four years at Wickham Market A.J. Morgan retired on 11th April, 1934 and was succeeded by R. Lees who gained promotion from Bentley. Unfortunately Morgan hardly had time to enjoy his retirement for he passed away on 20th October of the same year. N.G. Ruggles, who was promoted from Felsted on the Bishop's Stortford to Braintree line, replaced Lees in September 1945 to serve at the junction station. At the end of the following month station master Thomas Walter Simpson retired from Framlingham after nearly 50 years service with the GER and LNER, having originally been appointed to the terminal station on 29th May, 1933. At a ceremony driver Manthorpe, the driver in charge, presented Simpson with an inscribed silk umbrella and a pouch of his favourite tobacco on behalf of the branch station and motive power staff. He also received a cheque from local farmers and businessmen in appreciation of his work over the 12 years he was in charge. V.C. Boulton, who transferred from Barnham on the Bury St Edmunds to Thetford branch, replaced Simpson on 25th February, 1946 and remained at the terminus until December 1955. From February 1956 until January 1962 David Loft was station master at Framlingham being succeeded by B.L.S. Unsworth from September 1962 until December 1963. The last station master to serve at Framlingham was A.D. Bellhouse.

An example of the ornate cottages provided by the East Suffolk Railway for the crossing keepers on the Framlingham branch. This is the cottage at Broadwater crossing, No. 15 at 89 miles 73 chains from Liverpool Street, where the B1116 road bisected the railway between Parham and Framlingham.   *R. Powell*

The fireman of a Framlingham to Wickham Market passenger service opening the gates at Lime House level crossing, also known as Cornish crossing, for the passage of the train in 1937. This crossing had been trainmen-operated from 1923 when the working of the branch was rationalised and extra running time was allowed in the timetable. The gates were fitted with a special lock and key, similar to the crossings on the Hadleigh branch where workings were similarly rationalised.   *The late H.P. Lehmann*

Traffic Staff

The gatekeeper at Broadwater crossing in the early years was John Naylor, who had joined the GER in 1863 and served as a signalman at Tottenham and then Hoe Street before transferring to the Suffolk branch. Prior to joining the GER, he had served with the 6th Dragoons serving in the Crimea and India and returned to north-east London after his sojourn at Broadwater and died at Hoe Street at the grand age of 83 in 1912. Along the line at Marlesford, A.H. Crane commenced his career in 1883 as junior porter. He remained at the intermediate station for some years before seeking promotion and finally retired from a signalman's position at Ipswich on 19th November, 1933.

In March 1912 George Stannard the crossing keeper at Broadwater crossing died. He had worked as a horseman at Diss for over 30 years before transferring to take charge of the level crossing in 1904. James Winwright, a ganger replaced Stannard and he lived in the crossing keeper's cottage rent free in return for himself and his wife opening and closing the crossing gates for all trains. Similar arrangements were in operation at other crossings on the branch. In 1924 Walter Messenger, a grade 1 porter, occupied the station house at Marlesford with Walter Barnes, a grade 1 porter, at Parham station house. Messenger's son succeeded his father as porter at Marlesford and was there when the line closed to traffic.

In 1892 Edward E. Smith, who had commenced his career at Parham, was promoted to the post of porter/signalman but after a few years on the branch transferred to Orwell station on the Ipswich to Felixstowe line. W. Battle, a retired horseman at the Junction station, passed away in January 1928 at the age of 82. John Bennett, a long serving porter at Framlingham, retired on 16th January, 1940, whilst Ray Taylor was a porter at Parham in World War II.

The first signalman appointed to the box at Wickham Market Junction on the opening of the Framlingham branch was a Mr Charlton. He remained in the post, signalling trains and opening and closing the level crossing gates for 36 years when Henry (Harry) Barnabus Graystone took over. Graystone was equally long-serving in the Junction signal box before retiring on 14th February, 1931. Edward E. Everett, a signalman at Wickham Market for 43 of his 50 years' service, retired on 13th April, 1936 and was presented with an easy chair, a pipe and pouch of tobacco by his colleagues. As a lad he had travelled on a carrier's cart from Maldon to Burnham-on-Crouch to witness the opening of the New Essex Lines branch to Southminster in 1889. Another Wickham Market signalman, George Sawyer, died in retirement on 13th November, 1939. A long-serving signalman at Wickham Market was Harold John Copping, who commenced his service as a porter at Hadleigh before joining the relief staff in the Ipswich District in 1908. Eleven years later he was appointed to Wickham Market and was still at the Station signal box when he collapsed and died suddenly on 9th August, 1948. In 1914 Everett and Sawyer lived at No. 1 and No. 4 Railway Terrace respectively paying an annual rental of £6 10s. 0d. whilst Copping lived in the cottage attached to the Granary and paid £5 4s. 0d. Other residents of Railway Terrace were James Clark, a ganger at No. 2 and William George Whymark, a shunter, at No. 3. Henry Barnabus Grayston, signalman at

Wickham Market Junction, occupied the cottage adjacent to Blackstock crossing in 1914, where he lived rent free in return for himself and his wife opening and closing the level crossing gates. By 1924 Jesse Poole, a shunter, occupied No. 4 Railway Terrace. Another signalman at Wickham Market in the 1920s was Leonard Sewell. Arthur H. Catchpole was signalman at Framlingham in 1917 and retired after many years' service on the branch on 1st May, 1932, before passing away on 9th November, 1936.

Of the guards based at Framlingham, John Emms, son of the station master at Parham, transferred in a similar capacity to Saffron Walden in 1904. Richard Groom was recorded as a passenger guard in 1920 before transferring to a similar post at Brightlingsea. Stan Templar, one of Framlingham's guards, as well as performing staff haircuts in his turn of duty was also a 'ladies man' and during one passionate affair managed to get left behind at Hacheston Halt after signalling 'right away' to the engine crew. Fortunately a passenger noticed he had not joined the train and pulled the communiction cord. A breathless Templar quickly rejoined the train with another 'affair' ruined. 'Painter' Snowling was a porter at Parham before transferring as guard at Framlingham and was responsible for working the last passenger train. James Bennett, a porter for many years at Framlingham, retired on 4th May, 1940.

Regular staff dinners were held in January of each year at Framlingham until 1915 when up to 15 personnel sat down to a four course meal financed from funds donated by local tradesmen.

The down side platform at Wickham Market in 1950 showing the main station building fronted by an ornate canopy over the platform. Some station staff are gathered in front of the running-in station nameboard pronouncing 'Wickham Market (Campsey Ash) change for Marlesford, Parham and Framlingham'. There was no mention of Hacheston Halt.

Author's Collection

Chapter Seven

Timetables and Traffic

The Framlingham branch was built essentially as a feeder railway to the East Suffolk main line and to appease certain notaries of the town after the route of direct line from Ipswich to Yarmouth and Lowestoft had by-passed the area. It was hoped the new line would help expand trade and thereby generate an increase in the population. Like many other routes built or absorbed by the GER, however, the area served formed part of large agricultural estates and the majority of the populace was employed on the land. Local industry was almost non-existent and therefore passenger traffic tended to be spasmodic and long distance, with the only regular traffic conveyed on Tuesdays, which was Ipswich market day, supplemented by the arrivals and departures of students attending Framlingham College. It is therefore surprising the branch supported a service of between four and seven weekday trains for 94 years, when the population of the towns and villages served by the line was below 4,000 and had decreased by 24½ per cent by the time passenger services were withdrawn. The population of the places served by the line was as under.

	1851	1861	1871	1881	1891	1901	1911	1921	1931	1951	1961
Framlingham	2,450	2,252	2,569	2,518	2,525	2,526	2,400	2,397	2,101	1,943	2,005
Parham	532	470	477	446	477	375	338	337	310	339	285
Hacheston	510	526	476	435	436	442	463	390	361	367	389
Marlesford	428	412	410	334	375	354	388	379	337	308	285
Campsea Ash	371	379	374	383	340	345	341	401	366	351	340
Wickham Market	1,697	1,571	1,541	1,469	1,537	1,417	1,343	1,259	1,210	1,167	1,283
Total *	3,920	3,660	3,932	3,733	3,813	3,697	3,589	3,503	3,109	2,957	2,964
Total +	5,988	5,610	5,847	5,585	5,690	5,459	5,273	5,163	4,685	4,475	4,587

* excluding Wickham Market and Campsea Ash. + including Wickham Market and Campsea Ash.

As will be noticed, all the places listed had fewer inhabitants in 1961 than they had in 1851.

In the late 1840s and early 1850s Mr Bloss, the landlord at the Crown and Anchor, Framlingham ran a horse-drawn coach once a day to and from Wickham Market, to connect with the main coach service linking Yarmouth and Ipswich. With the opening of the railway, connections with the outside world were vastly enhanced and the initial timetable operated by the ECR on the Framlingham branch from 1st June, 1859 was:

Up		Weekdays				Sundays	
		am	am	pm	pm	am	pm
Framlingham	dep.	6.50	11.50	4.30	7.10	7.20	7.30
Parham	dep.	6.57	11.57	4.37	7.17	7.27	7.37
Marlesford	dep.	7.03	12.04	4.43	7.22	7.33	7.43
Wickham Market	arr.	7.10	12.11	4.50	7.30	7.40	7.50

Down		am	pm	pm	pm	am	pm
Wickham Market	dep.	7.43	12.53	3.15	7.35	8.53	8.43
Marlesford	dep.	7.49	12.59	3.22	7.42	8.59	8.49
Parham	dep.	7.54	1.04	3.28	7.48	9.04	8.54
Framlingham	arr.	8.00	1.10	3.35	7.55	9.10	9.00

January 1, 1863. 60

EAST SUFFOLK DISTRICT.—BRANCHES.

Down. Framlingham Branch.—(Single Line.)

Week Days. **Sundays.**

Miles from Wckhm M.	FROM	1 Pass 1 2 3	2 Parl. 1 2 3	3 Pass 1 2	4 Pass 1 2	5 Pass 1 2 3	6	7	8	9	10 Pass 1 2 3	11 Parl. 1 2 3	12	13	14
		a.m.	p.m.	p.m.	p.m.	p.m.					a.m.	p.m.			
—	Wickham Market......	7 40	12 40	3 12	5 10	7 43	...	...	...	...	8 50	8 36	...	...	...
1¾	Marlesford	7 48	12 48	3 20	5 18	7 50	...	...	...	...	8 58	8 45	...	...	...
4¼	Parham	7 56	12 54	3 26	5 27	7 57	...	...	...	...	9 6	8 54	...	...	...
6¼	Framlingham	8 5	1 0	3 35	5 35	8 5	...	...	...	...	9 15	9 0	...	...	...

On this Branch the load of the Branch Engine is not to exceed 10 Trucks, and the load of the regular Goods Trains is not to exceed 20 Trucks.
Goods will be worked by the ordinary Passenger Trains when necessary.

Up.

Week Days. **Sundays.**

Miles from Frmlghm	FROM	1 Parl. 1 2 3	2 Pass. 1 2	3 Pass 1 2	4 Pass 1 2 3	5 Pass 1 2 3	6	7	8	9	10 Parl. 1 2 3	11 Pass 1 2 3	12	13	14
		a.m.	noon	p.m.	p.m.	p.m.					a.m.	p.m.			
—	Framlingham	6 50	12 0	2 35	4 30	7 0	...	...	...	...	7 15	7 15	...	...	...
2¼	Parham	6 57	12 8	2 43	4 38	7 7	...	...	...	...	7 23	7 23	...	...	...
4½	Marlesford	7 4	12 16	2 52	4 45	7 15	...	...	...	...	7 32	7 32	...	...	...
6¼	Wickham Market......	7 14	12 24	3 0	4 55	7 25	...	...	...	...	7 40	7 40	...	...	...

When required the Framlingham Branch Engine will perform a Special Trip between 8.0 a.m. and 11.0 a.m., between Framlingham and Wickham Market, for the service of the Goods Traffic.
Third Class locally by all Trains between Framlingham and Wickham Market.

GER Working Timetable 1863.

GER Working Timetable 1870.

The Trains on this Branch are to be worked under the Train Staff and Train Ticket arrangements, as laid down in Special Order, No. 1223, dated October 1st, 1866.
No Engine or Train is to be run on this Branch without a Train Staff or Train Ticket. The Train Staff Stations are Wickham Market and Framlingham.

FRAMLINGHAM BRANCH.

Single Line.

Down Trains. **Week Days**

Miles from Wickham M.	FROM	1 Pass. 1 2 3	2 Parl. 1 2 3	3 A Pass. 1 2 3	4 B Pass. 1 2 3	5 Pass. 1 2 3	6	7	8	9	10	11	12
		a.m.	p.m.	p.m.	p.m.	p.m.							
—	**Wickham Market** dep.	8 0	12 58	3 5	5 20	7 58	...	...	...	...	...	...	...
1¾	Marlesford	8 8	1 0	3 12	5 28	8 6	...	...	...	...	...	...	...
4¼	Parham	8 16	1 10	3 22	5 37	8 15	...	...	...	...	...	...	...
6¼	**Framlingham** ......arr	8 25	1 18	3 30	5 45	8 23	...	...	...	...	...	...	...

A No. 3 runs on Thursdays only.
B No. 4 runs on Thursdays and Saturdays only.
Goods are worked by Passenger Trains when necessary.

Up Trains. **Week Days.**

Miles from Framlinghm	FROM	1 Parl. 1 2 3	2 Parl. 1 2 3	3 C Pass. 1 2 3	4 Pass. 1 2 3	5 D Pass. 1 2 3	6	7	8	9	10	11	12
		a.m.	noon	p.m.	p.m.	p.m.							
—	**Framlingham** ......dep.	6 55	12 10	2 30	4 40	6 55	...	...	...	...	...	...	...
2¼	Parham	7 2	12 16	2 37	4 48	7 2	...	...	...	...	...	...	...
4½	Marlesford	7 10	12 23	2 45	4 55	7 10	...	...	...	...	...	...	...
6¼	**Wickham Market** arr.	7 18	12 32	2 53	5 5	7 20	...	...	...	...	...	...	...

C No. 3 runs on Thursdays only.
D No. 5 runs on Thursdays and Saturdays only.
When required the Framlingham Branch Engine will perform a Special Trip between 8.30 a.m. and 11 a.m., between Framlingham and Wickham Market, for the service of the Goods Traffic.

Passenger trains worked goods traffic when necessary, although the branch engine was permitted to perform a special goods trip between Framlingham and Wickham Market between 8.00 am and 11.00 am. Within a short while the 11.50 am train from Framlingham was retimed to depart at 11.40 am and an additional train departed at 2.45 pm.

By 1862 the working timetable showed an increased service of five passenger trains in each direction, with two each way on Sundays and all conveying third class accommodation. Trains departed Framlingham at 6.50 am, 12.00 noon, 2.35, 4.30 and 7.00 pm returning from Wickham Market at 7.40 am, 12.40, 3.12, 5.10 and 7.43 pm. Up departures from Framlingham on Sundays were 7.15 am and 7.15 pm with the return from Wickham Market at 8.50 am and 8.36 pm. Goods traffic was worked by ordinary passenger services where necessary, although the branch engine, as before, could work a special goods trip from Framlingham to Wickham Market between 8.00 am and 11.00 am. On the branch the load of the branch engine was not to exceed 10 trucks and the load of regular goods trains not to exceed 20 trucks.

Except for minor alterations in timing the working timetable for 1865 continued to show five passenger trains each way on weekdays and two in each direction on Sundays. Up trains departed Framlingham at 6.50 am, 12.05, 2.35, 4.30 and 7.00pm on weekdays and 7.15 am and 7.15 pm on Sundays. Down departures from Wickham Market were 8.02 am, 12.50, 3.12, 5.10 and 7.52 pm on weekdays and 8.50 am and 8.35 pm on Sundays. Goods continued to be conveyed by passenger services.

As the years progressed it became evident to the GE authorities that the service provided on the Framlingham branch was on the generous side for the receipts earned, and in 1868 some services were altered to run on Thursdays and/or Saturdays only. Early in July 1869 the residents of Framlingham and the surrounding neighbourhood submitted a memorandum asking for the 3.15 pm Thursdays-only train from Wickham Market to Framlingham, which provided a connection off the 11.42 am train from London, to run daily. Robertson, the superintendent, duly investigated and reported to the Traffic Committee on 13th July that he thought it would be unremunerative to run the train every day and the request was subsequently declined.

The working timetable for 1870 showed three passengers trains in each direction on Mondays, Tuesdays, Wednesdays and Fridays, with four each way on Saturdays and five on Thursdays. Up trains departed from Framlingham at 6.55 am, 12.10, 2.50 (Thursdays only), 4.40 and 6.55 pm (Thursdays and Saturdays only), whilst down services returned from Wickham Market at 8.00 am, 12.53, 3.05 (Thursdays only), 5.20 (Thursdays and Saturdays only) and 7.58 pm. Trains were allowed 22 to 25 minutes for the 6 miles 37 chains journey, and passenger trains worked the goods traffic when necessary. In the event of any large consignments requiring to be moved the Framlingham branch engine was permitted to work a special goods trip between 8.30 and 11.00 am. The timetable was meagre in the extreme and the three-train service on Mondays, Tuesdays and Fridays offered no solace to passengers missing the 12.53 pm down departure from Wickham Market for they had to wait until 7.58 pm for the next service to Framlingham!

The Trains on this Single Line are worked by Train Staff and Train Staff Ticket, according to the "Train Staff Regulations" contained in the "Appendix" to this Working Time Book. No Engine or Train is to be run on this Branch without a Train Staff or Train Staff Ticket. The Train Staff Stations are Wickham Market and Framlingham.

FRAMLINGHAM BRANCH.—*Single Line.*

Down Trains—Week Days.

Miles from Wickham M.	FROM	1	2	3	4	5	6	7	8	9	10	11	12	13
		Pass.	Parl.	Pass.	Pass.	Pass.								
		a.m.	p.m.	p.m.	p.m.	p.m.								
—	**Wickham Mkt.** dep.	7 55	12 55	2 38	5 22	7 55	.....	.....	.....	.....	.....	.....	.....	.....
1¾	Marlesford .... "	8 3	1 2	2 45	5 29	8 3	...	...	...	...	...	...	...	...
4½	Parham .... "	8 11	1 11	2 53	5 37	8 11	.....	.....	.....	.....	.....	.....	.....	.....
6½	**Framlingham** ...arr.	8 20	1 20	3 2	5 45	8 20	...	...	...	...	...	...	...	...

Goods are worked by Passenger Trains when necessary.

Up Trains—Week Days.

Miles from Framlingham	FROM	1	2	3	4	5	6	7	8	9	10	11	12	13
		Parl.	Pass.	Pass.	Pass.	Pass.								
		a.m.	noon	p.m.	p.m.	p.m.								
—	**Framlingham** ..dep.	7 20	12 0	2 0	4 35	6 50	.....	.....	.....	.....	.....	.....	.....	.....
2¼	Parham .... "	7 26	12 6	2 6	4 42	6 57	...	...	...	...	...	...	...	...
4½	Marlesford .... arr.	7 32	12 12	2 12	4 49	7 4	.....	.....	.....	.....	.....	.....	.....	.....
	Marlesford .... dep.	7 34	12 14	2 14	4 51	7 7	...	...	...	...	...	...	...	...
6½	**Wickham Mkt.** arr.	7 42	12 22	2 22	4 58	7 15	.....	.....	.....	.....	.....	.....	.....	.....

When required, the Framlingham Branch Engine will perform a Special Trip between 8.30 a.m. and 11.0 a.m., between Framlingham and Wickham Market, for the service of the Goods Traffic.

Left: GER Working Timetable 1883.

FRAMLINGHAM BRANCH.

Junction with East Suffolk Main Line at Wickham Market.

WEEK DAYS.

Miles from Wickham M.	DOWN TRAINS. FROM		Tusdys only.			Saturdays only.		
		morn	morn	morn	even.		even.	even.
	LONDON (Lpool St.) dep.	5 10		10 0	12 0		3 20	5 0
	Colchester .... "	6 29		11 19	1 23		4 10	5 35
	Ipswich .... "	7 8		11 58	2 6		5 6	6 50
	Wickham Market ......arr.	7 46		12 27	2 44		5 37	7 29
	Yarmouth .... dep.	6 15	8 15	11 15	...		4 0	6 30
	Lowestoft .... "	6 20	8 17	11 17	...		3 50	6 27
	Beccles .... "	6 54	8 48	11 50	...		4 31	7 2
	Wickham Market ......arr.	7 51	9 36	12 47	...		5 19	7 53
	Wickham Market ...dep.	7 55	9 40	12 50	2 50		5 42	7 55
1¾	Marlesford	8 3	9 47	12 57	2 57		5 49	8 3
4½	Parham	8 11	9 55	1 6	3 5		5 57	8 11
6½	**Framlingham** ....arr.	8 20	10 4	1 15	3 15		6 5	8 20

WEEK DAYS.

Miles from Framlingham	UP TRAINS. FROM		Tusdy only.			Saturdays only.		
		morn	morn	noon	even.		even.	even.
	Framlingham ....dep.	7 20	9 5	12 0	2 10		4 47	7 0
2¼	Parham	7 26	9 11	12 6	2 16		4 54	7 6
4½	Marlesford	7 34	9 19	12 14	2 24		5 3	7 14
6½	**Wickham Market**	7 42	9 27	12 22	2 32		5 10	7 22
	Wickham Market ......dep.	7 46		12 27	2 44		5 37	7 29
31½	Beccles ....arr.	8 38		1 16	3 38		6 25	8 23
39¾	Lowestoft .... "	9 20		1 43	4 15		6 58	8 51
43¾	Yarmouth .... "	9 20		1 45	4 17		6 55	9 2
	Wickham Market ......dep.	7 51	9 36	12 47	3 39		5 19	7 53
72¼	Ipswich ....arr.	8 35	10 10	1 28	4 10		5 56	8 30
89	Colchester........ "	9 15	10 45	2 7	4 47		6 42	...
	LONDON (Lpool St.) "	10 30	12 15	3 25	6 0		8 0	...

Left: GER Public Timetable 1884.

The poor service resulted in George E. Jeafferson submitting a memorandum in the first week of November 1870 from the inhabitants of Framlingham and the surrounding parishes stating:

> ...there was a long felt feeling in the district that the present insufficient railway accommodation, especially during the winter months, as persons were unable to reach Framlingham and the neighbourhood from London except by an early and inconvenient train or by an evening train. It would be a great advantage if the Directors would give them accommodation every day of the week as formerly but this they only now enjoy on a Thursday by a connection off the 11.45 am train from London at Ash for Framlingham.

The superintendent was asked to investigate the matter on 23rd November and report his findings to the Traffic Committee meeting on 7th December. Robertson duly reported that the train referred to, the 3.05 pm train from Wickham Market to Framlingham, originally ran on a daily basis but was discontinued except on Thursdays in the spring of 1868 because of the small number of passengers conveyed. On average the train conveyed seven passengers whilst the corresponding up train from Framlingham conveyed only two passengers. He could not therefore recommend the expense of reinstating the train on a daily basis, as there was no expectation of greater numbers of passengers than in 1868. The findings were advised to Jeafferson and the application declined.

The working timetable for 1875 showed little improvement, save that five passengers trains now operated on Thursdays and Saturdays with three on other weekdays. Goods traffic continued to be worked by passenger train when necessary, whilst a path was still retained for the branch engine to convey heavier goods loads if necessary between 8.30 am and 11.00 am. Trains departed Framlingham at 6.50, 11.40 am, 2.30 (Thursdays and Saturdays only), 4.40 and 7.05 pm (Thursdays and Saturdays only) and returned from Wickham Market at 8.00 am, 12.43, 3.05 (Thursdays and Saturdays only), 5.20 (Thursdays and Saturdays only) and 8.00 pm.

The 1883 working timetable showed a service of five passenger trains in each direction on weekdays only across the branch, with goods being worked by these services as necessary. The special trip path for heavier goods loads was between 8.30 and 11.00 am. Up trains departed Framlingham at 7.20 am, 12.00 noon, 2.00, 4.35 and 6.50 pm returning from Wickham Market at 7.55 am, 12.55, 2.38, 5.22 and 7.55 pm.

By 1897 the branch was served by five passenger, one mixed and one goods train in each direction on weekdays and two passenger trains each way on Sundays. An additional path was booked for an express cattle train at 6.10 am from Framlingham on weekdays, if required, with a balancing down goods working from Wickham Market at 6.45 am. When operated, these trains were to be treated as specials with the Framlingham station master arranging and advising as necessary. The goods trains departing Framlingham at 1.20 pm and returning from Wickham Market at 2.00 pm only served Marlesford and Parham if required. In addition the Framlingham branch engine was permitted to work a special trip to Wickham Market for additional goods traffic. The two mixed trains, 7.53 am ex-Wickham Market and 4.50 pm ex-Framlingham, were permitted to work through goods traffic as a tail load. To cater for passengers attending Ipswich market, the 8.38 am from Framlingham ran as a through train to Ipswich, although it stood at Wickham Market from 8.56 am until 9.50 am before continuing its journey. The return working departed Ipswich at 10.40 am with departure from Wickham Market at 11.09 am and thence seven minutes later across the branch.

The full working timetable for 1900 showed the following weekdays-only service.

Up		R Ex Ct am	Pass am	D Pass am	Pass pm	SX Gds pm	SO Pass pm	SO Gds pm	SX Mxd pm	SO Mxd pm	Pass pm
Framlingham	dep.	6.10	7.15	8.40	12.10	1.20	2.10	3.25	4.42	4.52	7.10
Parham	dep.		7.21	8.46	12.16	*	2.16	*	4.49	4.59	7.16
Marlesford	dep.		7.26	8.51	12.21	*	2.21	*	4.55	5.05	7.21
Wickham Market	arr.	6.30	7.33	8.58	12.28	1.45	2.28	3.50	5.03	5.13	7.28

Down		R Gds am	Mxd am	Pass am	C Pass pm	Pass pm	SX Gds pm	SO Pass pm	SO Gds pm	Pass pm	Pass pm
Wickham Market	dep.	6.45	7.55	11.13	12.45	2.00	2.43	4.05		5.48	8.05
Marlesford	dep.		8.01	11.18	12.50	*	2.48	*		5.53	8.10
Parham	dep.		8.08	11.24	12.56	*	2.54	*		5.59	8.16
Framlingham	arr.	7.05	8.15	11.31	1.03	2.25	3.01	4.30		6.06	8.23

*	Calls only if required.
C	On Tuesdays starts from Ipswich 10.50 am and leaves Wickham Market for Framlingham at 11.20am.
D	On Tuesdays runs to Ipswich, leaving Wickham Market at 9.50 am, arriving Ipswich 10.29 am.
Ex Ct	Express cattle
R	Runs only when required. When run to be treated as Specials, Framlingham to arrange and advise forward.
SO	Saturdays only.
SX	Saturdays excepted.

When required, the Framlingham Branch Engine will perform a Special Trip between Framlingham and Wickham Market, for the service of Goods Traffic.

Between 1st July and 30th September, 1900 a Sunday service was operated as under:

Up		am	pm	Down		am	pm
Framlingham	dep.	8.20	5.55	Wickham Market	dep.	9.15	6.52
Parham	dep.	8.26	6.01	Marlesford	dep.	9.20	6.57
Marlesford	dep.	8.31	6.06	Parham	dep.	9.26	7.03
Wickham Market	arr.	8.38	6.13	Framlingham	arr.	9.33	7.10

By 1907 the through working to Ipswich had been withdrawn and the service provided on the branch was formed of five passenger, one mixed and one goods train in each direction on weekdays. An additional express cattle train departed Framlingham at 6.10 am on Tuesdays only with livestock for Ipswich market and returned as a goods train from Wickham Market at 6.45 am. This train also ran on other weekdays, when required, with the station master at Framlingham arranging and advising as necessary. The mixed trains departing Wickham Market at 7.55 am and Framlingham at 4.52 pm were permitted to work through traffic only between Wickham Market and Framlingham or vice versa, whilst the goods trains 10.05 am ex-Framlingham and 10.45 am ex-Wickham

Market only called if required at Marlesford and Parham. When the ordinary goods train was unable to clear traffic to or from Marlesford a special trip was run between Wickham Market and Marlesford departing at 5.20 pm, with the station master at the Junction station arranging as necessary. When required the branch engine could also perform a special trip from Framlingham to Wickham Market to clear urgent goods traffic. Sunday services continued with two passenger trains in each direction.

The timetable remained unchanged for the next few years and in 1910 the quickest journey from Framlingham to Liverpool Street was 2 hours 47 minutes afforded by the 8.38 am whose connection arrived in London at 11.25 am. Conversely, the slowest journey of 4 hours 21 minutes was offered off the last branch train of the day, the 7.00 pm whose connecting services arrived at Liverpool Street at 11.21 pm. In the down direction the fastest journey was made on the 10.27 am ex-Liverpool Street which connected with the 12.52 pm branch train giving a 2 hours 43 minute timing from London to Framlingham. The worst down timing was off the 5.00 pm from Liverpool Street, whose connection arrived at Framlingham 3 hours 30 minutes later.

The working timetable for 1913 was basically the same as that operated in 1907, with minor timing adjustments, the Tuesdays-only express cattle train departing Framlingham at 6.10 am and returning as a goods train at 6.45 am ex-Wickham Market. On other days it ran only as required. The mixed trains 7.55 am from Wickham Market and the 4.52 pm ex-Framlingham worked only through traffic between the junction and terminal or vice versa, whilst the goods trains at 10.05 am ex-Framlingham and 10.45 am from Wickham Market only served the intermediate station sidings if required.

By 1916 the service had increased to six passenger, one mixed and one goods train in each direction, weekdays only, augmented on Tuesdays only by the express cattle train which departed Framlingham at 6.00 am and returned as a goods train departing Wickham Market at 6.35 am. The path was available on other days for the running of goods trains, which if run, were treated as specials with the Framlingham station master arranging and advising forward. The mixed trains departing Wickham Market at 8.05 am and Framlingham at 4.32 pm were permitted to work through goods traffic only, whilst the booked goods services departing Wickham Market at 9.30 am and Framlingham at 12.00 noon only called if required at Marlesford and Parham. When required, the branch engine could run a special trip from Framlingham to Wickham Market to clear essential freight from the line. If the ordinary goods services were unable to clear traffic to or from Marlesford, a special trip could be run from Wickham Market departing at 5.00 pm to clear such traffic. Passenger services ran at a uniform time Mondays to Saturdays except the afternoon down working, which departed Wickham Market at 3.05 pm (Saturdays excepted) and 3.32 pm (Saturdays only).

The working timetable for 1917 showed a reduction in passenger services with the withdrawal of the last up and down trains 7.52 pm ex-Framlingham and the 8.20 pm return from Wickham Market. The only other alterations were the 11.11 am down passenger retimed to depart Wickham Market at 11.17 am, the 7.10 pm down passenger train retimed to depart at 7.36 pm and the 1.42 pm up passenger train from Framlingham, which was retimed to start at 2.02 pm.

FRAMLINGHAM BRANCH.—*Single Line.*

Only one Engine in steam (or two or more Engines coupled together) must be allowed on this Single Line at one and the same time. No Engine or Train must be run on this Branch without a Train Staff; no Tickets being used. The Train Staff Stations are Wickham Market Junction and Framlingham. For Regulations for working, see "Appendix" to this Working Time Book.

Down Trains.—Week Days. / Sundays.

Miles from Wickham Mkt. M.C.	FROM.	1 Gds.	2 Mxd.	3 Pass.	4 Gds.	5	6	7 Pass.	8 Pass.	9 Pass.	10	11 Pass.	12 Pass.
—	Wickham Market dep.	a.m. 6 45	a.m. 7 55		a.m.	a.m.	p.m.	p.m. 2 57	p.m.		p.m.	p.m. 9 40	p.m. 8 53
67	Wickham Market Junc.	6 48	7 57		9 33			2 59	5 56			9 42	8 59
1 61	Marlesford	…	…		9 35			3 0	5 58		8 10	9 44	9 4
4	Parham (arr.) (dep.)	…	…		9 36			3 5	5 59		8 15	9 45	9 7
5		…	8 11		*			3 9	6 5		8 17	9 51	9 11
58	Framlingham arr.	7 8	8 16		9 49	11 10	1 10	3 15	6 12		8 24	9 58	7 15

Up Trains.—Week Days. / Sundays.

Miles from Framlingham M.C.	FROM.	1 Exp. Cattle	Pass.	Pass.	Gds.	Pass.	Pass.	B Mxd.	Pass.	Pass.	Pass.	Pass.
—	Framlingham dep.	a.m. 6 10	a.m. 7 15	a.m. 8 30	a.m. 10	noon 5 12	p.m. 0 24	p.m. 4 52	p.m. 6 50	a.m. 8 15	p.m. 5 53	
3 33	Parham		7 30	*		12 11	1 35	4 59	6 56	8 21	6 59	
4 58	Marlesford		7 37	8 47	10	12 12	1 36	5 6	7 1	8 26	8 4	
5 32	Wickham Market Junc.	6 27	7 31	8 48	10 11	12 13	1 40	5 11	7 6	8 27	8 9	
6 39	Wickham Market arr.	6 30	7 33	8 54	10 30	12 18	1 42	6 13	7 9	8 35	6 11	

A No. 1 Down & No. 1 Up, To run on Tuesdays. On other days to run only when required. When req., except Thursday, to be treated as Appendix. Framlingham to arrange and advise forward.

B No. 1 Down and No. 2 Up may work Through Traffic only from Wickham Market to Framlingham, and Framlingham to Wickham Market, respectively.

N.B.—When the ordinary Goods is unable to clear traffic to or from Marlesford, a Special Trip is to be run between Wickham Market & Marlesford at 5.20 p.m. Wickham Market to arrange.

When required, the Framlingham Branch Engine will perform a Special Trip between Framlingham and Wickham Market, for the service of the Goods Traffic.

GER Working Timetable 1913.

GER Working Timetable 1916.

WICKHAM MARKET AND FRAMLINGHAM.

Single Line worked by Train Staff without tickets and by only one engine in steam (or two or more engines coupled together). For regulations for working, see Appendix.

DOWN WEEK DAYS.

Miles from Wickham Mkt. M.C.		1 Gds. TO	2 Mxd	3 Gds	4 Pass	5 Pass	6 Pass	7 NS Pass	8 SO Pass	9 Pass	10 Pass	11 Pass	12 Pass	13
—	Wickham Mkt. dep.	a.m. 6 35	a.m. 8 5	a.m. 9 30	a.m. 11	p.m. 12 37	p.m. 3 3	p.m. 3 32	p.m. 5 54	p.m. 7 10	p.m. 8 20			
67	Wickham M. Junc(S)	6 48	8 7	9 32	11 12	12 39	3 5	3 34	5 56	7 12	8 22			
1 61	Marlesford	…	8 11	*	11 16	12 42	3 10	3 37	5 59	7 15	8 31			
4	Parham	…	8 18	…	11 48	12 48	3 16	3 43	6 5	7 21	8 31			
6 39	Framlingham (S) arr.	6 55	8 25	9 55	11 29	12 55	3 23	3 50	6 12	7 28	8 38			

UP WEEK DAYS.

Miles from		1 Exp. Cattle TO	2 Pass.	3 Pass.	4 Pass.	5 Gds.	6 Pass.	7 noon Pass.	8 Pass.	9 Mxd.	10 Pass.	11 Pass.	12	13
—	Framlingham (S) dep.	a.m. 6 0	a.m. 7 10	a.m. 8 40	a.m. 10 38	p.m. 2 0	p.m. 4 32	p.m. 6 30	p.m. 7 52					
	Parham	…	7 16	8 10	10 44	*	4 39	6 36	7 58					
	Marlesford	…	7 22	8 10	10 50	*	4 46	6 42	8 4					
6 17	Wickham M. Junc(S)	6 17	7 26	8 50	10 54	2 22	4 51	6 46	8 8					
6 39	Wickham Mkt. arr.	6 20	7 28	8 58	10 56	2 30	4 53	6 48	8 10					

1 down and 1 up. To run on Tuesdays. On other days to run only when required. When run, except Tuesdays, to be treated as specials. Framlingham to arrange and advise forward.

1 up to run under class B regulations.

2 = down and 7 up may work through traffic only from Wickham Market to Framlingham, and Framlingham to Wickham Market respectively.

N.B. When the ordinary Goods is unable to clear traffic to or from Marlesford, a special trip is to be run between Wickham Market and Marlesford at 5.0 p.m. Wickham Market to arrange. When required, the Framlingham Branch engine will perform a special trip between Framlingham and Wickham Market, for the service of the goods traffic.

Three years later the 1920 working timetable showed five passenger, one mixed and one goods train in each direction, augmented by an express cattle train which ran on Tuesdays only departing Framlingham at 6.00 am and returning as a goods train from Wickham Market at 6.35 am. By now these trains only ran when required and were treated as specials with the Framlingham station master arranging and advising forward. The mixed trains departing Wickham Market at 8.05 am and Framlingham at 4.25 pm were only permitted to take through goods traffic whilst the two goods services departing Wickham Market at 9.30 am and Framlingham at 12.12 pm only called at Marlesford and Parham if required. The additional 'Q' (when required) goods working from Wickham Market to Marlesford was fully timetabled departing the junction station at 4.55 pm and returning from Marlesford at 5.30 pm.

The branch passenger service in 1922 showed the following five weekdays-only trains in each direction and connections with Liverpool Street.

Up		am	am	pm	pm	pm
Framlingham	dep.	7.20	8.30	12.40	4.25	6.30
Parham	dep.	7.26	8.36	12.46	4.32	6.36
Marlesford	dep.	7.32	8.42	12.52	4.39	6.42
Wickham Market	arr.	7.38	8.48	12.58	4.46	6.48
Liverpool Street	arr.	10.30	11.22	3.42	7.51	9.22

Down		am	am	am	pm	pm
Liverpool Street	dep.	5.00		10.20	3.18	4.55
Wickham Market	dep.	7.56	9.35	1.14 pm	5.52	7.10
Marlesford	dep.	8.02	9.41	1.19	5.57	7.15
Parham	dep.	8.09	9.48	1.25	6.03	7.21
Framlingham	arr.	8.16	9.55	1.32	6.10	7.28

By 1923 conductor guard working was in operation and the initial LNER passenger timetable showed all trains were allowed an extra four minutes running time for the additional stop at the newly opened Hacheston Halt and also to permit trainmen to operate the gates at Cornish level crossing between Marlesford and Hacheston. The passenger service consisted of five trains in each direction, Tuesdays excepted, six each way, Tuesdays only, whilst on Saturdays six down and five up trains ran.

Up				TO			
		am	am	am	pm	pm	pm
Framlingham	dep.	7.14	8.30	9.37	12.34	4.19	6.26
Parham	dep.	7.20	8.36	9.43	12.40	4.26	6.32
Hacheston Halt	dep.	7.23	8.39	9.46	12.43	4.30	6.35
Marlesford	dep.	7.32	8.45	9.55	12.52	4.39	6.44
Wickham Market	arr.	7.38	8.51	10.01	12.58	4.46	6.50
Ipswich	arr.	8.36	9.40	10.46	1.50	5.37	7.40
Liverpool Street	arr.	10.30	11.22	1.20	3.42	7.51	9.22

Down		M	MTO	MTX	TO	SO			
		am	am	am	am	am	am	pm	pm
Liverpool Street	dep.	5.00				8.15	10.20	3.18	4.55
Ipswich	dep.	7.07	8.20	8.50	8.50	10.37	12.30 pm	5.06	6.28
Wickham Market	dep.	7.56	9.03	9.35	10.15	11.50	1.14	5.52	7.10
Marlesford	dep.	8.02	9.08	9.41	10.21	11.55	1.19	5.57	7.15
Hacheston Halt	dep.	8.06	9.15	9.48	10.28	12.02	1.26	6.04	7.22
Parham	dep.	8.12	9.20	9.54	10.34	12.07	1.31	6.09	7.27
Framlingham	arr.	8.19	9.27	10.01	10.41	12.14	1.38	6.16	7.34

M - mixed train on the branch; MTO - Mondays & Tuesdays only; MTX - Mondays & Tuesdays excepted; SO - Saturdays only, TO - Tuesdays only.

WICKHAM MARKET AND FRAMLINGHAM.

Single Line worked by Train Staff without tickets and by only one engine in steam (or two or more engines coupled together). For regulations for working see Appendix.

Miles from Wickham Mkt. M. C.	DOWN WEEK DAYS.		1	2	3	4	5	6	7	8	9	10	11	12	13	14	15	16	17	18	19	20	21	22	SUNDAYS.	23	24	25	26	27
				Gds.		Mxd		Pass.		Mxd.		Mxd.		Pass.		Pass.		Gds.		Pass.		Pass.								
				TO				TO		NT		TO		SO																
				a.m.		a.m.		a.m.		a.m.		a.m.		a.m.		p.m.		p.m.		p.m.		p.m.								
	Ipswich	dep.																												
—	**Wickham Mkt.**	arr.																												
		dep.		*6 30*		7 56		9 3		9 35		10 15		11 50		1 14		*2 45*		5 52		7 10								
— 67	Wickham Mkt. Jnc. (S)	"		*6 33*		7 58		9 5		9 37		10 17		11 52		1 16		*2 48*		5 54		7 12								
1 61	Marlesford (NB)	"				8 2		9 8		9 41		10 21		11 55		1 19		*3 8*		5 57		7 15								
3 6	Hacheston Halt	"				8 6		9 15		9 48		10 28		12 2		1 26				6 4		7 22								
4 7	Parham (NB)	"				8 12		9.20		9 54		10 34		12 7		1 31		*		6 9		7 27								
6 39	**Framlingham** (NB) (S)	arr.		*6 55*		8 19		9 27		10 1		10 41		12 14		1 38		*3 25*		6 16		7 34								

2 down and 2 up. Run only when required. When run to be treated as specials. Framlingham to arrange and advise forward. 2 up to run under class **B** regulations.

=8 To work through trucks only Wickham Mkt. to Framlingham, but conveys brake goods to Marlesford and Parham. =20 May work, when required, not exceeding two trucks of cattle from Wickham Mkt. to Framlingham, if trucks are fitted with westinghouse brake pipes.

UP WEEK DAYS.		1	2	3	4	5	6	7	8	9	10	11	12	13	14	15	16	17	18	19	20	21	22	23	SUNDAYS.	24	25	26	27	28
			Exp. Catle.		Pass.		Pass.			Pass.			Catle		Pass.		Gds.		Mxd.		Pass.									
			TO							TO			SO																	
			a.m.		a.m.		a.m.			a.m.			a.m.		p.m.		p.m.		p.m.		p.m.									
Framlingham (NB) (S)	dep.		*5 50*		7 14		8 30			9 37			*11 12*		12 34		*1 45*		4 19		6 26									
Parham (NB)	"				7 20		8 36			9 43					12 40		*		4 26		6 32									
Hacheston Halt	"				7 23		8 39			9 46					12 43				4 30		6 35									
Marlesford (NB)	"				7 32		8 45			9 55			*		12 52		*		4 39		6 44									
Wickham Mkt. Jnc. (S)	"		*6 12*		7 36		8 49			9 59			*11 34*		12 56		*2 27*		4 44		6 48									
Wickham Mkt.	arr.		*6 15*		7 38		8 51			10 1			*11 37*		12 58		*2 30*		4 46		6 50									
	dep.																													
Ipswich	arr.																													

Passenger trains are worked on the "Conductor Guard" principle. All trains except 4 down and 6 up are allowed extra time between Marlesford and Hacheston Halt to permit trainmen to open and close crossing gates at Cornish level crossing.

12 Conveys pig traffic from Framlingham to Brettell Lane, G.W., to go forward from Wickham Market by 7.50 a.m. goods Halesworth to Ipswich.
=18 May work through traffic only from Framlingham to Wickham Market.

LNER Working Timetable 1924.

The 1924 working timetable showed a more complex service of four passenger Tuesdays excepted, five passenger Tuesdays only, one goods, one cattle Saturdays only and one mixed train in the up direction augmented by the Tuesdays-only express cattle train which ran only if required and departed Framlingham at 5.50 am. The 11.20 am Saturdays-only cattle train conveyed pig traffic from Framlingham *en route* to Brettell Lane on the Great Western Railway, and the wagons were taken forward from Wickham Market by the 7.50 am Halesworth to Ipswich goods. The daily goods train departing Framlingham at 1.45 pm continued to call only if required at Parham and Marlesford whilst the mixed train departing Framlingham at 4.19 pm was permitted to work through goods traffic from Framlingham to Wickham Market. In the down direction the service consisted of four passenger Saturdays excepted, five passenger Saturdays only, one mixed Tuesdays excepted, two mixed Tuesdays only and one goods train. The additional Tuesdays-only goods service, the return working of the up express cattle train ran only if required. The Tuesdays-excepted mixed service, which departed Wickham Market at 9.35 am, was permitted to work through truck load traffic between the junction station and Framlingham and also conveyed brake goods to Marlesford and Parham. The final passenger train of the day, departing Wickham Market at 7.10 pm was permitted to work, when required, not exceeding two trucks of cattle from Wickham Market to Framlingham provided the wagons were fitted with Westinghouse brake pipes.

Services on the Framlingham branch were reduced as a result of the 1926 coal strike and from 31st May, 1926 trains departed Framlingham at 7.14, 9.37 am (Tuesdays-only), 12.22 and 6.28 pm returning from Wickham Market at 7.56, 10.15 am (Tuesdays-only) and 1.00 pm, whilst the 7.10 pm was retimed to depart at 7.45 pm weekdays only. Within a few weeks the full timetable was restored.

The 1932 summer timetable showed the following passenger services, weekdays only, with connections to and from Liverpool Street.

Up

		am	am	TuO am	pm	pm	pm
Framlingham	dep.	7.10	8.30	9.41	12.34	4.19	6.27
Parham	dep.	7.17	8.36	9.47	12.40	4.26	6.33
Hacheston Halt	dep.	7.21	8.39	9.50	12.43	4.30	6.36
Marlesford	dep.	7.30	8.45	9.59	12.52	4.39	6.45
Wickham Market	arr.	7.37	8.51	10.05	12.58	4.46	6.51
Liverpool Street	arr.	10.30	11.15	1.13	3.42	7.52	9.24

Down

		am	TuO am	TuX am	TuO am	SO am	am	pm	pm
Liverpool Street	dep.	5.05				8.15	10.20	3.18	4.55
Wickham Market	dep.	7.55	9.07	9.37	10.20	11.50	1.14 pm	5.50	7.05
Marlesford	dep.	8.01	9.12	9.43	10.26	11.55	1.19	5.55	7.10
Hacheston Halt	dep.	8.05	9.29	9.50	10.33	12.02 pm	1.26	6.02	7.17
Parham	dep.	8.11	9.24	9.56	10.39	12.07	1.31	6.07	7.22
Framlingham	arr.	8.18	9.31	10.03	10.46	12.14	1.38	6.14	7.29

TuO - Tuesdays only; TuX - Tuesdays excepted; SO - Saturdays only.

WICKHAM MARKET AND FRAMLINGHAM.

Single Line worked by Train Staff without tickets and by only one engine in steam (or two or more engines coupled together).

For regulations for working see Appendix.

Miles from Wickham Mkt.	DOWN WEEK DAYS.		1	2	3	4	5	6	7	8	9	10	11
			Mxd		Mxd.		Pass.	Pass.	Pass.	Gds.	Pass.	Pass.	
								SX	SO				
M. C.			a.m.		a.m.		a.m.	a.m.	p.m.	p.m.	p.m.	p.m.	
—	Wickham Mkt.	dep.	7 58	....	9 40	....	11 32	11 50	1 14	3 5	5 44	7 4	....
— 71	Wickham Mkt. Jnc. Ⓢ	„	8 0	—	9 42	....	11 34	11 52	1 16	3 8	5 46	7 6	—
1 60	Marlesford (NB)	„	8 4	....	9 46	....	11 37	11 55	1 19	3 22	5 49	7 9	....
3 15	Hacheston Halt	„	8 8	—	9 53	....	11 44	12 2	1 26	—	5 56	7 16	—
4 8	Parham (NB)	„	8 12	—	9 57	....	11 47	12 5	1 29	*	5 59	7 19	....
6 37	Framlingham (NB) Ⓢ	arr.	8 18	—	10 4	—	11 53	12 11	1 35	3 45	6 5	7 25	

=3 To work through wagons only Wickham Mkt. to Framlingham, but conveys brake goods to Marlesford and Parham. =10 May work, when required, not exceeding two braked wagons of cattle from Wickham Mkt. to Framlingham.

Miles from Framlingham.	UP WEEK DAYS.		1	2	3	4	5	6	7	8	9	10	11
				Pass.	Pass.		Pass.	Cattle	Pass.	Gds.	Mxd.	Pass.	
								SX	SO				
M. C.				a.m.	a.m.		a.m.	a.m.	p.m.	p.m.	p.m.	p.m.	
—	Framlingham (NB) Ⓢ	dep.	....	7 19	8 36	....	10 40	11 12	12 36	1 45	4 23	6 30	....
2 29	Parham (NB)	„	—	7 25	8 42	—	10 46	—	12 42	*	4 30	6 36	
3 22	Hacheston Halt	„	—	7 27	8 44	—	10 48	....	12 44	....	4 33	6 38	
4 57	Marlesford (NB)	„	—	7 34	8 48	—	10 55	*	12 51	*	4 41	6 45	
5 46	Wickham Mkt. Jnc. Ⓢ	„	....	7 37	8 51	—	10 58	11 34	12 54	2 14	4 44	6 48	
6 37	Wickham Mkt.	arr.	—	7 39	8 53	—	11 0	11 37	12 56	2 17	4 46	6 50	

6 Conveys pig traffic from Framlingham for Brettell Lane, G.W.
8 Engine to shunt Wickham Market Yard and leave Up Road traffic for the return Snape Goods to attach in Up Siding.
=9 May work through traffic only from Framlingham to Wickham Market.

Passenger trains are worked on the "Conductor Guard" principle. All trains except 1 down and 3 up are allowed extra time between Marlesford and Hacheston Halt to permit trainmen to open and close crossing gates at Cornish level crossing.

LNER Working Timetable 1939.

In 1935 the working timetable showed a weekdays-only service of one mixed, Tuesdays excepted, and two mixed trains, Tuesdays only, five passenger trains Tuesdays and Saturdays excepted, and four passenger trains, Tuesdays and Saturdays only, one goods and one cattle train (Saturdays only) in the up direction and two mixed, four passenger and one goods trains in the down direction. The Saturdays-only cattle train departing 11.12 am from Framlingham called at Marlesford, if required and conveyed pig traffic *en route* to Brettell Lane. The train arrived at Wickham Market at 11.37 am and was worked forward by the 11.50 am goods train to Ipswich. The 1.55 pm goods train ex-Framlingham called at Parham and Marlesford only if required, whilst the 4.19 pm mixed train from Framlingham could only convey goods traffic direct to Wickham Market and was not permitted to collect wagons from the intermediate stations. On the down road the 9.40 am Tuesday-excepted service was only permitted to work through trucks from Wickham Market to Framlingham but could convey brake goods to Marlesford and Parham, whilst the 2.45 pm goods train ex-Wickham Market made a mandatory stop at Marlesford but only called at Parham if required. The last train of the day, the 7.08 pm passenger train ex-Wickham Market, was allowed to work, when required, not exceeding two braked wagons of cattle from Wickham Market to Framlingham. All trains except for the 7.56 am mixed ex-Wickham Market and the 8.32 am passenger train ex-Framlingham were allowed extra time between Marlesford and Hacheston Halt to permit trainmen to open and close the crossing gates at Cornish level crossing.

A similar service operated in 1937 with minor adjustments to timing but by 1939 the working timetable showed in the up direction the weekday service of one mixed train, five passenger, Saturdays excepted and four passenger, Saturdays only, one cattle train, Saturdays only, and one goods train, whilst in the down direction two mixed, four passenger and one goods train ran across the branch. The 11.12 am cattle train from Framlingham continued to convey pig traffic for Brettell Lane, whilst the branch engine working the 1.45 pm goods train from Framlingham was required to shunt Wickham Market yard and leave up road traffic ready for the return Snape goods train to attach wagons in the up yard. The 4.23 pm mixed train was only permitted to work through wagons from Framlingham to Wickham Market. In the down direction the same arrangements applied to the 9.40 am mixed train ex-Wickham Market as in 1935. Similarly the 7.04 pm passenger train ex-Wickham Market had the same stipulation as the 7.08pm, being the last train of the day, in 1935. As before all trains except the 8.36 am passenger train ex-Framlingham and the return 9.40 am mixed train ex-Wickham Market were permitted extra time for the trainmen to open and close the crossing gates at Cornish level crossing.

Following the outbreak of World War II on 3rd September, 1939, the LNER introduced an emergency timetable with effect from 2nd October, 1939 when the passenger services was reduced to three trains in each direction as follows:

WICKHAM MARKET AND FRAMLINGHAM (No Sunday Service)

Single line worked by Train Staff without tickets and by only one engine in steam (or two or more engines coupled together).
For regulations for working see Appendix.

DOWN — WEEK DAYS

Miles from Wickham Mkt. (M.C.)		Description → Class →	1 Mxd	2 Mxd	4	5 Mxd	Mxd
—	—	Wickham Market dep. (S)	9 30	1 14		6 22	8 2
—	71	Wickham Market Jc. (NB)	—	1 16			8 8
1	60	Marlesford (NB)	9 36	1 20			8 12
3	15	Hacheston Halt	9 43	1 27			8 15
4	8	Parham Halt	9 49	1 33		6 28	8 21
6	37	Framlingham (NB)(S) arr.	9 56	1 40		6 35	8 28

UP — WEEK DAYS

Miles from Framlingham (M.C.)		Description →	6 Mail, Cars	7 Mxd	Mxd
—	—	Framlingham (S) dep.	8 38 a.m.	3 15 p.m.	6 47
2	29	Parham Halt	8 45	3 22	6 54
3	22	Hacheston Halt	8 48	3 25	6 57
4	57	Marlesford (NB)	8 56	3 33	7 5
5	46	Wickham Market Jc. (S)	8 59	3 36	7 8
6	37	Wickham Market (NB)(S) arr.	9 1	3 38	7 10

5 On Mondays, Fridays and Saturdays to start at 8.4 p.m. and run 2 minutes later.

7 May convey goods traffic if necessary.

These trains are worked on the "Conductor Guard" principle. All trains are allowed extra time between Marlesford and Hacheston Halt and Hacheston Halt to permit trainmen to open and close crossing gates at Cornish level crossing and between Hacheston Halt and Parham Halt to permit trainmen to open Parham Crossing gates, which will be closed by the gatekeeper after the passing of trains.

WICKHAM MARKET AND FRAMLINGHAM
(NO SUNDAY SERVICE)

Single Line worked by Train Staff without tickets and by only one engine in steam (or two or more engines coupled together). For regulations for working, see Appendix.

DOWN — WEEKDAYS

Miles from Wickham Mkt. (M.C.)		No.	1	2	3	4	5	6
		Description	Mxd		Mxd		Mxd	Mxd
		Class	Q					
			am	am	PM	PM	PM	PM
—	—	Wickham Mkt.	9 30		1 17	4 15	6 8	8 0
—	71	Wickham M. Jc. (S)	9 32		1 19	4 17	6 11	8 2
1	60	Marlesford	9 36		1 23	4 24	6 15	8 13
3	15	Hacheston Halt	9 43		1 30		6 22	8 19
4	8	Parham Halt	9 49	10 53	1 36		6 28	8 26
6	37	Framlingham (S)	9 56	11 0	1 43		6 35	

UP — WEEKDAYS

Miles from Framlingham (M.C.)		No.	7	8	9	10	11	12
		Description	Mxd	Mxd	Mxd	Mxd	Mxd	Mxd
		Class			Q		Q	
			am	am	PM	PM	PM	PM
—	—	Framlingham (S)	8 38	10 30	12 30	3 15		6 57
2	29	Parham Halt	8 45	10 37	12 37	3 22		7 7
3	22	Hacheston Halt	8 48		12 40	3 25		7 7
4	57	Marlesford	8 56		12 48	3 33	4 45	7 15
5	46	Wickham M. Jc.(S)	8 59		12 51	3 36	4 48	7 18
6	37	Wickham Mkt.	9 1		12 53	3 38	4 50	7 20

These trains are worked on the "Conductor Guard" principle. All trains are allowed extra time between Marlesford and Hacheston Halt at Cornish level crossing and between Hacheston Halt and Parham Halt to permit trainmen to open Parham Crossing gates, which will be closed by the gatekeeper after the passing of trains.

Down		am	am	pm		Up		am	am	pm
Liverpool St.	dep.		10.00	4.00		Framlingham	dep.	8.40	10.00	4.00
Wickham Mkt	dep.	9.30	1.10 pm	7.15		Parham	dep.	8.47	10.07	4.07
Marlesford	dep.	9.36	1.16	7.21		Hacheston Halt	dep.	8.50	10.10	4.10
Hacheston Halt	dep.	9.40	1.20	7.25		Marlesford	dep.	8.58	10.18	4.18
Parham	dep.	9.44	1.24	7.29		Wickham Mkt	arr.	9.03	10.23	4.23
Framlingham	arr.	9.51	1.31	7.36		Liverpool St.	arr.	12.04	1.40	7.40

From December 1939 Parham was reduced in status to a halt as the platform was unattended for most hours of the day and subsequent public passenger timetables showed the revised designation. By 1940 the service had been further reduced by the withdrawal of one up train and the meagre branch service, with London connections was:

Down		am	am	pm		Up		am	pm
Liverpool St.	dep.	4.40	10.00	5.12		Framlingham	dep.	8.42	3.15
Wickham Mkt	dep.	9.30	1.10 pm	7.42		Parham Halt	dep.	8.49	3.22
Marlesford	dep.	9.36	1.16	7.48		Hacheston Halt	dep.	8.52	3.25
Hacheston Halt	dep.	9.43	1.23	7.55		Marlesford	dep.	9.00	3.33
Parham Halt	dep.	9.49	1.29	8.01		Wickham Mkt	arr.	9.05	3.38
Framlingham	arr.	9.56	1.36	8.08		Liverpool St.	arr.	11.35	6.51

This service of three down and two up passenger trains continued with only minor alterations in timing until 1943 when the service was increased to four down and three up trains.

Down		am	am	pm	pm	Up		am	pm	pm
Liverpool St.	dep.	4.33	10.00	3.40	5.10	Framlingham	dep.	8.42	3.10	6.41*
Wickham Mkt	dep.	9.30	1.08pm	5.59	7.53	Parham Halt	dep.	8.49	3.17	6.48*
Marlesford	dep.	9.36	1.11	6.05	7.59	Hacheston Halt	dep.	8.52	3.20	6.51*
Hacheston Halt	dep.	9.43	1.18	6.12	8.06	Marlesford	dep.	9.00	3.28	6.59*
Parham Halt	dep.	9.49	1.24	6.18	8.12	Wickham Mkt	arr.	9.05	3.33	7.04*
Framlingham	arr.	9.56	1.31	6.25	8.19	Liverpool St.	arr.	11.36	6.51	10.15

* Runs four minutes later Saturdays only.

The working timetable for 1945 showed the weekdays-only service of three mixed trains and one empty stock working in the up direction and four mixed trains on the down road. The mixed trains departed Framlingham at 8.38 am, 3.15 and 6.47 pm whilst the 11.30 am empty coaching stock was permitted to convey goods traffic if necessary and call at Parham and Marlesford if required. The mixed trains returned from Wickham Market at 9.30 am, 1.14, 6.09, 8.02 pm Mondays, Fridays and Saturdays excepted and the last train ran two minutes later on Mondays, Fridays and Saturdays only. The mixed trains conveyed all goods traffic and no freight trains ran across the branch. Trains were now permitted 26 minutes running time across the branch as trainmen now had to open the level crossing gates at Parham in addition to Cornish level crossing. However, the gates at Parham were closed by the gatekeeper after the passage of the train.

By 1947 the service had increased to four mixed trains each way with 'Q' paths as required for short freight trip workings between Framlingham and Parham and Wickham Market and Marlesford. Up services departed Framlingham at 8.38 am, 12.30, 3.15 and 6.57pm returning from Wickham

WICKHAM MARKET AND FRAMLINGHAM
(NO SUNDAY SERVICE)

Single Line worked by Train Staff without tickets and by only one engine in steam (or two or more engines coupled together). For regulations for working, see Appendix.

Miles from Wickham Mkt.	DOWN		WEEKDAYS					Miles from Framlingham	UP			WEEKDAYS				
	No.	1	2	3	4	5	6		**No.**	7	8	9	10	11	12
	Description	Mxd		Mxd		Mxd	Mxd		**Description**	Mxd		Mxd	Mxd		Mxd
	Class		D		D				**Class**		D		D		
M. C.		am	am	PM Q	PM Q	PM	PM	M. C.		am	am	PM Q	PM	PM Q	PM
— —	Wickham Mkt....	9 30	....	1 20	4 15	6 9	8 0	— —	Framlingham (S)	8 38	10 30	12 30	3 15	....	6 57
— 71	Wickham M. Jc. (S)	9 32	...	1 22	4 17	6 11	8 2	2 29	Parham Halt	8 45	10 37	12 37	3 22	..	7 4
1 60	Marlesford	9 36	...	1 26	4 24	6 15	8 6	3 22	Hacheston Halt ...	8 48		12 40	3 25	....	7 7
3 15	Hacheston Halt ..	9 43	..	1 33		6 22	8 13	4 57	Marlesford ..	8 56	..	12 48	3 33	4 50	7 15
4 8	Parham Halt.......	9 49	10 53	1 39	.....	6 28	8 19	5 46	Wickham M. Jc. (S)	8 59	....	12 51	3 36	5 53	7 18
6 37	Framlingham (S)	9 56	11 0	1 46	..	6 35	8 26	6 37	Wickham Mkt...	9 1	..	12 53	3 38	4 55	7 20

These trains are worked on the " **Conductor Guard** " principle. All trains are allowed extra time between Marlesford and Hacheston Halt to permit trainmen to open and close crossing gates at Cornish level crossing and between Hacheston Halt and Parham Halt to permit **trainmen to open** Parham Crossing gates, which will be **closed by the gatekeeper** after the passing of trains.

BR(ER) Working Timetable 1949.

BR(ER) Working Timetable 1950.

WICKHAM MARKET AND FRAMLINGHAM
(NO SUNDAY SERVICE)

Single Line worked by Train Staff without tickets and by only one engine in steam (or two or more engines coupled together). For regulations for working, see Appendix.

Miles from Wickham Mkt.	DOWN		WEEKDAYS					Miles from Framlingham	UP			WEEKDAYS				
	No.	1	2	3	4	5	6		**No.**	7	8	9	10	11	12
	Class	B	K	B	K	B	B		**Class**	B	K	B	B	K	B
	Description	Mxd		Mxd		Mxd	Mxd		**Description**	Mxd		Mxd	Mxd		Mxd
M. C.		am	am	PM Q	PM Q	PM	PM	M. C.		am	am	PM Q	PM	PM Q	PM
— —	Wickham Mkt....	9 30	....	1 25	4 15	6 9	8 0	— —	Framlingham (S)	8 44	10 30	12 30	3 10	....	6 57
— 71	Wickham M. Jc. (S)	9 32	..	1 27	4 17	6 11	8 2	2 29	Parham Halt	8 51	10 37	12 37	3 17	..	7 4
1 60	Marlesford	9 36	....	1 31	4 24	6 15	8 6	3 22	Hacheston Halt ...	8 54		12 40	3 20	....	7 7
3 15	Hacheston Halt ..	9 43	..	1 38		6 22	8 13	4 57	Marlesford ..	9 2	..	12 48	3 28	4 50	7 15
4 8	Parham Halt.......	9 49	10 53	1 44	.....	6 28	8 19	5 46	Wickham M. Jc. (S)	9 5	....	12 51	3 31	5 53	7 18
6 37	Framlingham (S)	9 56	11 0	1 51	..	6 35	8 26	6 37	Wickham Mkt...	9 7	..	12 53	3 33	4 55	7 20

These trains are worked on the " **Conductor Guard** " principle. All trains are allowed extra time between Marlesford and Hacheston Halt to permit trainmen to open and close crossing gates at Cornish level crossing and between Hacheston Halt and Parham Halt to permit **trainmen to open** Parham Crossing gates, which will be **closed by the gatekeeper** after the passing of trains.

Market at 9.30 am, 1.17, 6.09 and 8.00 pm. The 'Q' path permitted a freight trip to depart from Framlingham at 10.30 am, arriving at Parham at 10.37 am and after 16 minutes for shunting the return working departed at 10.53 am arriving at Framlingham at 11.00 am. The Marlesford trip departed Wickham Market at 4.15 pm with 9 minutes running time to the intermediate station. On completion of shunting the trip departed Marlesford at 4.45 pm and arrived back at Wickham Market at 4.50 pm. The branch engine made both trip workings.

The working timetable commencing 5th June, 1950 continued to show four mixed trains in each direction. Up trains departed Framlingham at 8.44 am, 12.30, 3.10 and 6.57 pm returning from Wickham Market at 9.30 am, 1.25, 6.09 and 8.00 pm. Twenty-three minutes running time was permitted for up trains and 26 minutes for down services over the 6 miles 37 chains journey. In between the running of these services a 'Q' path was available for a goods trip working departing Framlingham at 10.30 am to Parham, returning at 10.53 am with seven minutes running time in each direction. Another 'Q' path was available if required for a goods trip working from Wickham Market to Marlesford departing the junction station at 4.15 pm with arrival at Marlesford at 4.24 pm. The return trip was made at 4.50 pm with arrival at Wickham Market five minutes later.

The winter timetable commencing 25th September, 1950 showed the following passenger service running on weekdays only:

Up		am	pm	pm	
Framlingham	dep.	8.38	12.30	5.10	
Parham Halt	dep.	8.45	12.37	5.17	
Hacheston Halt	dep.	8.48	12.40	5.20	
Marlesford	dep.	8.56	12.48	5.28	
Wickham Market	arr.	9.01	12.53	5.33	
Down		am	pm	pm	pm
Wickham Market	dep.	9.30	1.25	6.09	8.00
Marlesford	dep.	9.38	1.31	6.15	8.06
Hacheston Halt	dep.	9.43	1.38	6.22	8.13
Parham Halt	dep.	9.49	1.44	6.28	8.19
Framlingham	arr.	9.56	1.51	6.35	8.26

The final working timetable to include passenger services operative from 15th September, 1952 showed four mixed trains in each direction together with 'Q' paths between Framlingham and Parham and return and Wickham Market and Marlesford and return. The mixed trains departed Framlingham at 8.38 am, 12.37 pm (Saturdays only), 12.47 pm (Saturdays excepted), 3.20 and 6.52 pm returning from Wickham Market at 9.25 am, 1.15pm (Saturdays only), 1.40 pm (Saturdays excepted), 6.09 and 8.00pm. Up trains were allowed 23 minutes running time whilst down trains were allowed 25 minutes. The 'Q' path running as a class 'K' goods train departed Framlingham at 10.30 am to Parham arriving 7 minutes later and returned from Parham at 10.53 am arriving at Framlingham at 11.00 am. The 'Q' path for a class 'K' goods train from Wickham Market departed at 4.15 pm arriving at Marlesford at 4.24 pm before returning at 4.50 pm and arriving back at Wickham Market at 4.55 pm.

The point-to-point running times used for branch passenger services after World War II was:

A sylvan East Anglian branch line setting as 'F3' class 2-4-2 tank locomotive No. 67127 trundles the morning branch mixed train from Wickham Market to Framlingham between Marlesford and Hacheston Halt in 1949. The six-wheel coaches used for conductor-guard working were replaced in 1940 by ex-GER bogie corridor vehicles, and the brake/third vehicle was similarly equipped with steps which were operated by the guard to enable passengers to alight and join the train at Hacheston Halt. *The late Dr Ian C. Allen*

After World War II nearly all services on the Framlingham branch operated as mixed trains and the heavy tail loads could often tax the branch locomotive. 'F6' class 2-4-2 tank locomotive No. 67220 rouses the echoes as she departs from Parham with a Framlingham to Wickham Market train in June 1950. The normal branch two-coach set is followed by a mixture of wagons, including two bulk grain wagons. No. 67220 was not normally associated with the Framlingham branch, and more often than not worked the neighbouring Aldeburgh branch. Note the absence of a disc to denote the class of train. No. 67220 was withdrawn from traffic in July 1955. *The late Dr Ian C. Allen*

Once clear of the branch at Wickham Market Junction, up Framlingham branch trains could sprint along the main line the short distance to Wickham Market. 'F6' class No. 67230 in charge of driver Jack Turner approaches the junction station with a mixed train in July 1950.

The late Dr Ian C. Allen

'F6' class 2-4-2 tank locomotive No. 67239 leaving Framlingham with an evening train in July 1952. Sister engine No. 67230 had earlier in the day become a total failure on the branch and No. 67239 had been sent from Ipswich to push the failed train and engine to Framlingham before taking over the branch workings. Normally all locomotives shedded at Framlingham worked chimney first down the branch, to ease the hand coaling at night, but in this instance the locomotive is 'wrong way round'. In addition to the two-coach branch conductor-guard set the leading vehicle is an ex-Great Central six-wheel goods brake van. *The late Dr Ian C. Allen*

M 50

WICKHAM MARKET AND FRAMLINGHAM

(NO SUNDAY SERVICE)

Single Line worked by Train Staff without tickets and by only one engine in steam (or two or more engines coupled together). For regulations for working, see Appendix.

DOWN   WEEKDAYS

Miles from Wickham Mkt.	No.	1	2	3	4	5	6	7
	Class	B	K		B	K	B	B
	Description	Mxd			Mxd		Mxd	Mxd
			Q			Q		
M. C.		am	am		PM	PM	PM	PM
— —	Wickham Mkt.	9 40			1 40	4 15	6 9	8 0
— 71	Wickham M. Jc. (S)	9 42			1 42	4 17	6 11	8 2
1 60	Marlesford	9 46			1 46	4 24	6 15	8 6
3 15	Hacheston Halt	9 53			1 53		6 22	8 13
4 8	Parham Halt	9 59	10 53		1 59		6 28	8 19
6 37	Framlingham (S)	10 6	11 0		2 6		6 35	8 26

UP   WEEKDAYS

Miles from Framlingham	No.	1	2	3	4	5	6	7
	Class	B	K	B		B	K	B
	Description	Mxd		Mxd		Mxd		Mxd
			Q				Q	
M. C.		am	am	PM		PM	PM	PM
— —	Framlingham (S)	8 38	10 30	12 37		3 20		6 52
2 29	Parham Halt	8 45	10 37	12 44		3 27		6 59
3 22	Hacheston Halt	8 48		12 47		3 30		7 2
4 57	Marlesford	8 56		12 55		3 38	4 50	7 10
5 46	Wickham M. Jc. (S)	8 59		12 58		3 41	4 53	7 13
6 37	Wickham Mkt.	9 1		1 0		3 43	4 55	7 15

These trains are worked on the " **Conductor Guard** " Principle. All trains are allowed extra time to permit trainmen to open and close crossing gates at Cornish level crossing, (between Marlesford and Hacheston Halt) and to permit **trainmen to open** Parham Crossing gates (between Hacheston Halt and Parham Halt), which will be **closed by the gatekeeper** after the passing of trains.

The epitome of an East Anglian branch mixed train. 'J15' class No. 65467 running tender-first with a train formed of a two-coach conductor-guard set and an assortment of wagons gets away from Framlingham and approaches Broadwater level crossing. Framlingham down fixed distant signal can be seen towards the rear of the train. Note the wooden tender cab sheet provided for the enginemen when working tender first. This Ipswich-made attachment was very necessary when 'J15' class engines were working the Framlingham, Snape, Aldeburgh and Eye branches and the Mid Suffolk Light Railway where no turntables were provided.

The late Dr Ian C. Allen

'D16/3' class 4-4-0 No. 62526 is the branch engine and is shown departing Parham with a Framlingham to Wickham Market mixed train formed of the two-coach conductor-guard bogie coaching stock, 12 wagons and a goods brake van. *The late Dr Ian C. Allen*

It was an extremely unusual occurrence when a locomotive became a total failure on the branch as it could usually limp along to reach its destination. However in July 1952 'F6' class 2-4-2 tank locomotive No. 67230 completely failed whilst working the branch train between Parham and Framlingham, when the fusible plug melted and the fire was hurriedly thrown out. A relief locomotive was requested from Ipswich and after much delay sister locomotive No. 67239 arrived to propel the stricken train into Framlingham, the passengers having already been dispatched to their destination by taxi. Here the cavalcade is approaching Framlingham. *The late Dr Ian C. Allen*

Driver Jack Turner on 'F6' class No. 67239 waits for the shunter to climb on the engine before shunting the Framlingham branch train from the up main line platform at Wickham Market to the down side ready to reform the stock for the return journey. *D. Trevor Rowe*

'J15' class 0-6-0 No. 65459 passing Blackstock Wood on the approach to Wickham Market Junction with the last up College special train. The engine is adorned with the College crest on the lamp iron by the chimney and carries an incorrect class headcode for the train. *The late Dr Ian C. Allen*

A Framlingham College special train formed of LNER Gresley- and Thompson-designed suburban stock makes for Wickham Market at the end of term hauled by 'J15' class No. 65467. The engine, which is crossing Hoggate Hill footpath crossing No. 16 at 90 miles 32 chains from Liverpool Street, is carrying the correct express passenger train headcode of a lamp above each buffer. *The late Dr Ian C. Allen*

'F6' class 2-4-2 tank locomotive No. 67230 getting into her stride away from Wickham Market Junction past Blackstock Wood with the branch train in April 1955. The train is strengthened to four coaches as it conveyed pupils returning to Framlingham College, who had changed from a main line service at Wickham Market. *The late Dr Ian C. Allen*

At certain times students at Framlingham College returning from Liverpool Street were only provided with through coaches, which were attached to a Liverpool Street to Yarmouth South Town main line service and detached at Wickham Market. The vehicles were then attached to the branch train and taken forward to Framlingham. 'F6' class No. 67230 is in charge of one such working, the six-coach train formed of the two-coach branch set and four ex-LNER Gresley corridor stock. On a dull day the train is clear of Blackstock Wood near Alder Carr crossing and is making for Marlesford. *The late Dr Ian C. Allen*

'F6' class 2-4-2T No. 67230 at the head of a Framlingham train train awaits departure in the down platform at Wickham Market in July 1952. The up side loading dock is to the left.

A. Forsyth

'F6' class 2-4-2 tank locomotive No. 67239 pauses at Marlesford with a Framlingham to Wickham Market train in 1952. *D. Trevor Rowe*

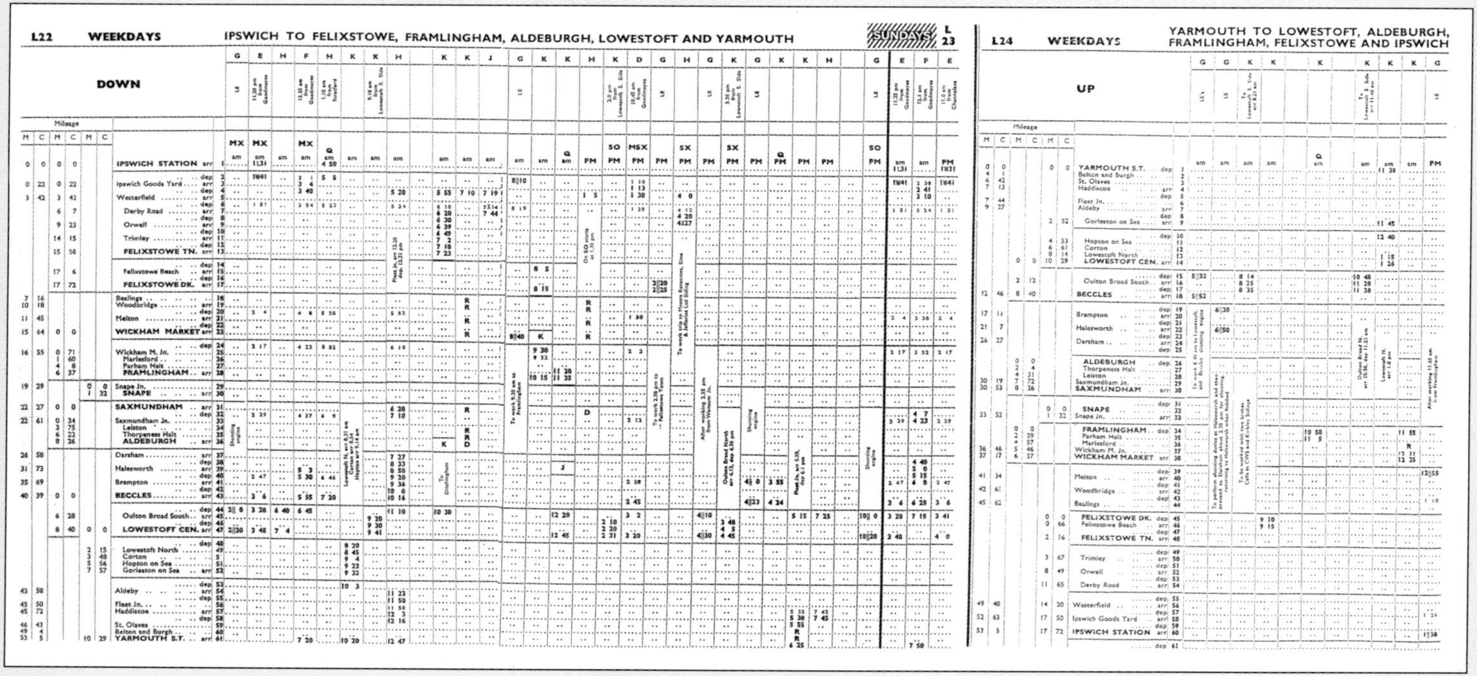

YARMOUTH TO LOWESTOFT, ALDEBURGH, FRAMLINGHAM, FELIXSTOWE AND IPSWICH

UP · WEEKDAYS

IPSWICH TO FELIXSTOWE, FRAMLINGHAM, ALDEBURGH, LOWESTOFT AND YARMOUTH

DOWN · WEEKDAYS

BR(ER) Working Timetable 1955.

	Pass to pass	Pass to stop	Start to pass	Start to stop
Wickham Market to Framlingham				
Wickham Market to Wickham Market Junction	-	-	2	-
Wickham Market Junction to Marlesford	-	3	-	-
Marlesford to Hacheston Halt	-	-	-	6
Hacheston Halt to Parham Halt	-	-	-	5
Parham Halt to Framlingham	-	-	-	6
Framlingham to Wickham Market				
Framlingham to Parham Halt	-	-	-	6
Parham Halt to Hacheston Halt	-	-	-	6
Hacheston Halt to Marlesford	-	-	-	7
Marlesford to Wickham Market Junction	-	-	3	-
Wickham Market Junction to Wickham Market	-	2	-	-

Thereafter one class 'K' freight train in each direction served the branch on weekdays only. In 1955 the engine to work the train ran light from Ipswich departing at 8.10 am arriving at Wickham Market at 8.40 am. After yard shunting the engine worked the down branch goods departing Wickham Market at 9.30 am with arrival at Framlingham at 10.15 am. If necessary a 'Q' path short trip working was then made to Parham to clear the yard of traffic or offload wagons, departing Framlingham at 10.50 am, arriving at 11.05 am, with the return departing Parham at 11.20 am with arrival at the terminus at 11.35 am. After more yard shunting the up branch goods train departed Framlingham at 11.55 am calling at Marlesford if required before arriving back at Wickham Market at 12.35 pm. After dropping the train off in the yard, the engine then ran light to Ipswich departing at 12.55 pm. Up road traffic was collected by the 'Bonus' goods trip from Snape to Ipswich goods yard Mondays and Saturdays excepted and on Saturdays by the 'bonus' goods working from Aldeburgh to Ipswich goods yard. Down road goods traffic for stations as far as Saxmundham was taken forward by the 1.05 pm 'bonus' goods ex-Ipswich goods yard to Saxmundham. All other down road traffic was sent via Ipswich. 'Bonus' workings for Ipswich footplatemen and guards entailed taking the train out and back as quickly as possible, running to Control instructions, the quicker the round trip the better the bonus.

The BR (ER) Working Timetable from 17th September, 1956 set the precedent for future operation of the branch and showed the 9.50 am Saturdays only, 11.12 am Saturdays excepted goods train ex-Ipswich goods yard running to Wickham Market and Framlingham, thence to Wickham Market and Saxmundham, returning to Snape Junction and Snape, and from Snape via Wickham Market and Woodbridge to Ipswich goods yard. No intermediate or arrival times were specified and the train ran as a 'bonus' working for the train crew who preferred to work the train with a steam brake-only 'J15' class locomotive, thereby making shunting at intermediate sidings easier. The departure times were unaltered until 17th June, 1957 when the Saturdays-only train departed Ipswich goods yard at 8.45 am. From 15th June, 1959 the Saturdays excepted departure time was altered to 11.20 am and yet again to 11.25 am from 2nd November, 1959.

After the withdrawal of steam traction and the closure of the Snape branch, the Framlingham branch freight continued 'bonus' trip working from and to Ipswich goods yard which ran at unspecified times. Occasionally special trip workings were made for sugar beet or malt traffic, again at short notice by local arrangement and at unspecified times.

Fares

On 27th June, 1861 it was resolved to issue market day return tickets to Framlingham from stations on the ESR at the rate charged for single fares prior to 1st June, 1860.

The tariff of fares from Liverpool Street to the branch stations in 1884 was:

	Single						Return					
	1st			2nd			3rd			1st		
	£	s.	d.	£	s.	d.	£	s.	d.	£	s.	d.
Wickham Market		15	10		12	0		7	1 ½	1	3	10
Marlesford		16	3		12	4		7	3	1	4	4
Parham		16	6		12	6		7	5 ½	1	5	0
Framlingham		17	0		13	0		7	8	1	5	6

	2nd			3rd		
	£	s.	d.	£	s.	d.
Wickham Market		19	0		14	3
Marlesford		19	6		14	6
Parham		19	11		14	11
Framlingham	1	0	5		15	4

By 1900 the following fares were operative from Framlingham:

to	1st single		3rd single		1st return		3rd return	
	s.	d.	s.	d.	s.	d.	s.	d.
Wickham Market	1	3	0	6 ½	1	10	1	1
Ipswich	4	3	1	10 ½	6	6	3	9
Liverpool Street	17	0	7	8	25	6	15	4

Fares from Liverpool Street to the branch stations in 1947 were:

to	1st single			3rd single			1st return			3rd return		
	£	s.	d.	£	s.	d.	£	s.	d.	£	s.	d.
Wickham Market	1	5	0		15	0	1	10	6	1	0	4
Marlesford	1	5	7		15	5	1	11	0	1	0	8
Hacheston Halt	1	5	11		15	7	1	11	3	1	0	10
Parham	1	6	3		15	9	1	11	6	1	1	0
Framlingham	1	6	11		16	1	1	12	6	1	1	8

Excursions

In the years the Framlingham branch was open for passenger traffic relatively few excursions were offered. Those that operated ran chiefly to East Anglian seaside resorts as well as to London, Ipswich, Norwich and Cambridge. The programme, like those of many other minor GER branch lines, was not as extensive as that provided for the more important stations or cross-country routes.

The first excursion offered in 1860 to Yarmouth attracted a large number of passengers and the *Framlingham Weekly News* reported,

> The various stations on our branch presented a very interesting appearance of hundreds of gaily dressed pleasure seekers who were determined to patronise the first cheap trip and spend a day at the seaside. Of the 2,500 that entered Yarmouth nearly a thousand were supplied by our branch line, including Campsea Ashe where about 500, with 300 at Saxmundham, had to join a second train.

Excursion fares were later extended to Felixstowe, Yarmouth, Clacton and Walton, with regular offerings for travel on a Monday to Aldeburgh.

In September 1862 a special train conveyed passengers from the branch stations to London for the Great Exhibition. A departure from Framlingham at

5.00 am with a 3½ hour journey and the return departing at 7.30 pm offered passengers nine hours in the capital. By the time the train reached Westerfield on the up journey over a thousand people were packed into the carriages.

As well as running their own special trains, the railway company provided facilities for private parties to travel by rail. The first schools excursion organised by the clergy of Worlingworth, Bedfield and Southolt ran from Framlingham to Aldeburgh in June 1865, with a return fare of 6d. Then in July 1876 Framlingham College became top school for pupils taking the Cambridge University Board examinations and to celebrate the event the Chairman of the Governors, Sir Edward Kerrison, paid for the hire of a 12-coach special train from Framlingham to Lowestoft and return.

London excursions were always popular and in 1865 a special train conveyed over 600 passengers, whilst a decade later, in September 1870, 150 passengers joined the train at Framlingham for a trip to the capital. The special traffic was however slow to materialise and patronage varied considerably according to the season, destination and not the least the weather. When the line opened the wages of agricultural workers were poor so it was to the middle and upper classes that the railway excursion appealed most. Gradually alterations were made and the introduction of paid holidays and additional leisure periods brought the price of the railway excursion within the pockets of most inhabitants served by the line. During the 1870s and 1880s the most popular destinations were Yarmouth, Lowestoft, Aldeburgh, Felixstowe and to a lesser degree Clacton, Walton and Cromer. Shorter half-day excursions were offered at one time to Suffolk resorts. For longer excursions, through coaches from the branch were attached to a main line train at Wickham Market. At other times passengers changed from the branch train to the connecting main line train at the junction. In the event of a late return, a special train connected with the main line train at Wickham Market to convey passengers to the branch stations.

In the years prior to the outbreak of World War I, the GER offered many excursion fares for cheap travel. In addition to those offered to branch stations, passengers were also offered five-, six- or eight-day excursion fares to Framlingham from Liverpool Street. These were the halcyon days for the excursion programme and cheap fares were made available to many exhibitions in London, including the annual Smithfield Show. Following the depressed years of World War I and the poor financial standing of the country in 1921, no excursion trains or fares were offered in 1921.

Between the two World Wars the excursion programme available to residents of Framlingham, Parham, Hacheston and Marlesford included the usual East Anglian destinations and in addition Spalding and Peterborough, although later the choice of destinations was drastically reduced. Day return fares continued to be offered to London and in 1937 the fare from Framlingham was 5s. 6d., raised to 5s. 9d. the following year. In the years before and after World War II, cheap fares were also offered to Ipswich for home games of Ipswich Town Football Club. In the late 1940s and until the closure of the branch to passenger traffic, a through excursion train ran from Framlingham to Liverpool Street and return at least once or twice a year.

A Framlingham to Liverpool Street Sunday excursion hauled by 'B12/3' class 4-6-0 No. 61564 negotiates the crossover from the branch via the down main line to the up main line at Wickham Market Junction in 1954. The gates of Blackstock level crossing can be seen to the right and the chimney of the signal box above the locomotive tender.   *The late Dr Ian C. Allen*

'D16/3' class 4-4-0 tender locomotive No. 62612 waiting to depart from Framlingham with the empty coaching stock of a return Sunday excursion from Liverpool Street formed of a mixture of Gresley and Thompson LNER corridor bogie stock and BR Mark I corridor coaches. The engine had just run round the stock prior to working back, and the correct class 'C' headcode is being exhibited on the tender lamp brackets.   *The late Dr Ian C. Allen*

Rousing the echoes 'J15' class 0-6-0 No. 65459 approaching Hoggate Hill crossing as she departs Framlingham with an eight-coach Sunday excursion bound for Liverpool Street. The 0-6-0 tender engine would have been replaced by a 'B12' class engine at Ipswich.

The late Dr Ian C. Allen

'J15' class 0-6-0 No. 65447 propels empty stock of a Sunday excursion to Liverpool Street back into the platform at Framlingham after running round the formation. This engine hauled the train forward as far as Ipswich, where it would have joined another section from Bury St Edmunds before the complete train was taken forward by a larger locomotive.

The late Dr Ian C. Allen

Brush type '2', 1,350 hp diesel-electric locomotive, later BR class '31', No. D5595 hauling the Liverpool Street to Framlingham ramblers' excursion train on Good Friday 12th April, 1963. The train, formed of a mixture of BR Mark I and Gresley and Thompson LNER corridor coaching stock, is passing over the two-arch River Ore underbridge No. 1105 between Parham and Framlingham. *The late Dr Ian C. Allen*

Brush type '2', 1,365 hp diesel-electric locomotive No. D5595 seen working the same train near Marlesford on Good Friday 12th April, 1963. This was the last occasion passengers were conveyed on the branch and the only time a diesel locomotive hauled a passenger train. *The late Dr Ian C. Allen*

Goods Traffic

Before the advent of the railway, the local carriers' carts were a common sight on the roads, linking the villages and towns of the area with market centres. Three carriers served Framlingham: Samuel Meen's carts travelled to Ipswich on Mondays, Wednesdays and Fridays and to Stradbroke on Tuesdays, Thursdays and Saturdays. James Sawyer journeyed to Ipswich on Mondays and Fridays and to Halesworth on Tuesdays and Saturdays whilst Thomas Coates also travelled to Ipswich and Halesworth on the same days. Edward Matlin provided a carrier service from Marlesford to Woodbridge in the 1860s. As the branch developed so the carriers provided an essential link from outlying villages and hamlets to the railheads at Framlingham and Wickham Market, bringing goods for onward dispatch by rail and delivering commodities brought by train to the branch station goods yards.

The initial freight handled confirmed the optimistic views of the promoters as barley, hay, wheat, straw and vegetable traffic were transferred from farm and carriers' carts to the railway for rapid transit to and from Ipswich, Lowestoft, Yarmouth, Norwich, Colchester and London markets. In addition to the root vegetable crops conveyed, including potatoes, swedes, carrots, turnips and mangold wurzels, from the early 1920s sugar beet was grown increasingly in East Suffolk, but as early as 7th November, 1914, Wilson of Cretingham sent 500 tons of beet from Framlingham to Cantley by rail. Considerable loads were transferred from farm carts and horse-drawn waggons to railway wagons at the branch goods yards for conveyance to the British Sugar Corporation factories at Ipswich, Cantley, Claydon and to a lesser extent Bury St Edmunds. By the late 1950s much of this traffic had transferred to road haulage for direct delivery from farm to factory, but until their closure in 1964 and 1965 respectively sugar beet was still loaded at Marlesford and Framlingham during the beet season from November to January.

By 1864 T.T. Buckmaster, advertising as a flour and corn merchant, miller, seed merchant, coal supplier, haulier of manure, salt and building materials was operating from the Victoria Road mill complex to and from Framlingham station whilst William Bone was a manufacturer of dressing and threshing machines near the station. Both used the railway extensively. The leading merchant for corn, wheat and barley traffic from the 1880s was E.G. Clarke & Sons Ltd who, at the peak of railway operation, was dispatching 20,000 tons in wagons after blending the product to provide the correct malt content. By 1932 ninety-two brewers and maltsters were receiving barley from Framlingham. Considerable grain traffic was conveyed by rail and in later years steel hopper wagons replaced covered vans, enabling larger tonnages to be conveyed. These were destined for Bass, Radcliffe and Gretton at Burton-on-Trent, Ind Coope throughout the country and Joshua Tetley at Leeds. Other consignments were sent to the Distillers Company in Glasgow and the Guiness Brewery, Dublin, via Bristol. Traffic was at its peak from December to June with the rate of over 100 wagon loads per month. Clarke's also sent wheat to Cranfield flour mills and were suppliers of animal feed, wheat, barley and mixed grass seed. The company also had sidings at Eccles Road on the Ely to Norwich main line and

FRAMLINGHAM DEPOT
No. 1.

arr. a.m.		dep. a.m.
	On Duty	{ 4 35 **T O** { 5 55 **T X**
	Loco	{ 5 20 **T O** { 6 40 **T X**
	Framlingham	5 50 **G T O**
6 15	Wickham Mkt.	6 30 **G T O**
6 55	Framlingham	7 14
7 38	Wickham Mkt.	7 56
8 19	Framlingham	8 30
8 51	Wickham Mkt.	9 3 **T O**
9 27	Framlingham	9 37 **T O**
10 1	Wickham	{ 10 15 **T O** { 9 35 **T X**
	Market	
T O 10 41 } **T X** 10 1 }	Framlinghm	11 12 Cattle **S O**
11 37	Wickh'm Mkt.	11 50 **S O**
p.m.		p.m.
12 14	Framlingham	12 34
12 58	Wickham Mkt.	1 14
1 38	Framlingham	1 45 **G**
2 30	Wickham Mkt.	2 45 **G**
3 25	Framlingham	4 19
4 46	Wickham Mkt.	5 52
6 16	Framlingham	6 26
6 50	Wickham Mkt.	7 10
7 34	Framlingham	L
	Loco	

Second set of men on duty **T X** 1.30 p.m.
T O 12.7 p.m.

Right: Locomotive and Enginemen's workings, Framlingham depot 1925.

Below: Locomotive diagram for Ipswich 'J15' class working Framlingham branch goods 1953.

Bottom: Consignments of pigs waiting to be loaded into cattle wagons at Framlingham in 1946.

Suffolk Record Office

IPSWICH DEPOT

Eng. Dia-gram No.	Engine M.P. Class	Engine Diagram			Days Run	Train Class	Reference to Trainmen's Workings	
							Enginemen	Guards
105	2 Fitted	a.m. 8 40 10 15 p.m. 12 59 2 20	Ipswich Wickham Mkt. Framlingham Wickham Mkt. Ipswich	a.m. 8 10 L 9 30 11 55 p.m. 1 45 L	EWD	 K K 	IPS 14 IPS 14 IPS 14 IPS 14	— IPS 8 IPS 8 —

Corpusty and Aylsham, both on the Midland & Great Northern Railway (M&GN). H.A. Walne Ltd also conducted an agricultural merchandising business at Framlingham and were the millers of barley for feed rather than malting. Gooderham and Hayward manufacturers of animal food compounds provided much traffic for the branch especially after the installation of the private siding to their mill at Marlesford in 1903.

Milk was regularly sent from all stations on the branch and conveyed to dairies at Ipswich in the then familiar 17 gallon churns. Two loads were dispatched during the summer months, one by the early morning train and then again in the late afternoon. Milk was only forwarded on the early morning train during the winter months. In the early years smaller quantities of milk were also sent to dairies in Yarmouth and Lowestoft. This area of Suffolk was not noted for its dairy farming and the relatively small amounts of traffic were quickly lost to road transport in the late 1930s, when milk churns were collected from the farms and delivered direct to the dairies.

Eggs became another significant commodity conveyed by rail from Framlingham. On 23rd June, 1900 the *Framlingham Weekly News* reported that the 4.42 pm train included a luggage van for the conveyance of 300 live cock pheasants from Jeptha Capon's pheasantries at Dennington *en route* to Germany. From then onwards consignments were regularly sent to other destinations. The Framlingham and District Agricultural Co-operative Society regularly dispatched eggs and complained in 1910 of the increase in charges made by the GER for conveyance of goods to London. By 1913 the Co-operative was the largest in England and 4,660,000 eggs had been sent out via Framlingham station in that year. The following year turkeys were dispatched and so trade continued to increase until, on 28th October, 1916, the GER Egg and Poultry train was exhibited at Framlingham station as part of a East Anglian tour to promote higher yields as part of the war effort. In the same month the Framlingham Co-operative announced that 479 tons of eggs had been dispatched via the branch, in 8,582,674 boxes containing 45,770,332 eggs. A further 1853 turkeys were sent by rail via Framlingham. Because of a shortage of staff arising from the war effort, in 1917 the GER asked the Framlingham Co-operative to take over the administration for the carrying of poultry produce in East Anglia and the transfer to Eastern Counties Farmers of all responsibility for running the Framlingham and Eastern Counties Co-operative Society Ltd goods depot, including the movement of grain. By 1921 the hub of the business had transferred to Ipswich and new properties had been bought at Debenham, Attleborough and Ipswich. From 1930 most of the conveyance of eggs had been transferred to road haulage and the railway saw little if any of that traffic thereafter.

Before the coming of the railway, drovers herded animals along the roads to and from market and prices fluctuated according to the condition of the beasts. The coming of the railway meant animals could be conveyed relatively quickly to local and London markets, arriving in much fresher condition and therefore gaining a higher price. From the outset livestock handled at the branch stations was two-way traffic. The potential of the railway for the speedy transportation of animals was soon realised and horses were regularly conveyed in wagons or horseboxes attached to passenger trains. Until World War II hunting horses

'J15' class 0-6-0 tender locomotive No. 65478 eases off the main line and on to the Framlingham branch at Wickham Market Junction with the branch goods train. The signal box and attendant Blackstock crossing keeper's cottage are to the right.   *The late Dr Ian C. Allen*

'J15' class 0-6-0 tender locomotive No. 65467 struggles with a heavy and extra long down goods train approaching Parham. The van behind the locomotive carried parcels and smalls traffic for local shops and was conveyed by at least one train each day across the branch after the withdrawal of passenger services in November 1952.   *The late Dr Ian C. Allen*

were conveyed to or from local hunt meetings on 24 hours notice being given to the forwarding stations. Cattle wagons were a common feature until the early 1950s and the branch was used to convey livestock to Ipswich and Norwich markets. Certain passenger trains were permitted to convey cattle wagons and this was especially useful on Tuesdays, Ipswich market day. Pigs and sheep were also conveyed by the branch freight service but trade declined with the relaxation of petrol rationing after World War II, when nearly all livestock traffic was lost to road transport.

On 29th January, 1898 Framlingham bacon factory was opened and pigs were brought by rail for slaughter, although some intrepid dealers from Parham and Hacheston persisted in driving their animals along the road to Framlingham; however, the premises closed in 1922. W. Hatcher, a local haulier, also collected pigs from local farms and these were subsequently divided into three categories, the smallest and fattest going to London by rail for slaughter. In the 1920s until World War II pigs were dispatched weekly to Brettell Lane, Staffordshire. For many years the railway employed horses for shunting duties and cartage and roan horse No. 3276, known locally at Wickham Market as 'Boxer', was in 1923 one of the oldest horses in service with the GER. The animal was then 18 years old having entered railway service in 1910 and was transferred from Ely to Wickham Market in June 1916.

Coal and coke traffic was handled at all stations with coal received from Newstead, Kirkley, Bestwood, Hucknall, Sheepbridge, Stanton, Shirebrook and Clipstone collieries. The wagons usually travelled via Peterborough where the Stanground sidings acted as a clearing house for empty wagons to the collieries and loaded ones returning to the branch. Other traffic came via the Great Northern and Great Eastern Joint Railway via Spalding and March. The coal loaded in colliery private owner wagons were then routed via Ely and Bury St Edmunds to Ipswich for onward delivery at the branch stations. In the 1920s and 1930s coke was also conveyed for horticultural purposes, but after World War II this commodity was taken by road. Fuel merchants handling traffic at the branch stations included W. Hayward at Marlesford, James Pepper Frost at Parham, who was also a timber and flour merchant, and W.E. Maulden, W. Hatcher and Fred Larter at Framlingham, the latter dealing with mainly steam coal. Other merchants included Edwin G. Clarke, corn, barley and coal merchants and Manby and Company, coal, corn and seed merchants. The reduction in the price of coal brought about by rail conveyance soon brought improvements when the local gas company supplied gas to Framlingham station. Three firemen were employed in the gasworks in the early days and a 20 ton load from the station goods yard was sufficient for four days. This coal was supplied from Wombwell colliery, South Yorkshire.

Of specific freight conveyed on the branch, Whitmore and Binyon manufactured machinery at Wickham Market but the establishment was closed in 1919. In the late 1920s and early 1930s many of the Suffolk roads remained unmetalled, dust tracks in summer and muddy morasses in winter. Suffolk County Council undertook a rolling programme of road improvements, which involved levelling the surface before covering with granite chippings and tarmacadam. Much of this material was delivered by rail to the branch station

On a dismal winter day 'B12/3' class 4-6-0 No. 61572 makes light work of the up branch freight leaving Framlingham and approaching Hoggate Hill crossing. No. 61572 is now preserved.

The late Dr Ian C. Allen

A complex shunting movement at Framlingham finds 'J15' class 0-6-0 tender locomotive No. 65389 with 16-ton all steel mineral wagons fore and aft. The quality of the coal in the locomotive tender is debatable, consisting of many large lumps and much dust. The rural nature of the Suffolk terminal is evident from the open fields beyond the railway.   *The late Dr Ian C. Allen*

goods yards from where the material was offloaded and taken to site by horse and waggon. The granite and tarmacadam was then levelled by steamroller.

The Anglo-American Oil Company, later to be taken over by Esso, created small storage depots at both Framlingham and Wickham Market stations whilst British Petroleum created a similar store at the junction station. Shell Marketing Ltd also had a store at Marlesford goods yard but the Wickham Market and Marlesford depots were closed in the early 1920s. These stores were established in the early 1900s using rail delivery to the yards before horse transport was employed to distribute lamp oil to surrounding villages. As motor transport became more reliable, and the speed limit was raised above 12 miles per hour, local distribution was made by road from Ipswich or Saxmundham.

In World War II the airfield at Parham, officially known as Framlingham, generated much traffic to and from between 1943 and 1945. Bombs, armaments and equipment for the USAF station were offloaded at Framlingham for onward conveyance by road. The ammunition was usually conveyed in open wagons, sheeted over to conceal the deadly cargo, although the prominent red flashed labels advised 'Shunt With Great Care' and 'Place As Far As Possible From The Engine, Brake Van and Wagons Labelled Inflammable'. Additional trains ran at night during the height of the allied bombing campaign against German cities.

For many years it was permitted for an engine to propel a brake van and no more than six wagons from Wickham Market along the down main line and then over the single line to Marlesford in order to deliver incoming goods traffic or clear the yard there of full or empty wagons. A suitable path was inserted in the working timetable. The working was cancelled in the latter years of the 1950s.

The following goods facilities were available at the branch stations:

Wickham Market
Loading gauges
Loading Dock
Fixed Crane 5 tons, later 6 tons capacity
Fixed Crane 1 ton 10 cwt capacity
Truck Weighbridge 18 tons, later 20 tons capacity
Weighing machine 1 ton 10 cwt, later 1 ton 12 cwt capacity
Goods Shed with capacity for storage of 50, later 75, quarters of grain
Lock Up for small packages
Three paved Cattle Pens with water supply
Also facilities for handling livestock, furniture vans on wheels and round timber also vans requiring crane power
Cartage conveyed by the GER Company

Marlesford
Loading gauge
Weighing machine 10 cwt, later 1 ton 2 cwt capacity
Lock Up for small packages
Facilities for loading livestock by special arrangement only

Parham
Loading gauge
Loading dock
Weighing machine 5 cwt capacity
Lock Up for small packages

'J15' class 0-6-0 No. 65478 trundles along the branch near Parham with the down branch 'bonus' freight on an early spring day.   *The late Dr Ian C. Allen*

A steam brake-only 'J15' class used on the branch and hence popular with train crews and shunters for working the 'bonus' goods train was No. 65361. Here she approaches Wickham Market Junction with a lengthy train of six covered vans, 10 open wagons, a LNER six-wheel passenger brake van and a former LMS brake van bringing up the rear.   *The late Dr Ian C. Allen*

Framlingham
Loading gauges
Loading Dock
Fixed Crane 5 tons capacity
Two Fixed Cranes 1 ton 10 cwt capacity
Truck Weighbridge 20 tons capacity
Weighing machine 1 ton 2 cwt capacity
Weighing machine 5 cwt capacity
Goods Shed with capacity for storage of 400 quarters of grain
Granary with storage capacity for 400 quarters of grain
Four paved Cattle Pens with water supply
Also facilities for handling livestock, furniture vans on wheels, round timber and for lifting vans requiring crane power

The latest time for the receipt of goods or livestock for forwarding by rail to ensure receipt at the destination station the following day was: Wickham Market 6.00 pm Saturdays excepted, 3.00 pm Saturdays only, Marlesford 4.00 pm, later 4.30 pm, Parham 4.30 pm and Framlingham 4.00 pm Saturdays excepted, 3.00 pm Saturdays only.

During GER days an appointed agent carted goods and parcels for the railway company at Framlingham, whilst local carriers' carts served the intermediate stations. Later the GER, LNER and BR carted goods.

The permitted load limit to be hauled by goods engines between Wickham Market and Framlingham in 1897 was:

	Goods Trucks loaded	*Coal Trucks loaded*
First Class Engines	-	-
Second Class Engines	30	26
Third Class Engines	25	21

Around the turn of the century the loads for goods engines was revised as under (numbers of trucks shown):

Class of	*Minerals*		*Goods*	
Locomotive	*Down*	*Up*	*Down*	*Up*
A	40	40	40	40
B	31	31	40	40
C	28	28	40	40
D	24	24	34	34
E	22	22	31	31
F	21	21	30	30
G	19	19	27	27
H	19	19	27	27

The following locomotives regularly allocated to the branch were classified as follows:

GE Class	*LNER Class*	*Classified*
Y14	J15	C
M15	F4	D
M15R	F5	D
G69	F6	D
C32	F3	E
Y65	F7	E
417	-	F
477	-	F
T26	E4	F
E22	J65	H

Shunting the 'bonus' goods at Framlingham. 'J15' class 0-6-0 tender locomotive No. 65389 backs a rake of covered vans and open wagons from the shed road to the main single line after taking water. To the right is H.A. Walne's Ltd granary. *The late Dr Ian C. Allen*

Brush type '2', 1,365 hp diesel-electric locomotive No. D5576 collecting three wagons from Marlesford goods yard on 22nd April, 1965. The local coal merchant had emptied all three wagons but when the last official goods train ran across the branch on Maundy Thursday 15th April, 1965 the leading vehicle was found defective. Once repairs were effected the Leiston to Ipswich goods train was delegated to collect the outstanding vehicles and here the shunter is preparing to couple the wagons to the locomotive as the guard waits by the ground frame to change the points, once the locomotive and wagons were back on the main single line. *The late Dr Ian C. Allen*

When the LNER reissued the loads book, freight trains on the Framlingham branch were not to exceed 40 wagons in length with individual loadings as follows:

Engine	Mineral	Goods	Empties
Class 1	26	39	40
Class 2	29	40	40
Class 3	32	40	40
Class 4	35	40	40
Class 5	39	40	40
Class 6	40	40	40

A class '3' goods engine was a 'J15' and a class '4' goods engine a 'J17'.

British Railways made slight amendments to the load book for class 'F', 'H', 'J' and 'K' class freight trains. Locomotives also had been reclassified, see below:

Load Group	Heavy	Goods	Empties
1	23	40	40
2	26	40	40
3	29	40	40
4	31	40	40
5	35	40	40

The following were the load groups for the various locomotive classes that worked across the Framlingham branch:

Tender	Group 1	Class D15+
		Class D16+
		Class E4*
	Group 2	Class J15
	Group 3	Class B12
	Group 4	Class J17
Tank	Group 1	F3*
		F4*
		F5*
		F6*

+ These classes to convey three heavy wagons or equivalent less than the loads shown for a Group 1 engine.
* These classes to convey five heavy wagons or equivalent less than the loads shown for Group 1 engines.

After dieselisation of freight services, a load limit of 35 wagons was placed on the branch services, with the undermentioned limits for individual classes of locomotive:

Class of Locomotive	Class of Train		
	4, 5, 6	7	8, 9
Class 15 8,00 hp	20	27	35
Class 21 1,100 hp	22	32	35
Class 24 1,160 hp	29	35	35
Class 31 1,250 hp	33	35	35

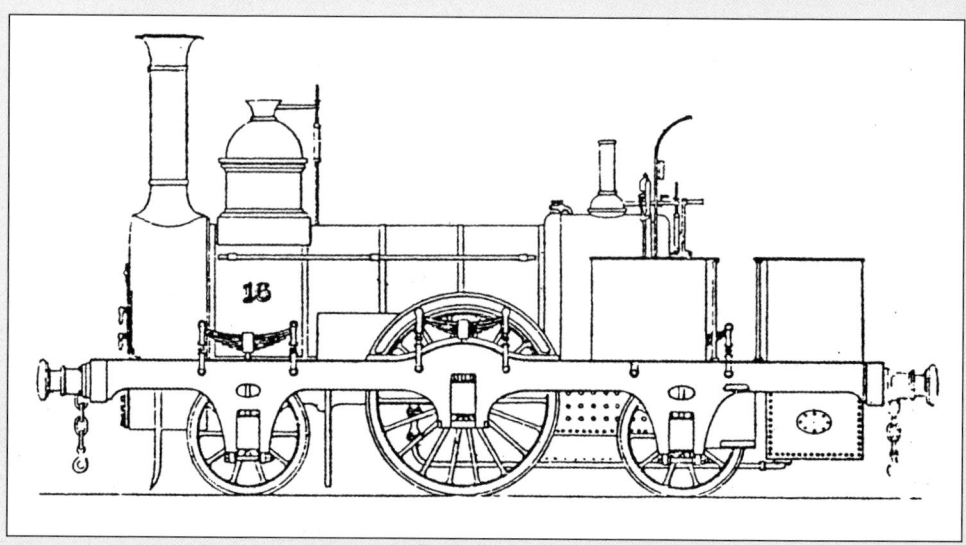

EUR 2-2-2 tank locomotive No. 16.

Gooch-designed ECR 'B' class 2-2-2 well tank locomotive.

Chapter Eight

Locomotives and Rolling Stock

The permanent way of the Framlingham branch was of light construction and only locomotives with low axle loading were permitted. The ECR, EUR and later GER fortunately possessed ample engines of low route availability to work the line. The LNER initially permitted class 'D1', 'D2', 'D13', 'D15', 'E4', 'J10', 'J11', 'J15', 'J17', 'J19' and 'J21' tender locomotives and 'C12', 'F1', 'F3', 'F4', 'F5', 'F6', 'F7', 'G5', 'J65', 'J66', 'J67', 'J68', 'J69', 'J70', 'Y1', 'Y3', 'Y5', 'Y6' and 'Y10' tank locomotives. The ex-Great Northern Railway 'D1' and 'D2' classes were only permitted subject to conforming to LNER loading gauge, whilst the 'D2', 'D13', 'D15', 'J19', 'C12', 'F6' and 'G5' classes were restricted to a speed limit of 30 mph on the branch. The LNER and later BR classified the branch to Route Availability 4 (RA 4) with additional classes with higher route availability 'C12', 'C13', 'D1', 'D15', 'D16', 'F2', 'J19', 'J27', 'N7' and 'N7/3' also permitted.

The following diesel locomotive classes were permitted across the Framlingham branch: BTH/Paxman 800 hp class '8/5' (RA4), NBL 1,100 hp class '11/4' (RA6), BR/Sulzer 1,160 hp class '11/1' (RA6), Brush 1,250 hp, 1,365 hp, 1,600 hp classes '12/2', '13/2' and '16/2' (RA6). All except the '8/5' class were restricted to 25 mph.

At an early stage it appears the decision was made to work the branch with a tank locomotive, which was capable of hauling the relatively lightweight passenger and mixed trains. It is almost certain the working of the Wickham Market to Framlingham branch was taken over by the trio of Eastern Union Railway 2-2-2 tank locomotives with one outbased at Framlingham at any one time. Built by Sharp Brothers of Manchester in 1854 (Works Nos. 765, 766 and 768) they were initially allocated the numbers 29, 30 and 31 but it is doubtful if these numbers were actually carried for they were delivered after the ECR had taken over the operation of the EUR. The new owners renumbered the 2-2-2 tank engines Nos. 13, 14 and 15 and they were well equipped to handle both passenger and freight traffic on the Framlingham branch. All were withdrawn for scrapping in November 1871 and the leading dimensions of the trio were:

Cylinders		14 in. x 18 in.
Heating	*tubes*	122 x 2 in.
	tubes surface	507.62 sq. ft
	firebox	54.00 sq. ft
	total	561.62 sq. ft
Leading wheels		3 ft 0 in.
Driving wheels		5 ft 0 in.
Trailing wheels		3 ft 0 in.
Wheelbase		13 ft 0 in.
Weight in working order		19 tons 0 cwt
Max. axle loading		8 tons

Working turn and turn about on the Framlingham line with the above trio was the former EUR 2-2-2 well tank locomotive No. 27, built by Sharp Brothers at Manchester (Works No. 595), and delivered in 1849. When the ECR took over the running of the EUR they renumbered the engine to 16 and she was withdrawn in February 1871. The principal dimensions were:

Cylinders		14 in. x 18 in.
Boiler	barrel length	10 ft 0 in.
	firebox	3 ft 6 in.
Heating	tubes	147 x 1⅞ in.
	tubes surface	704.7 sq. ft
	firebox	63.2 sq. ft
	total	767.9 sq. ft
Grate area		10.8 sq. ft
Leading wheels		3 ft 6 in.
Driving wheels		5 ft 6 in.
Trailing wheels		3 ft 6 in.
Wheelbase		12 ft 8 in.

Another class to be regularly outbased at Framlingham was the Gooch-designed 'B' class 2-2-2 well tank locomotives allocated to Ipswich. The class of six numbered 7 to 12 inclusive dated from 1853 and 1854 and before transfer to Suffolk worked the North Woolwich branch. No. 9 was certainly evaluated on the neighbouring Eye branch in 1867 and later worked on the Framlingham branch with No. 12. It must be assumed that others of the class worked on the line before scrapping. Nos. 10 and 11 were condemned in 1871, whilst Nos. 7, 9 and 12 were withdrawn in June, August and January 1874 respectively. No. 8 was converted to an inspection locomotive and was scrapped in March 1883. The leading dimensions of the 'B' class 2-2-2 well tank engines were:

Cylinders		12 in. x 22 in.
Boiler	max. diameter	3 ft 3½ in.
	length	10 ft
	firebox	3 ft 6 in.
Heating surface	tubes	127 x 1⅞ in.
	tubes surface	638.52 sq. ft
	firebox	69.17 sq. ft
	total	707.69 sq. ft
Grate area		9.41 sq. ft
Boiler pressure		110 psi
Leading wheels		3 ft 8 in.
Driving wheels		6 ft 6 in.
Trailing wheels		3 ft 8 in.
Wheelbase		12 ft 0 in.
Weight in working order		23 tons 19 cwt
Max. axle loading		9 tons 14 cwt

With the withdrawal of the various 2-2-2 tank classes the branch services were then taken over by Samuel Johnson's 'T7' class 0-4-2 tank locomotives especially built for light branch line traffic. Fifteen locomotives were built between 1871 and 1875, although the first three engines, Nos. 81, 82 and 83, were actually prototypes included in the class total. No record exists of all the individual locomotives outbased at Framlingham, but Nos. 12, 82 and 84 spent a period of time on the branch in 1878-1880. All locomotives were withdrawn by 1894 with No. 12 going for scrap in 1892, and No. 82 in 1892. The principal dimensions of the class were:

Cylinders		15 in. x 22 in.
Motion		Stephenson with slide valves
Boiler	*max. diameter*	3 ft 10 in.
	barrel length	9 ft 1 in.
	firebox	4 ft 4¾ in.
Heating surface	*tubes*	204 x 1½ in.
	tubes surface	754.0 sq. ft
	firebox	76.0 sq. ft
	total	830.0 sq. ft
Grate area		12.75 sq. ft
Boiler pressure		140 psi
Driving wheels		5 ft 3 in.
Trailing wheels		3 ft 7 in.
Length over buffers		23 ft 7 in.
Wheelbase		14 ft 6 in.
Weight in working order		33 tons 12 cwt
		30 tons 19 cwt*
Water capacity		750 gallons
		500 gallons*

* Nos. 81 to 83.

The last five engines Nos. 15 to 18 also differed in that the boiler contained 148 x 1¾ in. tubes with the boiler heating reduced to 636.9 sq. ft, firebox 74.43 sq. ft, giving a total of 711.12 sq. ft.

The introduction and condemnation dates of the 'T7' class were:

No.	Date new	Date condemned
81	March 1871	1892
82	March 1871	1891
83	April 1871	1892
84	June 1873	1892
85	June 1873	1893
86	September 1873	1892
13	November 1873	1891
14	December 1873	1894
11	December 1874	1893
12	December 1874	1892
15	April 1875	1894
16	April 1875	1894
17	May 1875	1893
18	May 1875	1891
19	June 1875	1894

As with so many of the GER branch lines, the 'T7' class worked turn and turn about with the 'K9' class 0-4-2 tank locomotives designed by William Adams. The latter class only totalled 10 in number and were all built in 1877 and 1878. Nos. 20, 24 and 25 are known to have worked on the Framlingham line at some time but all the class were withdrawn from service between 1903 and 1907. The 'K9' class were the only locomotives built at Stratford works during Adams' term of office. At first only a handbrake was fitted but the class was later equipped with the Westinghouse brake. A half-cab was originally provided when the locomotives were built, but a few years later weather plates were fitted at the back of the cab and later the roof was extended to cover the footplate completely. No. 20 was transferred to the duplicate list in 1902 and renumbered 020 before being scrapped in 1906. Nos. 24 and 25 were condemned in 1905. The leading dimensions of the 'K9' class were:

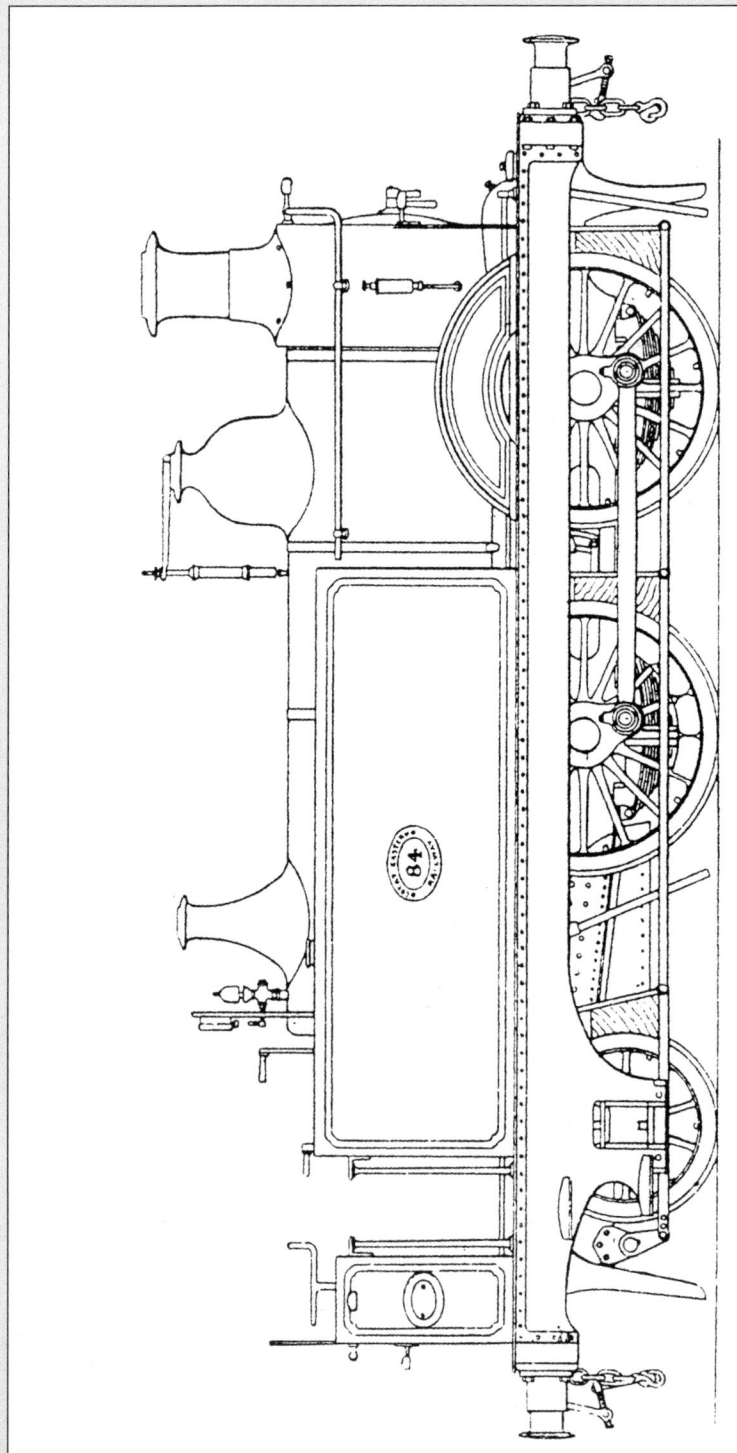

Samuel Johnson's 'T7' class 0-4-2 tank locomotive.

S.W. Johnson's 'T7' class 0-4-2 tank locomotives were introduced into traffic between 1871 and 1875 for light branch line duties. Nos. 12, 82 and 84 spent some time on the Framlingham branch. No. 84 built in 1873 was withdrawn from traffic in 1892.   *Author's Collection*

Working turn and turn about with the Johnson 'T7' class on the Framlingham branch were representatives of the 'K9' class 0-4-2 tank locomotives introduced by William Adams in 1877. No. 25 outbased on the Suffolk line for a short period, later worked the initial services on the Kelvedon and Tollesbury Light Railway in Essex in 1904 and is shown at Norwich in 1905 just before withdrawal from traffic.   *LCGB/Ken Nunn*

Cylinders		15 in. x 22 in.
Motion		Stephenson with slide valves
Boiler	max. diameter	4 ft 2 in.
	barrel length	9 ft 1 in.
Heating	tubes	203 x 1¾ in.
	tubes surface	874.87 sq. ft
	firebox	75.43 sq. ft
	total	950.30 sq. ft
Grate area		12.30 sq. ft
Boiler pressure		140 psi
Driving wheels		4 ft 10 in.
Trailing wheels		3 ft 8 in.
Wheelbase		14 ft 0 in.
Weight in working order		38 tons 11 cwt
Water capacity		850 gallons
Coal capacity		15 cwt

In 1889 James Holden introduced 10 six-coupled passenger tank locomotives into service for light branch duties and classified the engines 'E22'. The first six were sent to work on the Fenchurch Street to Blackwall services with the result that they quickly earned the nickname of the 'Blackwall Tanks'. The subsequent engines on release to traffic were allocated to Braintree and Buntingford. A further 10 locomotives with detailed differences were built in 1893 and whilst some were allocated to Blackwall the remaining locomotives were reallocated to various GER country depots. It was during this period that one of the representatives allocated to Ipswich was outstationed at Framlingham. For a short period No. 153 was the regular branch engine, but later replaced by Nos. 247 and 248. These engines never monopolised the branch services and in the latter years worked alongside the 'K9' class. They survived on branch duties until 1909 when they were ousted by the 'Y65' class 2-4-2 tank locomotives. The locomotives regularly used on the branch included:

In 1889 James Holden introduced into service 10 six-coupled passenger tank locomotives of class 'E22' for light branch duties followed by a further 10 engines in 1893. Soon after introduction of the second batch a member of the class was outbased from Ipswich to work the Framlingham branch to displace the 'T7' 0-4-2 tank engines and work alongside the 'K9' class 0-4-2 tank engines. The 'E22' class, later reclassified to 'J65' by the LNER, was ousted from the branch as early as 1909. No. 7248 as GER No. 248 was one of the class which worked the branch.   *LCGB/Ken Nunn Collection*

GER No.	LNER 1924 No.	LNER 1946 No.	BR No.	Withdrawn
153	7153			September 1931
156	7156			August 1937
247	7247	8213		February 1948
248	7248			May 1936
250	7250	8214	68214	October 1956
253	7252	8215		May 1949

The leading dimensions of the class were:

Cylinders		14 in. x 20 in.
Motion		Stephenson with slide valves
Boiler	max. diameter	4 ft 2 in.
	barrel length	9 ft 1 in.
	firebox	4 ft 6 in.
Heating	tubes	227 x 1⅝
	tubes surface	909.40 sq. ft
	firebox	78.00 sq. ft
	total	987.40 sq. ft
Grate area		12.40 sq. ft
Boiler pressure		160 psi
Driving wheels		4 ft 0 in.
Tractive effort		11,106 lb.
Length over buffers		27 ft 2 in.
Wheelbase		13 ft 4 in.
Weight in working order		36 tons 11 cwt
Max. axle loading		13 tons 3 cwt
Water capacity		650 gallons
Coal capacity		2 tons 10 cwt

The next class associated with the Framlingham branch was the 'Y65' class 2-4-2 tank locomotives designed by S.D. Holden and introduced into service in 1909-1910. Built especially for light branch passenger duties, they were the least successful of Holden's tank engines and after a time they were relegated to auto-train working and service on minor branch lines. Nos. 1300 to 1311 were constructed at Stratford works and their small boiler and enormous cab soon earned them the nickname 'Crystal Palaces'. Nos. 1300, 1309, 1310 and 1311 were allocated to Ipswich and regularly outbased at Framlingham to work the branch. Other duties of Ipswich-based locomotives included the Felixstowe line and short periods on the Hadleigh, Aldeburgh and Brightlingsea branches. The class never gained the monopoly of the Framlingham branch, being underpowered for the mixed trains, which were a regular feature of the line, and by 1913 was displaced by the larger 'C32' class 2-4-2 tank locomotives. After leaving the Ipswich district No. 1310 was subsequently allocated to Ramsey High Street. No. 1311 was converted to auto-train trials in 1914 on the Cambridge to Mildenhall and Somersham to Ramsey High Street branches before working on the reintroduced Churchbury loop line service between White Hart Lane and Cheshunt during World War I. The LNER redesignated the 'Y65s' to class 'F7' and renumbered them to 8300 to 8311 inclusive. No. 8310 was transferred to Scotland in 1931 with two other members of the class to work the Gifford, Lauder and Selkirk branches and the Galashiels to Peebles line. There she was renumbered in 1942 to 7598 and again under the 1946 scheme to 7094. With the former 8308, by then renumbered 7093, she was scrapped as joint last member of the class in November 1948. Details of the Framlingham branch engines were:

GER No.	LNER 1924 No.	LNER 1942 No.	LNER 1946 No.	Condemned
1300	8300			August 1938
1304	8304	7594		March 1944
1309	8309			January 1931
1310	8310	7598	7094	November 1948
1311	8311			September 1931

The principal dimensions of the 'Y65'/'F7' class were:

Cylinders	2 inside		15 in. x 22 in.
Motion			Stephenson with slide valves
Boiler		max. diameter	3 ft 11½ in.
		barrel	9 ft 1 in.
		firebox	4 ft 6 in.
Heating		tubes	199 x 1⅝ in.
		tubes surface	797.2 sq. ft
		firebox	75.7 sq. ft
		total	872.9 sq. ft
Grate area			12.2 sq. ft
Boiler pressure			160 psi
Leading wheels			3 ft 6 in.
Driving wheels			4 ft 10 in.
Trailing wheels			3 ft 6 in.
Tractive effort			11,607 lb.
Length over buffers			30 ft 11 in.
Wheelbase			19 ft 6 in.
Weight in working order			45 tons 14 cwt
Max. axle loading			14 tons 3 cwt
Water capacity			1,000 gallons
Coal capacity			2 tons

For a short while the 'Y65' class 2-4-2 tank locomotives, designed by S.D. Holden and introduced into service in 1909-10, were used on the Framlingham branch. The class never gained a monopoly on the workings, being underpowered for mixed trains and by 1913 they had been displaced by the larger 'C32' class 2-4-2 tank locomotives. No. 1311 shown at Ipswich was later converted for auto-train working in 1914 and was withdrawn from traffic as LNER 'F7' class No. 8311 in September 1931.   *LCGB/Ken Nunn*

GER 'C32' class 2-4-2 tank locomotives, later designated 'F3' by the LNER worked the Framlingham branch for several decades and were instantly recognisable by the large brass axleboxes on the leading and trailing axles. No. 8072 is in the plain unlined LNER black livery. *Author's Collection*

J. Holden's 'C32' class 2-4-2 tank locomotives, with 5 ft 8 in. driving wheels, soon replaced the 'Y65s' on the branch workings. They were built between 1893 and 1902 at Stratford works. A total of 50 engines were introduced into traffic, principally for use on the longer distance semi-fast services and initially they worked on the Liverpool Street to Bishop's Stortford semi-fasts. Later they ran from Liverpool Street to Southend and Southminster but soon after the turn of the century many were displaced and sent to GER country depots. Framlingham shed had two of the class outbased at one time but this was later reduced to one engine. The 'C32s' were reclassified 'F3' by the LNER after the grouping and remained the mainstay of the branch for many years. The engines based at Ipswich also worked the Felixstowe, Aldeburgh, Brightlingsea and Hadleigh branches. Locomotives known to have worked from Framlingham shed included:

GER No.	LNER 1924 No.	LNER 1946 No.	BR No.	Withdrawn
1041	8041	7142		April 1947
1042	8042	7143		July 1948
1049	8049	7150		October 1949
1064	8064	7137		November 1947
1065	8065			March 1938
1066	8066	7138		August 1947
1068	8068	7140		March 1949
1070	8070	7121		April 1947
1071	8071	7122		November 1947
1072	8072	7123		March 1947
1073	8073			November 1938
1076	8076			March 1937
1077	8077			August 1947
1079	8079	7127	67127	April 1953
1081	8081	7128	67128	December 1950

The Framlingham branch train normally used the down main line platform at Wickham Market before setting off on its journey. Here 'F3' class 2-4-2 tank locomotive No. 7140 waits with a mixed train in the down reception siding for a connecting down main line service to pass in 1946. Wickham Market goods shed and the shed road siding are to the right. No. 7140 carries the single disc for a stopping passenger services on the lamp bracket by the chimney. *The late Dr Ian C. Allen*

The branch down home signal arm is showing clear as 'F3' class 2-4-2 tank locomotive No. 67127 approaches Wickham Market Junction with steam shut off and blower on hauling the two-coach Framlingham branch train. As usual the guard's compartment of the ex-GER brake/third is in the middle of the formation, which enabled ease of passengers alighting and descending at Hacheston Halt and for the guard to check tickets on the journey. *The late Dr Ian C. Allen*

The principal dimensions of the class were:

Cylinders		17½ in. x 24 in.
Motion		Stephenson with slide valves
Boiler	max. diameter	4 ft 4 in.
	barrel length	10 ft 0 in.
	firebox	5 ft 5 in.
Heating	tubes	242 x 1⅝ in.
	tubes surface	1063.8 sq. ft
	firebox	100.9 sq. ft
	total	1,164.7 sq. ft
Grate area		18.0 sq. ft
Boiler pressure		160 psi
Leading wheels		4 ft 0 in.
Driving wheels		5 ft 8 in.
Trailing wheels		4 ft 0 in.
Tractive effort		14,700 lb.
Length over buffers		34 ft 10 in.
Wheelbase		23 ft 3 in.
Weight in working order		58 tons 12 cwt
Max. axle loading		15 tons 6 cwt
Water capacity		1,460 gallons
Coal capacity		3 tons 5 cwt

The 'F3' class was gradually superseded by members of S.D. Holden's 'G69' class reclassified by the LNER to 'F6'. These 2-4-2 tank locomotives represented the final development of the 2-4-2 wheel arrangement on the GER. They were originally put to work on the London suburban services but with the arrival of the GER 'L77' class 0-6-2 tank locomotives, redesigated class 'N7' by the LNER,

'F3' class 2-4-2 tank locomotive No. 67127 trundles off the Framlingham branch at Wickham Market Junction in June 1949 having worked a shuttle to Marlesford. As there is no goods traffic the engine is returning to Wickham Market to resume passenger working, hauling a 15-ton, six-wheel former Great Central Railway goods brake van, which for some time was the allocated branch goods brake. The East Suffolk main line can be seen following a straight course away towards Snape Junction and Saxmundham. The fireman has the single line Train Staff ready to hand to the signalman. *The late Dr Ian C. Allen*

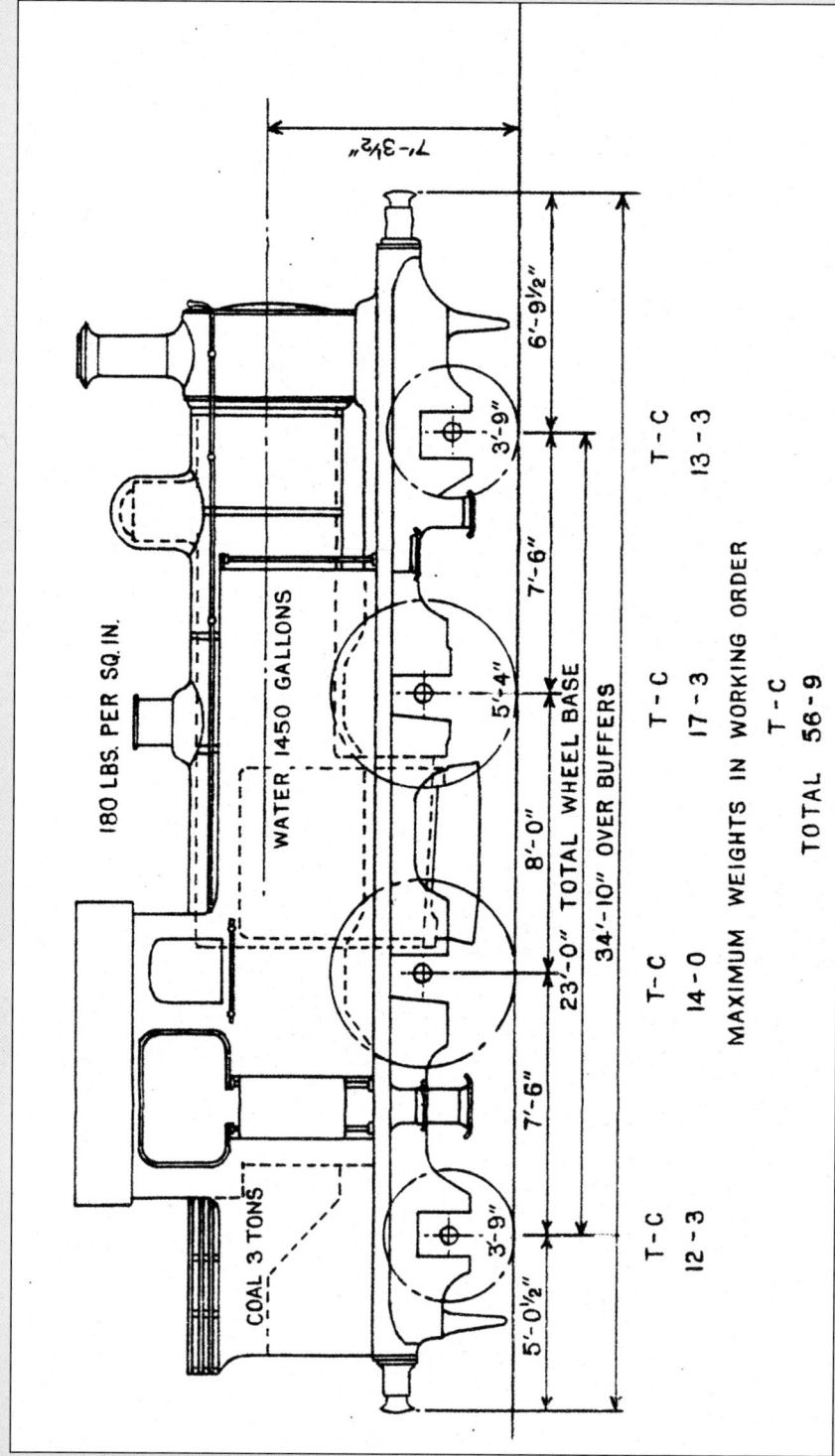

180 LBS. PER SQ. IN.

WATER, 1450 GALLONS

COAL 3 TONS

7'-3½"

6'-9½"

3'-9"

7'-6"

5'-4"

8'-0"

23'-0" TOTAL WHEEL BASE

34'-10" OVER BUFFERS

7'-6"

3'-9"

5'-0½"

T-C	T-C	T-C	T-C	T-C
12-3	14-0	17-3	13-3	

MAXIMUM WEIGHTS IN WORKING ORDER

T-C

TOTAL 56-9

S.D. Holden's GER 'G69' class, later LNER 'F6' class, 2-4-2 tank locomotive.

were gradually ousted as more of the 0-6-2 locomotives were introduced. The 'F6s' gradually migrated to country depots and worked out their days on rural branches. The Ipswich district allocation was usually outbased at Aldeburgh and Framlingham where they worked both passenger and mixed trains. The first of the class to arrive on the branch on 14th December, 1949 was No. 67220, which disgraced itself by developing valve trouble. Normally a 'J15' class 0-6-0 from Ipswich would have been provided as a replacement, but as this locomotive was required for the Mid Suffolk Light Railway No. 67220 was again pressed into service working with two coaches only, and the branch goods traffic was cancelled for the day. A relief 'F6' class locomotive No. 67228 was sent to Framlingham the following day and worked the branch complete with a destination board on the smokebox proclaiming 'Enfield Town'. In the last weeks of the passenger service the former regular engine No. 67220 was rarely seen on the branch and was usually working from Aldeburgh. Thus the branch was left in the hands of Nos. 67230 and 67239, the latter working the passenger services on the last day. Locomotives regularly allocated to Framlingham included:

GER No.	LNER 1924 No.	LNER 1946 No.	BR No.	Withdrawn
1	7001	7230	67230	May 1958
10	7010	7239	67239	December 1955
61	7061	7220	67220	July 1955
69	7069	7228	67228	April 1958

The principal dimensions of the 'F6' class were:

Cylinders	2 inside	17½ in. x 24 in.
Motion		Stephenson with slide valves
Boiler	max. diameter outside	4 ft 2 in.
	barrel length	10 ft 2½ in.
Firebox length outside		5 ft 5 in.
Heating surface	firebox	96.7 sq. ft
	tubes	227 x 1⅝ in.
	tubes surface	1,018.0 sq. ft
	total	1,114.7 sq. ft
Grate area		15.2 sq. ft
Boiler pressure		180 psi
Leading wheels		3 ft 9 in.
Coupled wheels		5 ft 4 in.
Trailing wheels		3 ft 9 in.
Tractive effort		17,571 lb.
Length over buffers		34 ft 10 in.
Wheelbase		23 ft 0 in.
Weight in working order		56 tons 9 cwt
Max. axle loading		17 tons 3 cwt
Water capacity		1,450 gallons
Coal capacity		3 tons

During World War II, 15 'F4' class and one 'F5' class 2-4-2 tank locomotives were loaned to the Government for hauling coastal defence armoured trains. The initial 40 members of the 'M15' class had entered service between 1884 and 1887 to the designs of T.W. Worsdell. Between 1903 and 1909 a further 120 locomotives were built, and from 1911 until 1920 the GER rebuilt 30 engines

S.D. Holden's 'G69' class, later reclassified 'F6' by the LNER, represented the final development of the 2-4-2 wheel arrangement on the GER. They originally worked London suburban services but were ousted from 1947 by Hill's 'L77' class 0-6-2Ts, later LNER 'N7' class. LNER No. 7061 was one of many that were transferred to country depots and was outbased from Ipswich to work on the Framlingham and Aldeburgh branches. No. 7061 was renumbered 7220 by the LNER and later 67220 by BR before withdrawal in July 1955.   *Author's Collection*

As it is a Sunday, 'F6' class 2-4-2 tank locomotive No. 67230 stands out of steam on the shed road at Framlingham, with an attendant locomotive coal wagon behind the bunker. If the wagon was almost full of coal the cleaner delegated to coal the engine on nights shovelled the fuel straight from the wagon into the bunker. Once the coal level dropped the coal was transferred to the adjacent coal stage. The water tank behind the locomotive was endorsed 'R. Garrett and Sons, Leiston, Suffolk 1859'.   *The late Dr Ian C. Allen*

'F6' class 2-4-2 tank locomotive No. 67230 was regularly outbased as the Framlingham branch engine. Here with fireman Ray Moore looking out of the cab she gets away from Wickham Market Junction passing Blackstock Wood with her two-coach train formed of ex-GER bogie brake/third to diagram 527 and bogie composite to diagram 227-1. *The late Dr Ian C. Allen*

With smoke obliterating most of the station, 'F6' class 2-4-2 tank engine No. 67230 waits departure at Framlingham in July 1952. The ornate canopy covering the single platform was drastically cut back in the latter years of the line. *A. Forsyth*

In the late 1940s and early 1950s the working timetable showed 'Q' path (as and when required), goods workings between passenger/mixed services. These ran from Framlingham to Parham and return and Wickham Market to Marlesford and return and obviated the necessity for mixed trains to shunt at the intermediate stations. 'F6' class 2-4-2 tank locomotive No. 67220 is approaching Parham with one such working in 1950.   *Author's Collection*

A view from the cab spectacle of 'F6' class 2-4-2 tank locomotive No. 67230 standing in the shed road at Framlingham, with the signal box and station in the distance and goods yard to the right. Note the allotments on the left.   *The late Dr Ian C. Allen*

with higher boiler pressure and designated them 'M15R'. The earliest built locomotives were all condemned by 1929, whilst the LNER reclassified the 'M15s' to class 'F4' and the rebuilt engines class 'F5'. They were nicknamed 'Gobblers' because the original engines had a voracious appetite for coal and, although improvements were made, the name persisted. Between June 1940 and July 1943 the Framlingham branch, together with the neighbouring Snape and Aldeburgh lines, was regularly patrolled by the coastal defence trains, initially by train 'D' powered by 'F4' class No. 7178 based at Ipswich, and then by train 'C' hauled by 'F4' class No. 7214. After returning from patrols in Cornwall, train 'D' resumed its activities on Essex and Suffolk coastal branches until disbanded in July 1943. They were not new to the branch, for occasional use had been made of these classes on the branch before the war deputizing for the usual 'F3' engines and at least four had been outbased at Framlingham in the period after Grouping. The following 'F4' and 'F5' class locomotives travelled across the Framlingham branch:

GER No.	LNER 1924 No.	LNER 1946 No.	BR No.	Condemned
74	7074	7182	67182	January 1953
144	7144	7191	67191*	November 1955
147	7147	7193	67193*	November 1957
178	7178	7173		April 1948
214	7214	7162	67162	August 1955
665	7665			August 1926

* F5 class

During World War II, two members of the LNER 'F4' class 2-4-2 tank locomotives, suitably modified with armour plating, worked Coastal Defence Armoured Trains over East Anglian lines including the Framlingham branch. Train 'C' which was disbanded in 1943 was hauled by No. 7214, which survived hostilities and with its armour plating removed was renumbered 7162 in the 1946 renumbering scheme. As BR No. 67162 she is shown just before withdrawal in 1955. *Author's Collection*

The leading dimensions of the 'F4' class were:

Cylinders	*2 inside*	17½ in. x 24 in.
Motion		Stephenson with slide valves
Boiler	*max. diameter outside*	4 ft 2 in.
	barrel length	10 ft 2½ in.
Firebox length outside		5 ft 5 in.
Heating surface	*firebox*	98.4 sq. ft
	tubes	227 x 1⅝ in.
	tubes surface	1,018.0 sq. ft
	total	1,116.4 sq. ft
Grate area		15.3 sq. ft
Boiler pressure		160 psi
Leading wheels		3 ft 9 in.
Coupled wheels		5 ft 4 in.
Trailing wheels		3 ft 9 in.
Tractive effort		15,618 lb.
Length over buffers		34 ft 10 in.
Wheelbase		23 ft 0 in.
Weight in working order		51 tons 11 cwt
Max. axle loading		14 tons 18 cwt
Water capacity		1,200 gallons
Coal capacity		3 tons 10 cwt

The detailed differences of the 'F5' class were:

Heating surface	*firebox*	96.7 sq. ft
	total	1,114.7 sq. ft
Grate area		15.2 sq. ft
Boiler pressure		180 psi
Tractive effort		17,571 lb.
Weight in working order		53 tons 19cwt
Max. axle loading		16 tons 0 cwt

'F5' class 2-4-2 tank locomotive No. 7147 worked on the Framlingham branch in the 1920s. She was renumbered 7193 in the 1946 renumbering scheme and became BR No. 67193 before withdrawal in November 1957.   *Author's Collection*

In the early years tank locomotives outbased at Framlingham normally handled the freight traffic, but special and out-of-course goods workings brought a variety of tender locomotives to the line. Locomotives known to have worked the East Suffolk main line and branch freight trains included five 0-6-0 goods engines built by Stothert & Slaughter for the ECR in March and April 1846. They were originally numbered 97 to 101 but were soon renumbered 155 to 159 and were delivered with six-wheel tenders. In 1858 the tenders received new tanks giving greater water capacity and although the first two were early casualties for scrapping, Nos. 157 to 159 were placed on the duplicate list in 1864 becoming 1570, 1580 and 1590 respectively. The first two were rebuilt with new boilers in 1866 and were sent away to Cambridge to work goods trains to Colchester via Sudbury and the Colne Valley & Halstead Railway. No. 1590 was scrapped in April 1873, No. 1580 in August 1880 and No. 1570 in October 1883. The leading dimensions of the class were:

Cylinders		16 in. x 24 in.
Boiler	outside diameter	3 ft 9 in.
	length	10 ft 2 in.
Firebox		4 ft 8 in.
Heating surface	tubes	152 x 1⅞ in.
Driving wheels		5 ft 0 in.
Wheelbase	locomotive	13 ft 8 in.
Water capacity		1,350 gallons
Weight in working order		24 tons 18 cwt*
Max axle loading		10 tons 3 cwt*

* after rebuilding

Another class used in the early years was Robert Stephenson & Company's 'Long Boiler' 2-4-0 tender locomotives, delivered to the ECR between March and September 1847. Numbered in the series 71 to 77, they regularly worked on the East Suffolk line in the first decade after opening. They were the subject of several modifications and rebuildings, Nos. 71 to 77 receiving new boilers in 1860 and Nos. 72 and 75 being rebuilt in June 1867. Several were placed on the duplicate list, Nos. 71, 72 and 75 becoming 710, 720 and 750 respectively in 1876. The locomotives were scrapped as follows: No. 710 in May 1878, 720 in September 1877, 73 in November 1869, 74 in April 1859, 750 in April 1881, 76 in July 1868 and 77 in August 1871.

The principal dimensions of the class as modified by Sinclair, the ECR locomotive superintendent, were:

Cylinders		15 in. x 22 in.
Boiler	max. diameter	3 ft 8 in.
	length	13 ft 8½ in.
Firebox		4 ft 2 in.
Heating surface	tubes	123 x 1⅞ in.
	tubes surface	838.5 sq. ft
	firebox	67.6 sq. ft
	total	906.1 sq. ft
Grate area		10.8 sq. ft
Boiler pressure		110 psi
Leading wheels		3 ft 6 in.
Coupled wheels		6 ft 0 in.
Wheelbase		11 ft 7 in.

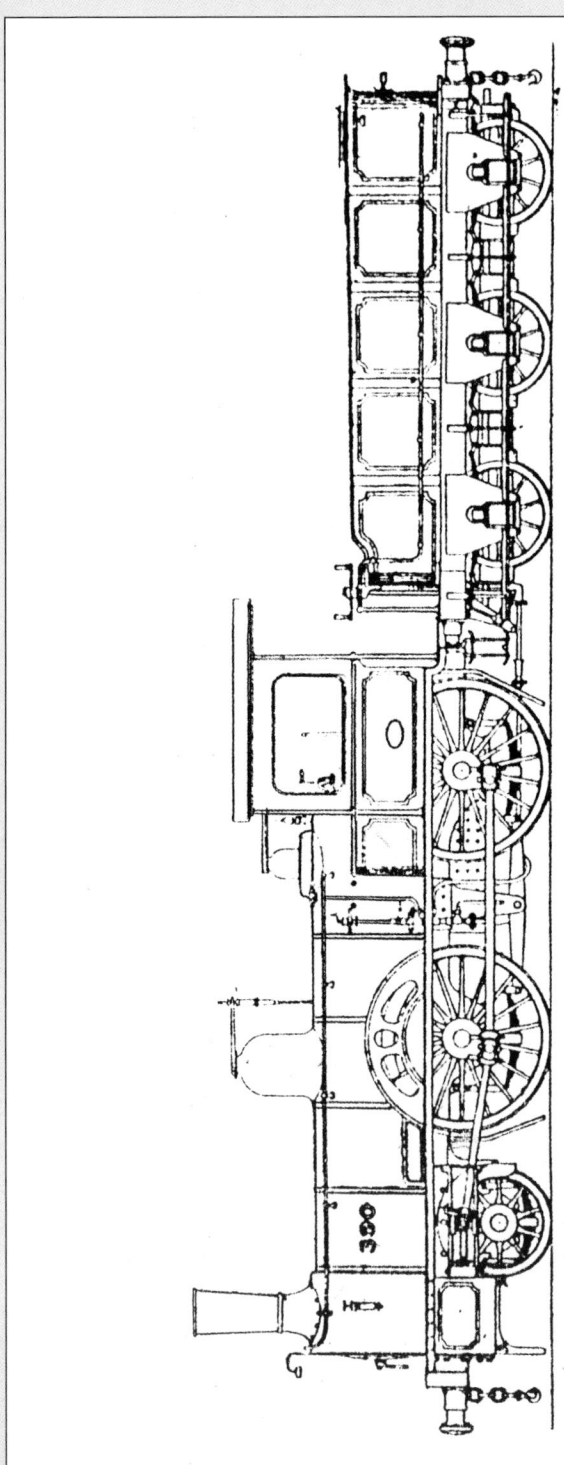

Sinclair 'Y' class 2-4-0 tender locomotive.

Between 1854 and 1855 Gooch introduced into service five 6-coupled goods engines with fairly new boilers taken from five large Crampton singles which were scrapped through lack of adhesion. The five, numbered 233 to 237, were built at Stratford works and had outside bearings. They served at Ipswich for a while and worked the East Suffolk goods services. New boilers designed by Sinclair were fitted to Nos. 234 and 236 in October 1867, whilst Johnson rebuilt the remaining three locomotives in 1869 and 1870. The five engines were placed on the duplicate list in 1880 by having a cipher added to their running number but only survived a few more years in service, No. 234 being scrapped in April 1882, Nos. 233 and 235 in January 1883, No. 237 in October 1883 and 236 in November 1884. The leading dimensions of the Johnson rebuilt engines were:

Cylinders		16 in. x 24 in.
Boiler	max. outside diameter	4 ft 0 in.
	length	9 ft 11¼ in.
Firebox		5 feet 1¾ in.
Grate area		15.5 sq. ft
Heating surface	tubes	157 x 2 in.
	tubes surface	841.5 sq. ft
	firebox	89.65 sq. ft
	total	931.15 sq. ft
Boiler pressure		140 psi
Driving wheels		5 ft 0 in.
Wheelbase	engine	14 ft 6 in.
	tender	10 ft 2 in.
Weight in working order	engine	27 tons 7 cwt
	tender	17 tons 1 cwt
	total	44 tons 8 cwt
Max. axle loading		10 tons 15 cwt

The next locomotives to work the branch were Sinclair's celebrated 'Y' class 2-4-0 goods engines. Between July 1859 and August 1866 one hundred and ten were introduced into service from a variety of makers, Neilson & Company building Nos. 307 to 326, Robert Stephenson & Company Nos. 327 to 341, R. & W. Hawthorn Nos. 342 to 356, Kitson & Company Nos. 357 to 381, Vulcan Foundry Nos. 382 to 406 and Schnider et Cie of Creusot Nos. 407 to 416. Each batch had detailed differences and engine No. 327 was displayed at the Exhibition held in Hyde Park, London in 1862. The engines worked all over the GER system on passenger, goods and mixed traffic services and those allocated to Ipswich spent considerable time on express and trip goods diagrams. Over the years most were rebuilt and a number were converted into 4-4-0 tender locomotives for passenger work. Scrapping of the class commenced in 1882 and after 1888 surviving engines were placed on the duplicate list by having a '0' placed before the running number. The class only saw service on the Framlingham branch in their declining years. The final batch of four locomotives was condemned for scrapping in 1894.

The leading dimensions of the 327 to 356 batch of locomotives as built were:

Cylinders		17 in. x 24 in.
Boiler	max. diameter outside	4 ft 0 in.
	length	11 ft 5¾ in.
Firebox		4 ft 8 in.

Heating surface	tubes	192 x 1¾ in.
	tubes surface	968.52 sq. ft
	firebox	72.36 sq. ft
	total	1,040.88 sq. ft
Grate area		13.75 sq. ft
Boiler pressure		120 psi
Leading wheels		3 ft 7 in.
Coupled wheels		6 ft 1 in.
Tender wheels		3 ft 7 in.
Wheelbase	engine	15 ft 1 in.
	tender	11 ft 5 in.
Weight in working order	engine	30 tons 16 cwt
	tender	21 tons 15 cwt
	total	52 tons 11 cwt
Water capacity		1,600 gallons

From the 1880s, Samuel Johnson's '417' class 0-6-0 tender locomotives, originally introduced between 1867 and 1869, and built by Neilson & Company and the Worcester Engine Company, worked some of the goods services. The 60 built were numbered 417 to 476 inclusive and initially worked main line goods trains but on the introduction of the '477' class and 'Y14' class 0-6-0 tender locomotives were relegated to pick-up freight and branch line work. The various members of the class allocated to Ipswich depot worked out their last years on the East Suffolk line, which included trips to Framlingham. The leading dimensions of the class were:

Cylinders	2 inside	16½ in. x 24 in.
Motion		Stephenson with slide valves
Boiler	max. dia outside	4 ft 2 in.
	length	10 ft 0 in.
Firebox		5 ft 5 in.
Heating surface	tubes	203 x 1¾ in.
	tubes surface	957.6 sq. ft
	firebox	94.9 sq. ft
	total	1052.5 sq. ft
Grate area		15.27 sq. ft
Boiler pressure		140 psi
Driving wheels		5 ft 3 in.
Tender wheels		3 ft 7 in.
Wheelbase	engine	15 ft 3 in.
	tender	9 ft 0 in.
Weight in working order	engine	30 tons 15 cwt
	tender	21 tons 17 cwt
	total	52 tons 12 cwt
Max axle loading		11 tons 5 cwt
Water capacity		1,740 gallons

The first of the class was withdrawn in 1888 and scrapping continued every year, with the exception of 1897, until 1899. The survivors after 1891 were placed on the duplicate list by having a '0' prefix added to the number.

The next class associated with goods services on the branch was the '477' class 0-6-0 tender locomotives, designed by Samuel Johnson and dating from 1871 to 1873. Numbered in the series 477 to 526, the class came from several builders: Beyer, Peacock; Robert Stephenson; Dübs; Nasmyth, Wilson; and the Yorkshire Engine Company. All were rebuilt between 1888 and 1895 and, by the time they appeared on the Framlingham branch, the engines had reliquished their main line goods turns and were relegated to branch line and secondary duties. Nos. 477 to 496 were placed on the duplicate list by having a prefix '0' added to the running number in 1894, whilst Nos. 497 to 506 were similarly treated in 1896. The remaining locomotives still in service were added to the duplicate list in 1899, and the survivors were withdrawn between 1897 and 1902. The leading dimensions of the class were:

Cylinders	2 inside	17 in. x 24 in.
Motion		Stephenson with slide valves
Boiler	max. diameter outside	4 ft 2 in.
	barrel length	10 ft 0 in.
Firebox outside length		5 ft 5 in.
Heating surface	tubes	223 x 1⅝ in.
	tubes surface	980.0 sq. ft
	firebox	94.9 sq. ft
	total	1,074.9 sq. ft
Grate area		15.27 sq. ft
Boiler pressure		140 psi
Coupled wheels		5 ft 2 in.
Tender wheels		3 ft 8 in.
Wheelbase	engine	15 ft 6 in.
	tender	12 ft 0 in.
Weight in working order	engine	32 tons 13 cwt
	tender	26 tons 5 cwt
	total	58 tons 18 cwt
Max axle loading		12 tons 6 cwt
Water capacity		2,038 gallons

After the withdrawal of the '477' class the freight traffic, when not handled by the branch locomotive, was placed in the hands of the GER 'Y14' class 0-6-0 tender locomotives designed by T.W. Worsdell. Introduced in 1883, these small engines were later classified 'J15' by the LNER. Such was the success of the design that building continued until 1913 with all except 19 of the class of 289 built at Stratford works, the others being built by Sharp, Stewart & Company. Because of their low RA1 route availability this ubiquitous class was ideal for branch line traffic and in the latter years often deputised on passengers services on the Framlingham branch in the event of a shortage of 'F3' or 'F6' class 2-4-2 tank locomotives. After the withdrawal of the passenger services a 'J15' class worked the Framlingham goods diagram out and back from Ipswich but later the 'J15' locomotive working the Snape 'bonus' goods train worked the freight services across the branch. This continued until March 1960 when the Snape goods line closed. Locomotives known to have worked on the Framlingham line included:

GER No.	LNER 1924 No.	LNER 1946 No.	BR No.	Condemned
37	7037			August 1923
38	07038			September 1932
39	07039			March 1933
40				October 1922
509	7509	5429		November 1950
510	7510	5430	65430	January 1956
516	7516	5435	65435	October 1956
525	7525			October 1935
537				August 1923
538	7538			December 1938

'J15' class 0-6-0 No. 65454 of Stratford shed standing in the dock siding at the back of Framlingham station together with a low-sided wagon and two Gresley condemned suburban coaches before the special exercise at Framlingham on 10th May, 1959.

The late Dr Ian C. Allen

GER No.	LNER 1924 No.	LNER 1946 No.	BR No.	Condemned
542	7542	5470	65470*	December 1959
545	7545	5473	65473*	March 1960
546	7546	5474	65474*	February 1960
550	7550	5478	65478*	October 1961
556	7556	5454	65454*	May 1959
559	7559	5457	65457*	February 1962
561	7561	5459	65459*	February 1960
566	7566	5464	65464*	September 1962
568	7568	5466	65466*	July 1958
569	7569	5467	65467*	February 1959
570	7570	5468	65468*	September 1959
592	7592			August 1928
593	7593			December 1926
594	7594			July 1926
595	7595			June 1929
596	7596			November 1932
597	7597			April 1928
598	7598			September 1926
599	7599			May 1931
641	7641	5441	65441*	October 1958
642	7642	5442	65442*	May 1958
647	7647	5447	65447*	April 1959
693	7693			July 1928
694	7694			October 1931
836	7836	5361	65361	September 1962
866	7866	5377		February 1951
875	7855	5382		March 1952
883	7883	5388	65388	May 1959
886	7886	5389	65389	April 1960
897	7897	5396		March 1951
910	7910	5404	65404	October 1956
914	7914	5407	65407	April 1951
915	7915	5408	65408	December 1951
923	7923			October 1934
933	7933			March 1936
934	7934	5421		March 1948
936	7936			April 1937
937	7937	5422	65422	July 1955
939	7939			February 1936
940	7940	5423		November 1950
941	7941	5424	65424*	December 1959
942	7942	5425	65425	October 1956
943	7943	5426	65426	May 1951

* Westinghouse and Vacuum brake fitted for working passenger trains.

The leading dimensions of the 'J15' class were:

Cylinders		17½ in. x 24 in.
Motion		Stephenson with slide valves
Boiler	Max. diameter	4 ft 4 in.
	Barrel length	10 ft 0 in.
Firebox		6 ft 0 in.
Heating Tubes		242 x 1⅝ in.
	Surface	1063.8 sq. ft
	Firebox	105.5 sq. ft
	Total	1,169.3 sq. ft
Grate area		17.9 sq. ft
Boiler pressure		160 psi
Driving wheels		4 ft 11 in.
Tractive effort		16,942 lb.
Length over buffers		47 ft 3 in.*
Wheelbase		35 ft 2 in.*
Weight in working order		37 tons 2 cwt
Max. axle loading		13 tons 10 cwt
Tender wheelbase		12 ft 0 in.
Tender wheel diameter		4 ft 1 in.
Tender weight in working order		30 tons 13 cwt
Water capacity		2,640 gallons
Coal capacity		5 tons

* Engine and tender

On the few occasions when a 'J15' class 0-6-0 tender locomotive was not available to work the 'bonus' freight train service to Framlingham, Snape and Saxmundham, a 'J17' class 0-6-0 tender locomotive was substituted. The running foreman at Ipswich was loathe to take this step as the 'J17' class was restricted from the Snape branch and thus required the Framlingham branch engine to cover and take the wagons from Snape Junction to Snape and back, a time consuming and costly process. Ipswich depot had few 'J17' class engines allocated and they were regularly diagrammed to work freight services on the Aldeburgh, Felixstowe and Hadleigh

The pride of Norwich depot, highly polished 'J15' class 0-6-0 tender locomotive No. 65469 fitted with a stovepipe chimney and complete with express train headcode hauls the Eastern Region General Manager's Officer's special train across the Framlingham branch in April 1961. Participants enjoyed a lunch during an extended stop at Parham. *The late Dr Ian C. Allen*

'J15' class 0-6-0 tender locomotive No. 65389 in charge of a mixed train gets away from Wickham Market Junction, with the East Suffolk main line seen through the branches of the tree. The suburban coaching stock conveyed on this train was for use in a special exercise at Framlingham on 10th May, 1959.   *The late Dr Ian C. Allen*

On occasions when a 'J15' class 0-6-0 tender locomotive was not available to work the 'bonus' freight train diagram to Framlingham and Snape, the running foreman at Ipswich shed had to substitute a 'J17' class 0-6-0 tender locomotive for the job. Whilst this was acceptable for the Framlingham branch, the 'J17' class engines were restricted from the Snape line because of weak timber bridges and wagons had to be left at Snape Junction for the Framlingham branch engine to work down to Snape. As this was time consuming and caused delays it was thus rare to find a 'J17' class engine on the 'bonus' working. On one such occasion steam brake-only 'J17' class No. 65510 works a lengthy train away from Framlingham near Hoggate Hill crossing in the summer of 1954.   *The late Dr Ian C. Allen*

branches so any substitution on the 'bonus' job caused problems elsewhere. The 'J17s' built to the design of J. Holden were originally introduced from 1900 as GER class 'F48' with round-topped fireboxes. A further batch of 30 engines was produced with Belpaire fireboxes as class 'G58' from 1905 to 1911. Thereafter some of the earlier engines were rebuilt with Belpaire fireboxes and reclassified. After Grouping the 'F48s' became LNER class 'J16' and the 'G58s' LNER class 'J17' but by 1932 all the round-topped firebox locomotives had been rebuilt with Belpaire fireboxes as class 'J17' and the 'J16' class became extinct. Locomotives known to have worked on the Framlingham branch included:

GER No.	LNER 1924 No.	LNER 1946 No.	BR No.	Withdrawn
1160	8160	5510	65510	March 1956
1162	8162	5512	65512	December 1959
1163	8163	5513	65513	March 1961
1210	8210	5560	65560	June 1962
1211	8211	5561	65561	December 1959
1228	8228	5578	65578	March 1962

The principal dimensions of the 'J17' class were:

Cylinders	2 inside	19 in. x 26 in.
Motion		Stephenson with slide valves
Boiler	max. diameter outside	4 ft 9 in.
	barrel length	11 ft 9 in.
Firebox outside length		7 ft 0 in.
Heating surface	tubes surface	863.5 sq. ft
	flues	282.7 sq. ft
	firebox	117.7 sq. ft
	total evaporative	1,263.9 sq. ft
	superheater	154.8 sq. ft
	total	1,418.7 sq. ft
Tubes		156 x 1¾ in.
Flues		18 x 5 in.
Elements		18 x 1⅛ in.
Grate area		21.24 sq. ft
Boiler pressure		180 psi
Coupled wheels		4 ft 11 in.
Tender wheels		4 ft 1 in.
Tractive effort		24,340 lb.
Length over buffers		50 ft 6 in.*
Wheelbase	engine	17 ft 8 in.
	tender	12 ft 0 in.
	total	38 ft 0 in.
Weight in working order	engine	45 tons 8 cwt
	tender	38 tons 5 cwt
	total	83 tons 13 cwt
Max axle loading		16 tons 11 cwt
Water capacity		3,500 gallons
Coal capacity		5 tons

* Engine and tender

Occasional use was made of the 'T26' class 2-4-0 tender locomotives, which were later designated class 'E4' by the LNER. The 100 locomotives were built at Stratford works to the design of J. Holden between 1891 and 1902 and were nicknamed 'Intermediates'. The engines were used on cross-country routes and mixed traffic workings and often worked on the East Suffolk main line. Details

The use of 'E4' class 2-4-0 tender locomotives on the branch in the latter years was very rare. No. 62789 deputising for the usual 2-4-2 tank locomotive makes heavy weather of the eight-coach train formed of four ex-GER bogie coaches, normally allocated for branch use and four Gresley LNER corridor stock, near Wickham Market Junction on an extremely dull day. The rear four coaches were being worked through to Framlingham for a Sunday excursion the following day.

The late Dr Ian C. Allen

A busy time at Framlingham as 'J15' class 0-6-0 tender locomotive No. 65447 trundles along the goods loop line passing branch engine 'E4' class 2-4-0 tender locomotive No. 62789 stabled out of steam on the shed road by the water tank and coaling dock. The 'J15' was working a Sunday excursion from Framlingham with the corridor coaching stock seen to the right of the picture. The 'E4' has a tender backplate to protect enginemen from the elements when running tender first.

The late Dr Ian C. Allen

of engines known to have worked to Framlingham included, in the latter years, Nos. 62782 and 62789 which acted as branch locomotives in lieu of the usual tank engine.

GER No.	LNER 1924 No.	LNER 1946 No.	BR No.	Withdrawn
413	7413			October 1931
421	7421			November 1938
465	7465			July 1928
466	7466	2782	62782	November 1954
467	7467			April 1937
468	7468			August 1929
469	7469			June 1929
470	7470			May 1934
471	7471			September 1929
472	7472			May 1938
473	7473			December 1935
474	7474			April 1929
475	7475			May 1931
476	7476			March 1937
497	7497	2789	62789	December 1957

The leading dimensions of the 'E4' class were:

Cylinders		17½ in. x 24 in.
Motion		Stephenson with slide valves
Boiler	max. diameter	4 ft 4 in.
	barrel length	10 ft 0 in.
Firebox		6 ft 0 in.
Heating surface	tubes	242 x 1⅝ in.
	tubes surface	1,063.8 sq. ft
	firebox	100.9 sq. ft
	total	1,164.7 sq. ft
Grate area		18.0 sq. ft
Boiler pressure		160 psi
Leading wheels		4 ft 0 in.
Driving wheels		5 ft 8 in.
Tractive effort		14,700 lb.
Length over buffers		48 ft 2 in.*
Wheelbase		16 ft 6 in.
Weight in working order		40 tons 16 cwt
Max. axle loading		14 tons 3 cwt
Tender	wheelbase	12 ft 0 in.
	wheel diameter	4 ft 1 in.
	weight in working order	30 tons 13 cwt
	water capacity	2,640 gallons
	Coal capacity	5 tons

* Engine and tender

As excursion traffic increased, members of the LNER 'D13' class 4-4-0 tender locomotives made occasional visits to the Framlingham branch from around Grouping until 1935. Originally built as GER class 'T19' 2-4-0 tender engines, 110 were constructed between 1886 and 1897. Sixty were rebuilt as 4-4-0s between 1905 and 1908 and 50 of these entered service with the LNER. Ipswich depot had an allocation of five in 1923 but they were gradually transferred or scrapped until the last one was withdrawn from the depot in 1937. Like all tender classes the engine usually worked tender first down the branch for excursion destinations

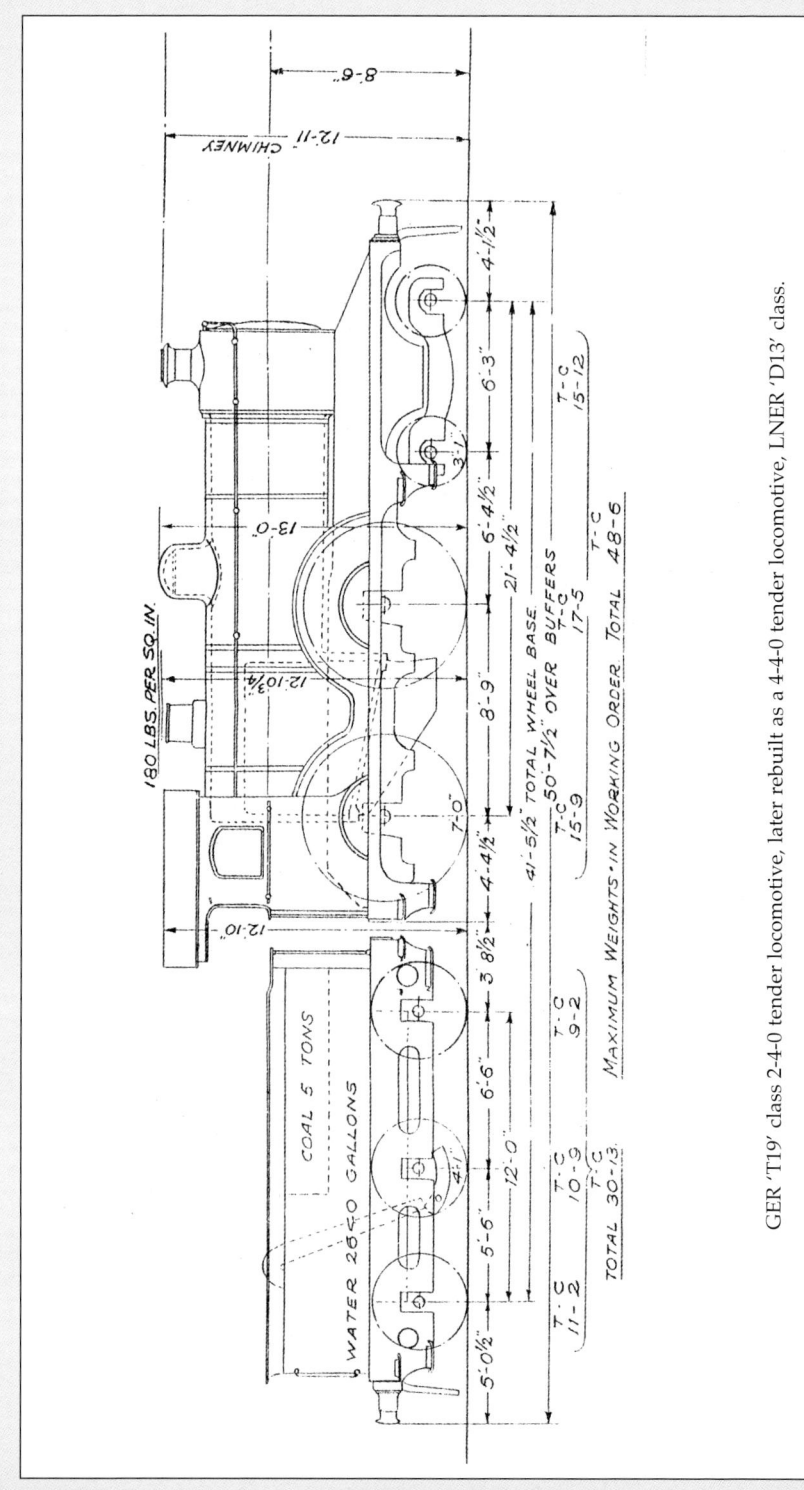

GER 'T19' class 2-4-0 tender locomotive, later rebuilt as a 4-4-0 tender locomotive, LNER 'D13' class.

south of Wickham Market or engine first when final destinations were north of Wickham Market. Locomotives known to have worked across the branch included:

GER No.	LNER 1924 No.	Withdrawn
700	7700	October 1935
731	7731	August 1931
737	7737	April 1933
738	7738	July 1931
741	7741	December 1935
744	7744	April 1935
765	7765	January 1930
1025	8025	October 1937
1037	8037	December 1934

The leading dimensions of the 'D13' class were:

Cylinders	2 inside	18 in. x 24 in.
		18 in. x 25 in.*
Motion		Stephenson with slide valves
Boiler	Max. dia. outside	4 ft 9 in.
	Barrel length	10 ft 0 in.
Firebox outside length		7 ft 0 in.
Heating surface (saturated)	tubes	282 x 1¾ in.
	firebox	117.7 sq. ft
	tubes surface	1,335.0 sq. ft
	total evaporative	1,452.7 sq. ft
Heating surface (superheated)	tubes	158 x 1¾ in.
	flues	18 x 5 in.
	elements	18 x 1⅖ in.
	firebox	117.7 sq. ft
	tubes surface	748.0 sq. ft
	flues surface	241.1 sq. ft
	total evaporative	1,106.8 sq. ft
	superheater	136.8 sq. ft
	total	1,243.6 sq. f t
Grate area		21.6 sq. ft
Boiler pressure		180 psi
Leading wheels		3 ft 1 in.
Coupled wheels		7 ft 0 in.
Tender wheels		4 ft 1 in.
Tractive effort		14,165 lb.
		14,753 lb.*
Length over buffers		50 ft 7½ in.
Wheelbase	engine	21 ft 4½ in.
	tender	12 ft 0 in.
	total	41 ft 5½ in.
Weight in working order	engine	48 tons 6 cwt
	tender	30 tons 13 cwt
	total	78 tons 19 cwt
Max. axle loading		17 tons 5 cwt
Water capacity		2,640 gallons
Coal capacity		5 tons 0 cwt

* Nos. 7731 and 7765 only.

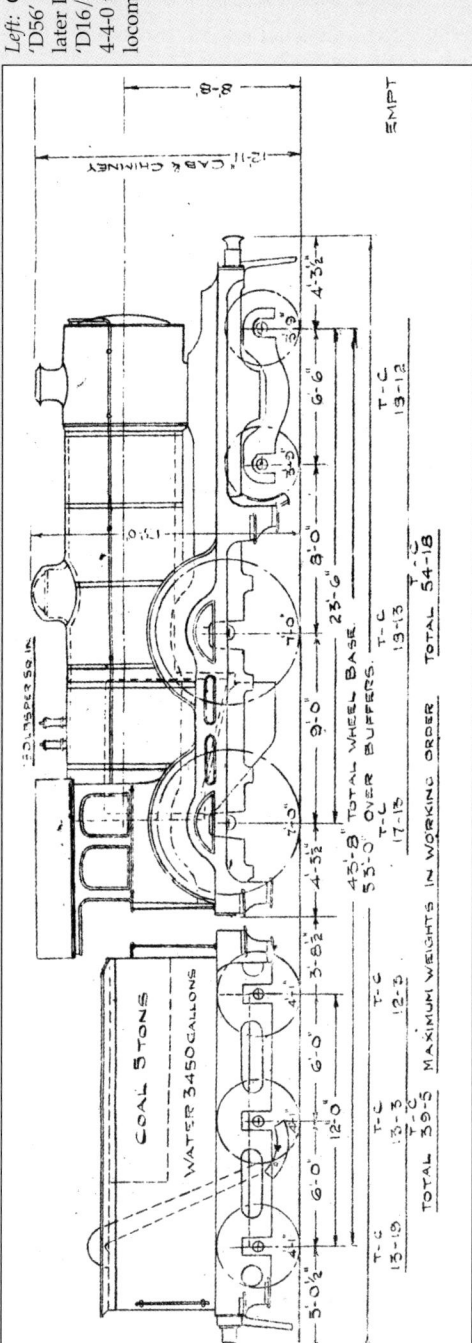

Left: GER 'D56' class, later LNER 'D16/2' class 4-4-0 tender locomotive.

Left: LNER 'D16/3' class 4-4-0 tender locomotive.

The LNER 'D14', 'D15' and 'D16' class 4-4-0 tender locomotives also made sporadic visits to the branch, usually with excursion trains but on a few occasions they substituted for the usual tank locomotive and worked the normal services. The 111 GER 'S46' and 'D56' classes, later LNER 'D14' and 'D15' class locomotives, dated from 1900, with the last 10 emerging as class 'D16' in 1923. Throughout the years many were rebuilt and the majority that survived into BR ownership formed the 'D16/3' sub-class. In 1936 No. 8855 deputised for a failed 'F3' locomotive on the branch duties. On Sunday 22nd October, 1950 'D16/3' class No. 62526 worked a through train from Liverpool Street across the branch, even stopping at Hacheston Halt to allow passengers to alight. The locomotive was fitted with a tender equipped with M&GN token exchange mechanism. 'Super Claud' class 'D16/2' No. 62590 once ran across the branch with an excursion train and then worked the branch services, whilst on 21st July, 1954 'D16/3' class No. 62612 of Ipswich worked a special public excursion train from all stations on the branch to Felixstowe.

GER No.	LNER 1924 No.	LNER 1946 No.	BR No.	Withdrawn
1875	8875	2526	62526	May 1957
1855	8855	2546*	62546	June 1957
1841	8841	2552	62552	October 1955
1819	8819	2590	62590	January 1952
1800	8800	2591	62591	April 1950
1781	8781	2612	62612	November 1959

* Named *Claud Hamilton* in 1947.

The principal dimensions of the 'D16/3' class were:

Cylinders	2 inside	19 in. x 26 in.
Motion		Stephenson and slide valves
Boiler	max. diameter	5 feet 1⅛ in.
	barrel length	11 ft 9 in.
	firebox	7 ft 0 in.
Heating surface	tubes	957.1 sq. ft
	firebox	126.0 sq. ft
	flues	346.3 sq. ft
	total evaporative	1,429.4 sq. ft
	superheater	302.5 sq. ft
	total	1,731.9 sq. ft
Tubes		172 x 1¾ in.
Flues		21 x 5¼ in.
Elements		21 x 1¼ in.
Grate area		21.0 sq. ft
Boiler pressure		180 psi
Leading wheels		3 ft 9 in.
Coupled wheels		7 ft 0 in.
Tender wheels		4 ft 1 in.
Length over buffers		53 ft 2 in.
Weight in working order	engine	53 tons 18 cwt
	tender	39 tons 5 cwt
	total	95 tons 3 cwt
Max. axle loading		18 tons 14 cwt
Water capacity		3,450 gallons
Coal capacity		5 tons 0 cwt

In the years following World War II, Gresley's rebuild of Holden's 'S69' 4-6-0 tender engines the 'B12/3' class were increasingly used on the branch, usually on excursions, school trains for Framlingham College and weedkilling trains. After the withdrawal of passenger services, the class continued to be used until the full

A down branch train, unusually hauled by 'D16/2' 4-4-0 tender locomotive No. 62591, waits at
Brick Lane crossing for the guard to rejoin his brake van after closing the gates.

The late Dr Ian C. Allen

'D16/2' class 4-4-0 tender locomotive No. 62590 deputising for the normal tank locomotive
stands at Parham with a down branch train from Wickham Market to Framlingham. The level
crossing gates have already been closed across the railway behind the train by the station staff.

The late Dr Ian C. Allen

'D16/3' class 4-4-0 tender locomotive No. 62612 running tender first hauling the empty coaching stock of a Sunday excursion from Liverpool Street near Hoggate Hill footpath crossing. These trains were popular in the latter years of the branch passenger workings. *The late Dr Ian C. Allen*

'D16/3' class 4-4-0 tender locomotive No. 62526 approaching Parham with a four-coach excursion train formed of LNER Gresley corridor stock. The engine has lost the ornate valencing above the driving wheels. *The late Dr Ian C. Allen*

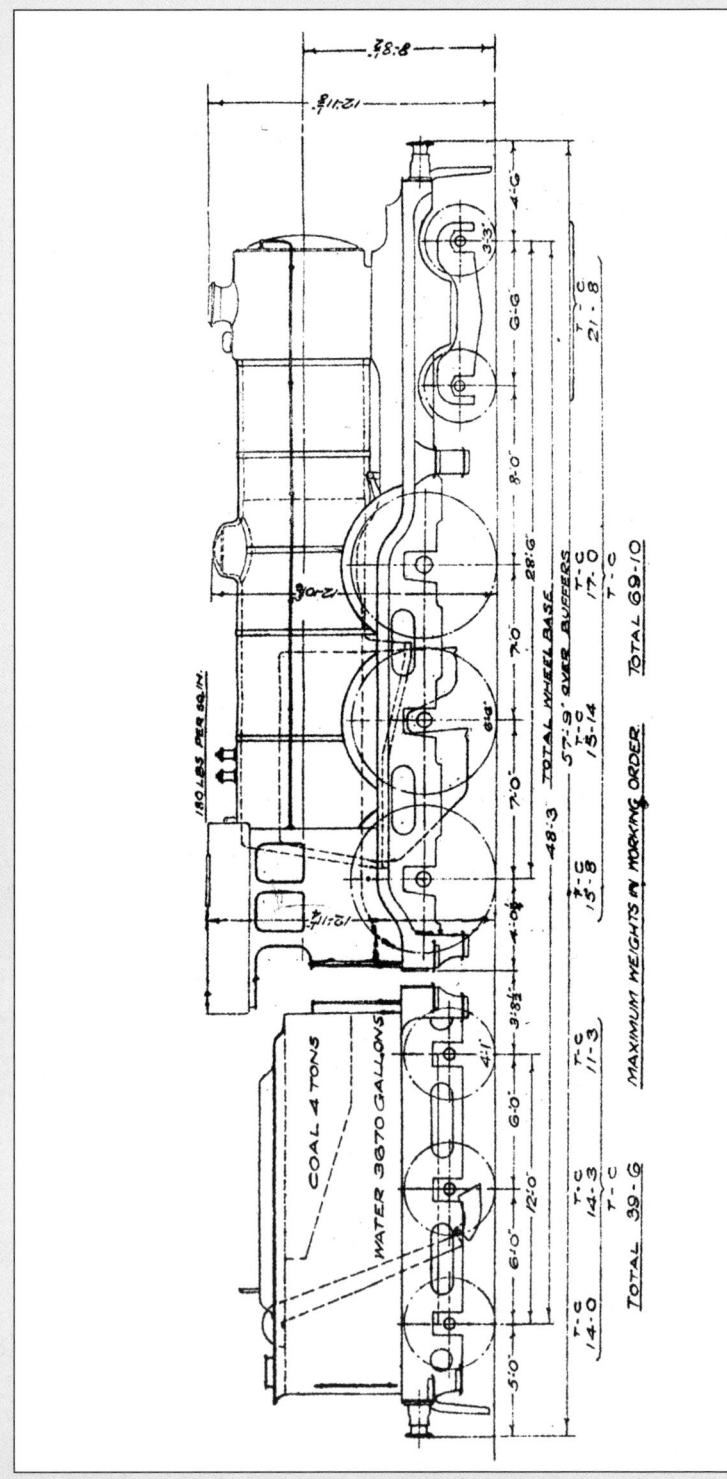

GER 'S69' class 4-6-0 tender locomotive, later rebuilt by the LNER to 'B12/3' class.

withdrawal of steam traction. The locomotives were first introduced in 1911 when the GER authorities were finding the 'Claud Hamilton' 'D15' and 'D16' class 4-4-0 tender locomotives struggling with the ever-increasing heavy trains. Known as the '1500s' from the number of the initial engine, a total of 71 was built to 1921 although one of these was totally written off after a fatal crash at Witham. After Grouping the locomotives were allocated to class 'B12' and a further 10 engines were introduced. With the introduction of the Gresley 'B17' class three-cylinder 4-6-0 locomotives from 1928, and a general improvement in motive power availability, the LNER found several 'B12s' could be made available for use on other sections of their system. Accordingly between 1931 and 1942 several of the class migrated to the Great North of Scotland section working trains from Aberdeen to Keith and Elgin. Most of the class that remained on the GE section were subsequently rebuilt between 1932 and 1944 with a larger boiler and other alterations and were designated to class 'B12/3'. Ipswich depot had a large allocation and it was usually one of these that visited the Framlingham branch. Those known to have worked on the line included:

GER No.	LNER 1924 No.	LNER 1946 No.	BR No.	Condemned
1533	8533	1533	61533	November 1959
1535	8535*	1535	61535	December 1959
1537	8537	1537	61537	April 1957
1561	8561	1561	61561	December 1958
1562	8562*	1562	61562	August 1955
1564	8564	1564	61564	November 1958
1566	8566	1566	61566	January 1959
1568	8568*	1568	61568	August 1959
1569	8569	1569	61569	January 1957
1570	8570	1570	61570	March 1958
–	8571	1571	61571	December 1959
–	8572	1572	61572	September 1961
–	8577*	1577	61577	December 1959

* The following were also renumbered in the 1942 scheme: 8535 - 7449; 8562 - 7476; 8568 - 7482; 8577 - 7491.

The leading dimensions of the 'B12/3' class were:

Cylinders	2 inside	20 in. x 28 in.
Motion		Stephenson with 10 in. piston valves
Boiler	max. diameter	5 ft 6 in.
	barrel length	12 ft 7½ in.
Firebox	outside length	10 ft 1½ in.
Heating surface	firebox	154.0 sq. ft
	tubes	979.0 sq. ft
	flues	426.0 sq. ft
	total evaporative	1,559.0 sq. ft
	superheater	315.0 sq. ft
	total	1,874.0 sq. ft
Tubes		143 x 2 in.
Flues		24 x 5¼ in.
Elements		24 x 1⅛ in.
Grate area		31.0 sq. ft
Boiler pressure		180 psi
Leading wheels		3 ft 3 in.
Coupled wheels		6 ft 6 in.
Tender wheels		4 ft 1 in.
Length over buffers		57 ft 9 in.
Wheelbase	engine	28 ft 6 in.
	tender	12 ft 0 in.
	total	48 ft 3 in.

'B12/3' class locomotive No. 61564 eases round the curve from Wickham Market Junction and makes for Framlingham with a special train from Liverpool Street conveying students to Framlingham College at the beginning of the September 1955 term. After the withdrawal of passenger services, Gerald Leedham, a former General Manager of the Cheshire Lines Committee and an inhabitant of Framlingham, persuaded BR to operate special trains for students of Framlingham College at the beginning and end of each term, as petrol was still rationed. These special trains operated to and from Liverpool Street each term between 1954 and 1958 and through tickets to Framlingham were also issued at the London terminus to any members of the public who wished to travel. *The late Dr Ian C. Allen*

A local service to Wickham Market awaits departure from Framlingham behind 'B12/3' class 4-6-0 tender locomotive No. 61561 in June 1951. The three-coach train was at the limit of the platform as other vehicles were standing by the buffer stops. The dock siding is to the right. *The late Dr Ian C. Allen*

Weight in working order	*engine*	69 tons 10 cwt
	tender	39 tons 6 cwt
	total	108 tons 16 cwt
Max. axle loading		17 tons 0 cwt
Coal capacity		4 tons 0 cwt
Water capacity		3,670 gallons

With the gradual introduction of diesel traction BTH/AEI 800 hp '8/5' class Bo-Bo diesel electric locomotive, later BR class '15', worked occasionally across the branch. The principal dimensions were:

Type	Bo-Bo
Weight in working order	68 tons
Tractive effort – maximum	38,000 lb.
Wheelbase	31 ft 0 in.
Wheel diameter	3 ft 3½ in.
Bogie wheelbase	8 ft 6 in.
Bogie pivot centres	22 ft 6 in.
Width overall	9 ft 2 in.
Length overall	42 ft 3⅜ in.
Height overall	12 ft 6 in.
Minimum curve negotiable	4 chains
Maximum permitted speed	60 mph
Fuel tank capacity	Main tank 400 gallons
Brakes	Oerlikon/Davies & Metcalfe compressed air brake and hand brakes on locomotive. Vacuum brake equipment giving proportional air braking on the locomotive.
Power equipment	16-cylinder diesel engine Davey-Paxman type 16 YHXL 800 hp at 1260 rpm
Traction motors - 4	D8200-10 GEC forced ventilated type '137 AZ'
	D8211-43 GEC forced ventilated type '137 BZ'

The weekdays-only goods train to Framlingham was hauled indiscriminately by classes '15', '21', '24' or '31' diesel-electric locomotives between 1960 and 1965. The smallest of the quartet was the BTH/Paxman, '8/5' class, later class '15' 800 hp Bo-Bo locomotives. Here No. D8215 is shunting a brake van, a van and an open wagon on the main single line at Framlingham on a dull day in November 1963.   *The late Dr Ian C. Allen*

Another diesel-electric class used for a short period after introduction in 1959 was the North British Locomotive Company (NBL) 1,100 hp of which Nos. D6110 to D6137 were allocated to Stratford and Ipswich depots. After a short period in service in East Anglia, major technical difficulties were experienced and by September 1960 all were re-allocated to the Scottish Region, enabling them to be nearer the NBL Works for rectification. The leading dimension of the class '21' locomotives were:

Type	Bo-Bo
Weight in working order	72 tons 10 cwt
Tractive effort – maximum	45,000 lb.
Wheelbase	37 ft 0 in.
Wheel diameter	3 ft 7 in.
Bogie wheelbase	8 ft 6 in.
Bogie pivot centres	28 ft 7 in.
Width overall	8 ft 8 in.
Length overall	51 ft 6 in.
Height overall	12 ft 8 in.
Minimum curve negotiable	4½ chains
Maximum permitted speed	75 mph
Fuel tank capacity	460 gallons
Brakes	Vacuum
Power equipment	NBL/MAN 12 cylinder diesel engine

North British Locomotive Co. 1,100 hp diesel-electric locomotive, later BR class '21', No. D6117 standing with a 'Toad D' brake van at Framlingham. On this occasion there was no outgoing freight traffic from the terminus.   *The late Dr Ian C. Allen*

On a wintry January day BR/Sulzer type '2' No. D5040 waits at Marlesford for the gates across the A12 main road to be opened. There are no wagons in the goods yard to the right where the entry points at the Framlingham end of the station had been removed. The siding could thus only be shunted by trains working in the up direction or by trains propelling from Wickham Market. Any such propelling movements were restricted to six wagons. The Wickham Market Junction repositioned up fixed distant signal is on the down side of the line just beyond station limits.   *The late Dr Ian C. Allen*

Ipswich depot also used BR Sulzer type '2' locomotives, initially classified '11/1', later class '24', on the Framlingham branch, although the allocation only operated for a relatively short period. The leading dimensions of Nos. D5036 to D5049 were:

Type	Bo-Bo
Weight in working order	75 tons
Tractive effort - maximum	40,000 lb.
Wheelbase	36 ft 6 in.
Wheel diameter	3 ft 9 in.
Bogie wheelbase	8 ft 6 in.
Bogie pivot centres	28 ft 0 in.
Width overall	9 ft 1⅞ in.
Length overall	50 ft 6 in.
Height overall	12 ft 8 in.
Minimum curve negotiable	4½ chains
Maximum permitted speed	75 mph
Fuel tank capacity	630 gallons
Brakes	Oerlikon type, compressed air and hand brakes on the locomotive. Vacuum brake equipment giving proportional air braking on the locomotive.
Power equipment	6-cylinder diesel engine. Sulzer 4-stroke type '6LDA28' 1,160 hp at 750 rpm.
Traction motors	BTH type 137BY 4-pole force ventilated.

The class '11/1s' worked turn and turn about with the Brush type '2', class '13/2', later '31/1', diesel-electric locomotives on the freight services. As well as working main line passenger and freight trains, the allocation at Ipswich, D5520-24, D5526-29, D5537-44 and D5548-54, also worked various branch freight services including the Framlingham branch. The principal dimensions of the Brush '13/2' locomotives were:

	Mirlees Engine		English Electric Engine
Type		A1A-A1A	
Weight in working order	104 tons		106 tons
Tractive effort maximum		42,000 lb.	
Wheelbase		42 ft 10 in.	
Wheel diameter		3 ft 7 in.	
Bogie wheelbase		14 ft 0 in.	
Bogie centres		28 ft 10 in.	
Width overall		8 ft 9 in.	
Length overall		56 ft 9 in.	
Height overall		12 ft 7½ in.	
Minimum curve negotiable		4½ chains	
Maximum permitted speed		D5520-D5534, 80 mph	
		D5535-D5699, 90 mph	
		D5800-D5862, 90 mph	
Fuel tank capacity		550 gallons	
Brakes		Compressed air and handbrakes on the locomotive. Vacuum brake equipment giving proportional air braking on the locomotive.	
Power equipment	Mirlees 12 cyl diesel engine JVs 12T 1,250 hp at 900 rpm		English Electric diesel engine 12SVT 1,470 hp at 850 rpm
Traction motors - 4		Brush DC type 'TM 73-68' 4-pole force ventilated	

The details quoted are those extant at the time the '13/2' class operated on the Framlingham branch. Many alterations were subsequently made.

Brush type '2', 1,365 hp diesel-electric locomotive No. D5595 stands at the head of the ramblers excursion train at Framlingham, waiting to depart with the return working to Liverpool Street on Good Friday 12th April, 1963.   *The late Dr Ian C. Allen*

Facilities and Staff

Ipswich motive power depot, later coded 32B by British Railways, supplied motive power for the branch. The locomotive allocated to Framlingham was stabled in a brick built shed measuring 55 ft long by 20 ft wide, just large enough to accommodate a 2-4-2 tank locomotive. The building was situated on the down side of the main single line, south-east of the station. From the mid-1940s the shed was rarely used by the locomotive in the spring and summer months, which usually stood by the coaling stage, but with the onset of adverse winter weather the opportunity was taken to stable the engine in the shed.

Water for locomotives was obtained from a water crane fed from the storage tank raised above the pump house and located alongside the shed road. The tank was supplied by Richard Garrett of Leiston in 1859. Water from the well was pumped into the storage tank by means of a water-raising pump fed from a cock fitted to the locomotive, and all engines working the branch services were required to be fitted with this equipment. It was usual for the branch engine to stand pumping water at the end of the daily diagram in order to replenish the tank. Later an external pump was fitted. The tanks and tenders of locomotives working the branch had to be replenished at Framlingham, there being no water facilities available at Wickham Market.

A cleaner or coalman on nights carried out the coaling of engines at Framlingham, from the open coaling stage located alongside the water tank. The fireman was responsible if the bunker or tender required replenishment during the day. In order to facilitate coaling the branch locomotive usually worked engine first to Framlingham and bunker or tender first to Wickham Market.

When the line opened to traffic, only one driver and fireman were employed at Framlingham covering the full 12 hours of working. A pumpman or coalman was also employed and one of these disposed of the engine after the day's duty and prepared it for the following day's service. As a result of legislation over enginemen's hours, two sets of men were later stationed at the shed, assisted initially by a coalman/labourer and later by an engine cleaner who was booked on nights to coal and water the engine for the following day's diagram. This work could be a lonely vigil, especially in winter when the bangs and creaks caused by the stabled heated locomotive reacting in the cold air could set one's hair on end. At least one Framlingham cleaner suffered a mental breakdown and was committed for psychiatric treatment.

During World War I the number of staff at Framlingham depot consisted of driver-in-charge, acting driver, fireman, acting fireman and cleaner. The fireman booked on duty at 1.30 am to light up the fire and raise steam on the branch locomotive. The driver-in-charge signed on at 6.00 am and, after checking the engine and oiling round, worked the first up train at 7.10 am with the fireman as his mate. After returning from Wickham Market the men worked another trip to the junction station before returning with the down goods, which shunted at Marlesford and Parham. The acting driver worked the middle shift relieving the fireman who then proceeded to clean the ash pit and tidy the locomotive shed yard before signing off duty at 11.30 am. At 3.00 pm the acting fireman signed on duty and the acting driver took over driving duties. After the last trip of the day the engine was connected to the water-raising cock to pump water into the storage tank, a process that took all of two hours. On one occasion the engine was moved whilst still attached to the water-raising cock and as it took a considerable time to obtain spares, water had to be hand-pumped into the tank. To obviate any further mishap, an acting fireman made a wooden wedge to fit across the regulator so that it could not be opened by accident.

During the coal shortage after World War I the cleaner was delegated to make briquettes from coal dust and cement to supplement the meagre coal supplies and cut up old sleepers to light up the fire in the firebox. The cleaner also offloaded coal from wagons on to the coaling stage. The junior driver or senior fireman performed tube cleaning on locomotives at the rural depot, and received four hours Sunday rate of pay for the work. Boiler washing and other running repairs and maintenance were carried out when the locomotive returned to Ipswich shed. Engines were normally changed over on a Monday morning, with Ipswich men bringing down the relieving engine and taking back the relieved engine, the changeover being made at Wickham Market.

By 1925 the two sets of men worked regular turns, the first set signing on at 4.35 am, Tuesdays only, and 5.55 am, Tuesdays excepted, preparing the engine before working four or five round trips to Wickham Market and back, depending on the day, before being relieved by the second set of men at 12.07 pm, Tuesdays only, or 1.30 pm, Tuesdays excepted. These men worked the rest of the services for the day before disposing of the locomotive on shed and handing over to the cleaner and/or coalman to water and coal the engine during the night.

The senior of the two drivers at Framlingham was designated locomotive foreman, later driver-in-charge, and received a half-day's additional pay per week for administrative duties, including the submission of driver's tickets and coal and oil returns to the locomotive shed master at Ipswich. The majority of drivers based at Framlingham 'signed the road' for the branch and the main line to Ipswich. Some also signed for the main line between Wickham Market Junction and Snape Junction and for the Snape goods branch. The footplate staff based at Framlingham were not provided with accommodation and lived away from the railway, in the town. The two sets of men based at the shed when the depot closed on 1st November, 1952 travelled with the engine to Ipswich before taking up alternative duties, initially at Ipswich but some moved to other depots. Ipswich depot men provided cover for Framlingham footplate staff during absence due to annual leave or sickness and these men 'signed the road' for the branch. However, on one occasion when a Framlingham driver was taken ill prior to working the last train on a dark winter's night, the only replacement Ipswich driver was not familiar with the route. He was not overly concerned with stopping at the intermediate stations as a slight miscalculation would not be catastrophic but asked advice from the fireman as to where he should apply the brake on the approach to Framlingham. He was duly advised that when entering the straight section of track on the approach to the terminus and passing the sewerage farm he should fully apply the brakes. The information was spot on for after inhaling the pungent smell the visiting driver made a full application of the brake and halted the train six inches from the buffer stops! Footplate crews were renowned for supplying lumps of coal to crossing keepers along the line, the odd lump often ill flighted and timed from the moving engine, breaking a pane of glass before reaching terra firma. Scrumping was another pastime as crews stripped apples or other fruit from any convenient lineside tree including those in gardens backing on to the line. Watercress was collected from the stream at Marlesford, whilst more than one intrepid driver carried a shotgun on the footplate and bagged rabbits or pheasants on the adjacent embankment or fields to be collected on the return journey.

Drivers at Framlingham included Ted Manthorpe and Ernie Finbow with firemen Jack Dale and A. Chittock. Often at GER branch line depots the firemen were older than the drivers as they settled into a routine at the small shed and did not wish the upheaval of moving away to get promotion as a driver. One such fireman at Framlingham was John Kettley who retired on 19th September, 1927, having started his railway career at Ipswich in 1884 and transferring as a fireman to Framlingham in 1894. The local staff presented him with a purse full of money as a retirement gift. Others joined the railway at the country shed and quickly moved on promotion. Harry R. Stannard started his footplate career at the age of 18 as an engine cleaner at Framlingham on 25th March, 1875 but just over a year later on 25th July, 1876 he was promoted to a fireman's position at Ipswich. Robert Dalby, a driver, retired on 15th July, 1927 and was presented with a money and wallet by local staff. He had started with the GER at Ipswich in March 1884, later served at Parkeston and transferred to Framlingham in 1912. The last footplate staff to serve at Framlingham included driver Jack Turner and his fireman Ray 'Pony' Moore. There was a vacancy for a driver on the other turn and as there were no applicants the work was covered by one of three Ipswich drivers, Harry Double, Frank Nock or 'Jammy' Garnham. Another Ipswich man, Tim or 'Tiger' Schofield, occasionally worked the branch, his claim being that he 'signed the road' for the whole of the former GER lines. In the latter years a cleaner was sent out nightly from Ipswich to Framlingham to clean the engine, raise steam, load ashes and coal the engine. When the branch closed to passenger traffic the shed was closed and Jack Turner transferred to Ipswich, taking up duties in the goods link. Ray Moore also transferred to Ipswich and completed his career at the shed.

Initially the engine working the booked branch services carried no headlamp by day and only one white light at the base of the chimney by night. Special trains only carried lights at night with the engine displaying a white light at the base of the chimney and another on the buffer beam, if fitted with a lamp bracket, or if not presumably attached to the coupling. By 1875 the headcode for ordinary trains was the same but special trains carried a white disc at the base of the chimney by day and two white lights at night. The headcode carried by locomotives hauling the branch trains in later GER days was a red light at the top of the smokebox by the chimney and a white light on the buffer beam. During daylight hours a circular disc, red centre with white rim, was carried by the chimney. Special trains carried an additional white light by night or white disc by day on the buffer beam. By 1890 a red disc with white rim was carried under the chimney by day, and a red light

'F6' class 2-4-2T No. 67230 rests in the down yard at Wickham Market, awaiting its next departure to Framlingham. On the footplate are fireman A. Chittock and driver Jack Turner.

The late Dr Ian C. Allen

Footplate staff at Framlingham, an Ipswich fireman and driver Jack Turner stand by 'F6' class 2-4-2T No. 67239 in the shed road. *The late Dr Ian C. Allen*

under the chimney and a white light on the left-hand end of the buffer beam by night. Special trains then carried a red disc with a white rim under the chimney and a white disc in the centre of the buffer beam by day, whilst at night, a red lamp under the chimney and white lights on the left- and right-hand ends of the buffer beam were stipulated. In 1903 the headcode for the single line was again changed to a red disc with white rim under the chimney during daylight hours and red lamp under the chimney and green lamp on the left-hand end of the buffer beam by night. From 1910, ordinary and special trains carried the same code, red disc with white outer rim or red lamp under the chimney, and a green disc with white outer rim or green lamp over the left hand end of the buffer beam. After Grouping, the LNER phased out the green lights and discs as a possible source of danger and replaced them with purple lights. From 1925 the standard stopping passenger train code of a white light or white disc at the base of the chimney was used on the Framlingham branch trains and remained so until the withdrawal of passenger services. Freight trains on the branch then carried the appropriate Railway Clearing House class headcode.

The following whistle codes were applicable to the branch in GER days:

Wickham Market Junction
Main Line   1 distinct sound
Framlingham Branch   3 distinct sounds

The LNER and BR issued no specific whistle codes for the branch.

In the event of a mishap or breakdown, the Ipswich breakdown vans, later breakdown crane and vans, covered the Framlingham branch, latterly using GER 20 ton capacity steam crane No. 5A dating from 1908. It was later renumbered by the LNER to 961603 in the 1938 renumbering scheme, and then by BR to No. 132 before being withdrawn in 1967.

Coaching Stock

The GER placed no weight or loading gauge restrictions for coaching stock on the Framlingham branch and conventional stock was utilised. Initially, coaching stock was very primitive four-wheel vehicles with first, second, third and Parliamentary accommodation offered, the latter travelling in third class. The first class vehicles had fully upholstered seats in the compartments, whilst at the other end of the spectrum the third class and Parliamentary passengers were subjected to sitting on bare wooden boards. Until the early 1900s coaching stock was exclusively four-wheeled, provided with oil lighting and only latterly equipped with the Westinghouse brake.

During the 1860s and 1870s, the stock allocated to the branch was of Sinclair's design for the ECR with four-compartment first/second composites to diagram 33, five-compartment thirds to diagram 34 , both with 24 ft body length, and full brake van to diagram 39 with a 21 ft length body. The branch train usually comprised four vehicles with one composite, two full thirds and one brake van as the normal formation. On Ipswich market day, an additional full third was attached. The leading dimensions of these vehicles were:

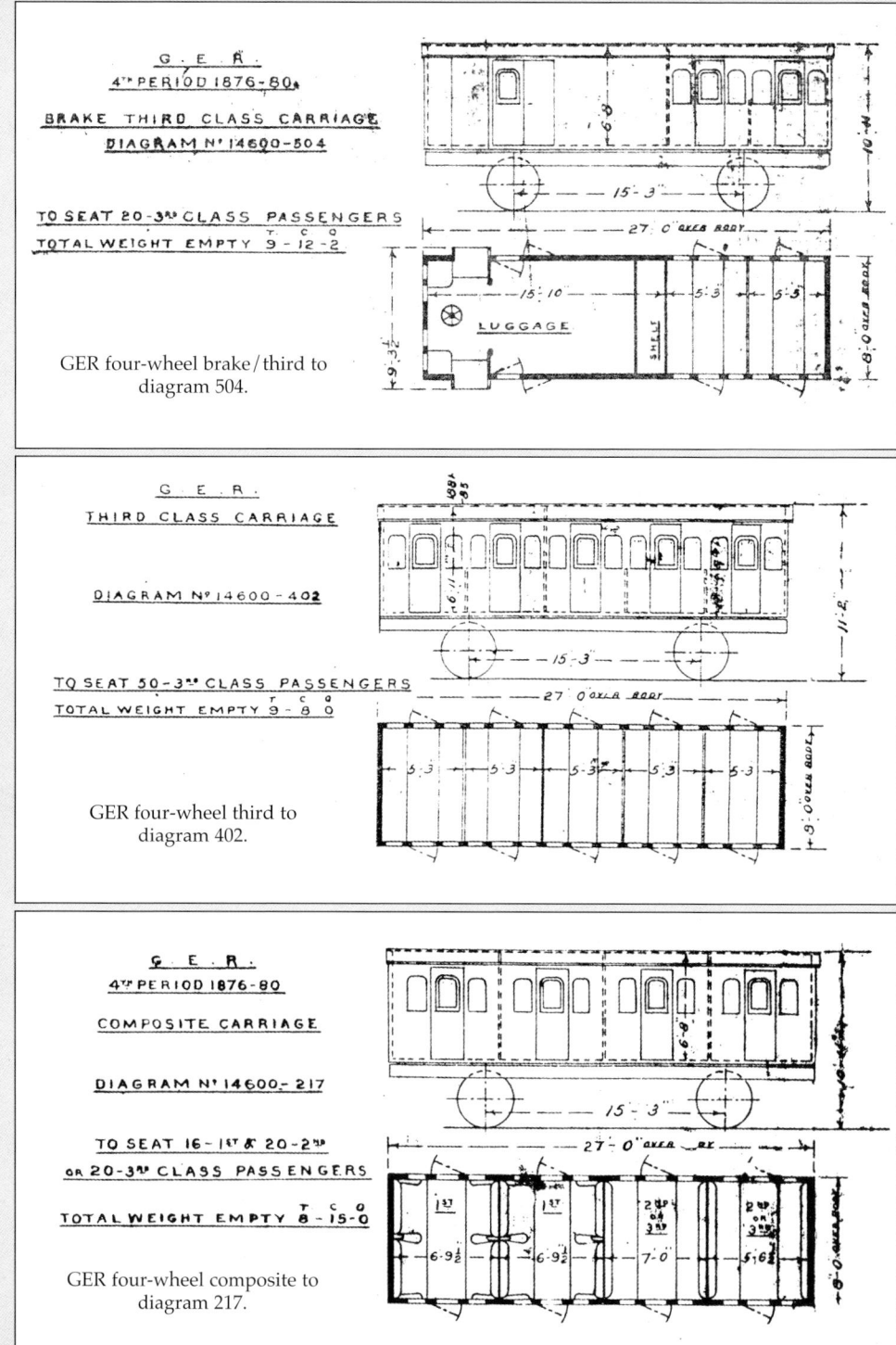

GER four-wheel brake/third to
diagram 504.

GER four-wheel third to
diagram 402.

GER four-wheel composite to
diagram 217.

GER diagram number	33	34	39
Type	4-wheel composite	4-wheel third	4-wheel brake
Length over body	24 ft 0in.	24 ft 0 in.	21 ft 0 in.
Body height	6 ft 1¾ in.	6 ft 5¾ in.	6 ft 2½ in.
Wheelbase	13 ft 6 in.	13 ft 6 in.	12 ft 0 in.
Seating 1st class	16	-	-
3rd class	20*	50	-
Weight empty	8 tons 2 cwt	7 tons 5 cwt	7 tons 17 cwt

* Second or third class.

From the early 1880s, the GER began drafting in four-wheel vehicles, 27 ft in length, originally built for main line services during the 1870s. Trains were usually formed of up to five coaches, two being third class, one second class, one composite and a brake third. These vehicles served on the Framlingham branch until the early 1900s and the leading dimensions were:

Diagram	217	302	402	504
Type	Composite	Second	Third	Brake/Third
Length over body	27 ft 0 in.	27ft 0¾ in.	27 ft 0 in.	27 ft 0 in.
Max. height	10 ft 11 in.	10 ft 11 in.#	11 ft 2 in.	10 ft 11 in.
Body height	6 ft 8 in.	6 ft 8¼ in.	6 ft 11 in.	6 ft 8 in.
Max. width	8 ft 0 in.	8 ft 0 in.	8 ft 0 in.	9 ft 3½ in.+
Wheelbase	15 ft 3 in.	15 ft 3 in.	15 ft 3 in.	15 ft 3 in.
Seating First class	16	-	-	-
Second class	20	30	-	-
Third class	*	-	30	20
Total weight empty	8 tons 15 cwt	9 tons 18 cwt	9 tons 8 cwt	9 tons 12 cwt

* Also 16 x first, 20 x third. # Also 11 ft 2 in. + Over guard's lookout.

The introduction of bogie stock on the principal GER trains from the late 1890s was a gradual process and the use of four-wheel coaching stock outside the London suburban area continued for many years. When replacement of stock was finally made on the branch, the six-wheel vehicles dated from 1879 onwards and varied in length from 32 ft for a full brake to 34 ft 6 in. for a six-compartment third. The branch train was then usually formed of a composite, two thirds and a brake third, strengthened at busy periods by either a composite or full third vehicle. During the early years of the 20th century trains were formed of a mixture of four- and six-wheel stock. The principal dimensions of the six-wheel coaching stock used on the Framlingham services were:

Diagram	219	404	422	514
Type	Composite	Third	Third	Brake/Third
Length over buffers	35 ft 1½ in. 37 ft 7½ in.	37 ft 4½ in.	37 ft 7½ in.	37 ft 7½ in.
Length over body	32 ft 0 in.	34 ft 6 in.	34 ft 6 in.	34 ft 6 in.
Height overall	11 ft 2 in.	11 ft 3 in.	11 ft 7 in.	11 ft 3 in.
Body height	6 ft 11 in.	7 ft 0 in.	7 ft 4 in.	7 ft 0 in.
Width over body	8 ft 0 in.	8 ft 0 in.	8 ft 0 in.	8 ft 0 in.
Width over guard's lookout	-	-	-	9 ft 3½ in.
Wheelbase	20 ft 0 in.	21 ft 0 in.	22 ft 6 in.	20 ft 0 in.
Seating first	12	-	-	-
third	20	60	60	30
Luggage	15 cwt	-	-	2 tons
Weight empty	12 tons 16 cwt	13 tons 3 cwt	18 tons 3 cwt	12 tons 16 cwt

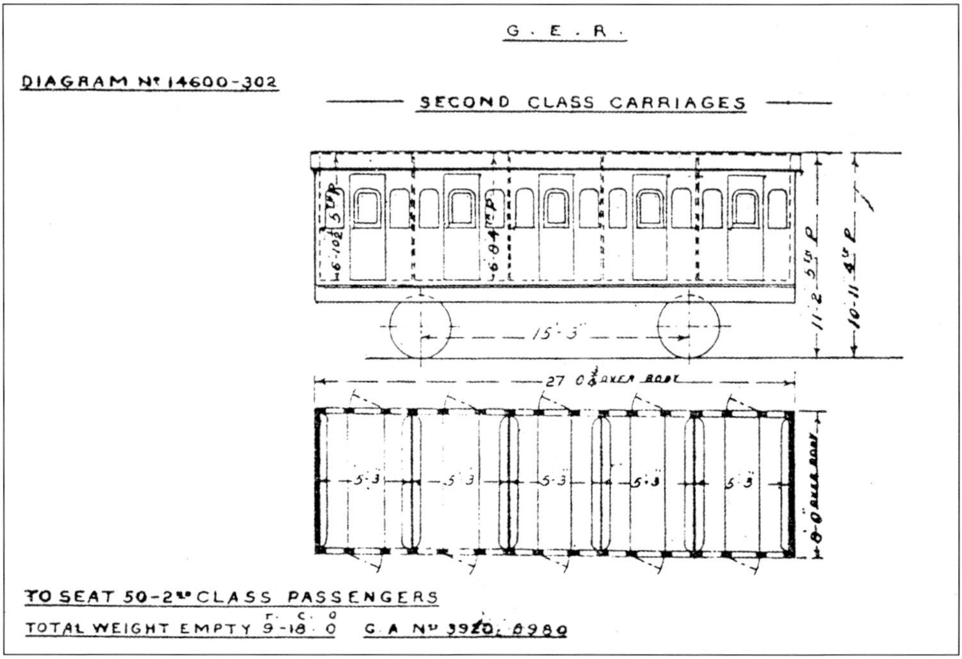

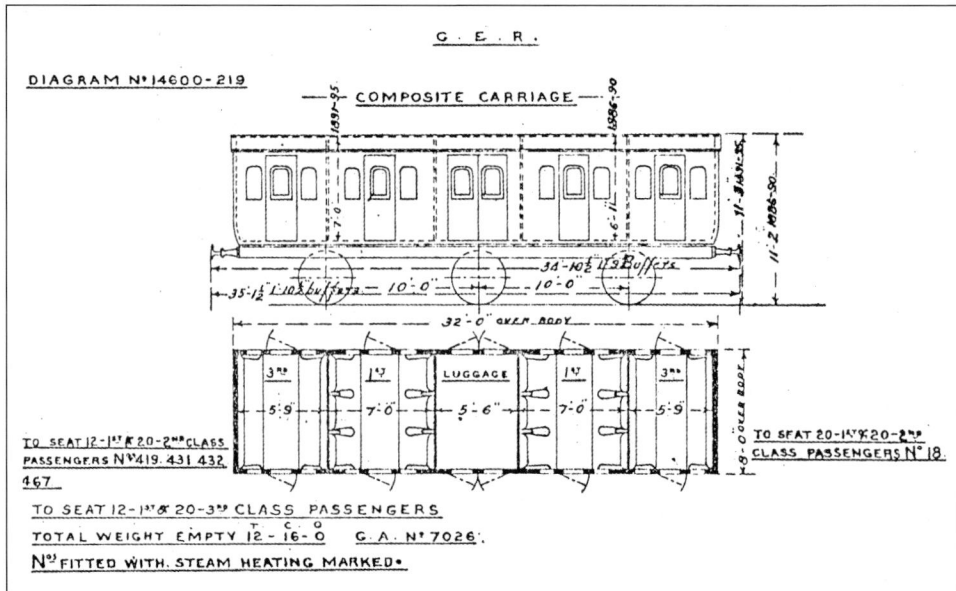

GER four-wheel second to diagram 302.

GER six-wheel composite to diagram 219.

Increasing competition from motor bus services in the early 1920s led to the GER authorities seeking ways of making economies in the operation of its branch lines, whilst at the same time bringing improvements to services. After investigation, it was decided to introduce conductor-guard working and at the same time provide cheaply built halts at suitable locations, in conjunction with specially adapted rolling stock to serve the halts as well as existing stations. As part of the programme, conductor-guard working was introduced on the Framlingham branch in the autumn of 1922 together with a new ground level halt at Hacheston between Marlesford and Parham.

The existing rolling stock was withdrawn and replaced by specially adapted three-coach sets comprising a brake third, full third and first/third composite coaches. Each coach had a centre gangway and connecting doors at each end of the full third and composite coaches and at the non-brake end of the brake third vehicle. The gangway was intended for the guard's use only, to enable him to gain access between the vehicles to collect the fares. On the brake third retractable steps were provided, essentially to serve the rail level halt at Hacheston. The guard operated the steps on the side of the vehicle by pulling a lever in the guard's compartment to extend the steps and pushing it to bring the steps back in line flush with the side of the vehicles. Direct access could be obtained to all coaches at the branch stations except that only the end doors were used as the remaining doors were sealed off. Passengers joining or leaving the train at the halt had to use the brake third and the following notice was exhibited inside the coach, 'Passengers for Hacheston Halt must not attempt to alight until the steps have been fixed and the guard has opened the door'. The brake third also carried a notice on the exterior panel of the vehicle, 'This car for Hacheston Halt'.

The carriage sets used for the conductor-guard working were converted from ordinary main line stock and appeared in the crimson livery adopted by the GER in 1919. In due course the LNER painted the stock in the more familiar teak or brown livery. The conductor-guard sets used on the Framlingham branch comprised vehicles of three types: brake thirds GER diagram 552 converted from main line diagram 514; full third diagram 440 converted from thirds to diagrams 404 or 422; and first/third composites to GER diagrams 246 and 248, converted from main line vehicles diagrams 219, 404 and 422.

No specific numbers of coaches used on the branch are known but brief details of conversions were:

Full third diagram 440	Converted from main line thirds built 1889 to 1892 (diagram 404), built 1893/4 (diagram 422); 22 vehicles converted, 10 in 1922, 12 in 1923; 6 withdrawn in 1932-3 and 16 withdrawn in 1940.
Brake third diagram 552	Converted from main line brake thirds built 1888 to 1896 (diagram 514); 18 vehicles converted, four in 1922, 14 in 1923; 5 withdrawn in 1932-3, one withdrawn in 1937 and 12 withdrawn in 1940.
First/third composite Diagrams 246 and 248	Two converted from composites built in 1890/1 (diagram 219) converted 1922 and withdrawn 1933 and 1935. 18 converted from main line thirds built 1892 (diagram 404), and 1893/4 (diagram 422), nine converted in 1922, nine converted in 1923. Two vehicles withdrawn in 1932, one withdrawn 1934 and the remaining 15 withdrawn in 1940.

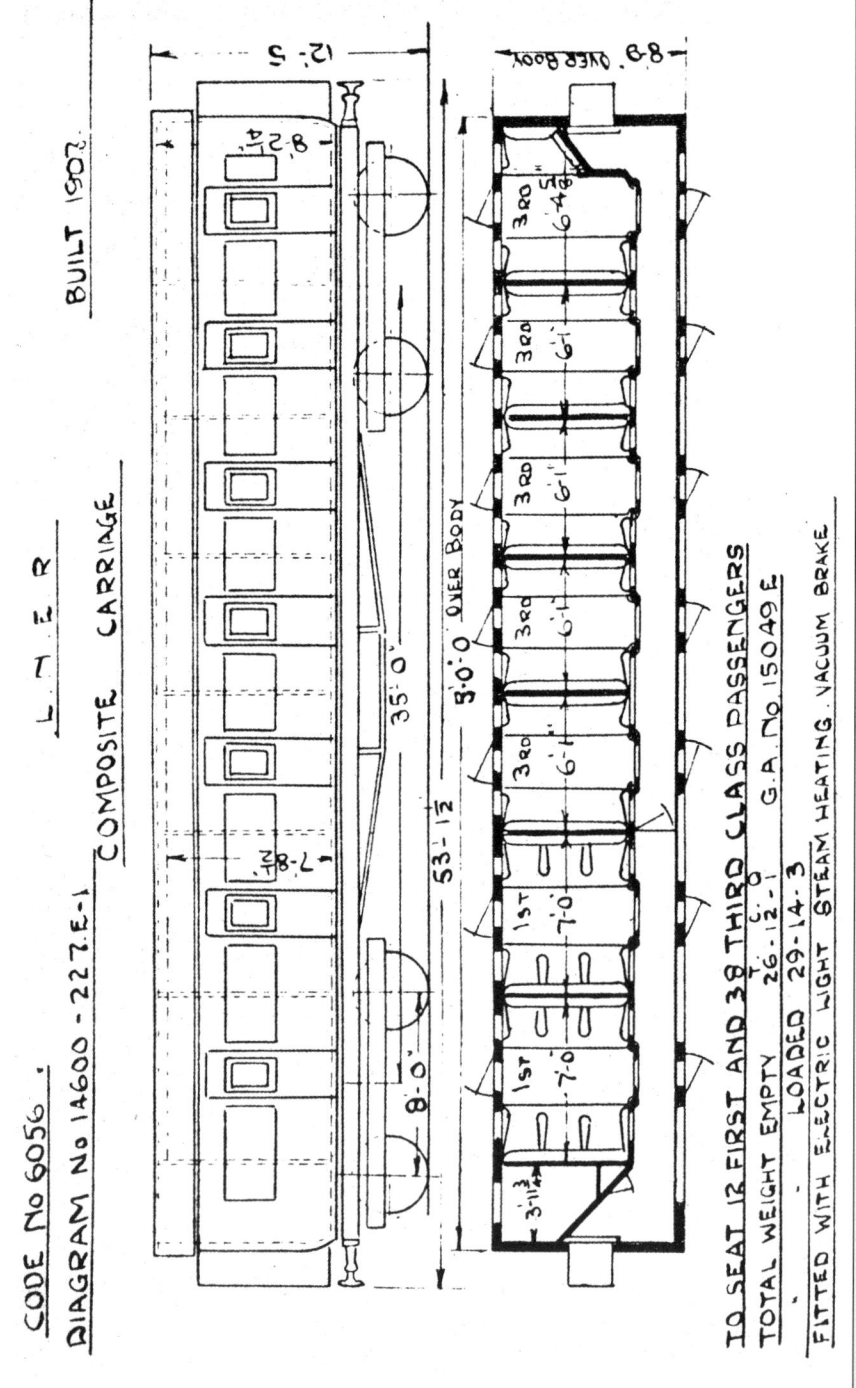

GER bogie composite to diagram 227-1 for conductor-guard working.

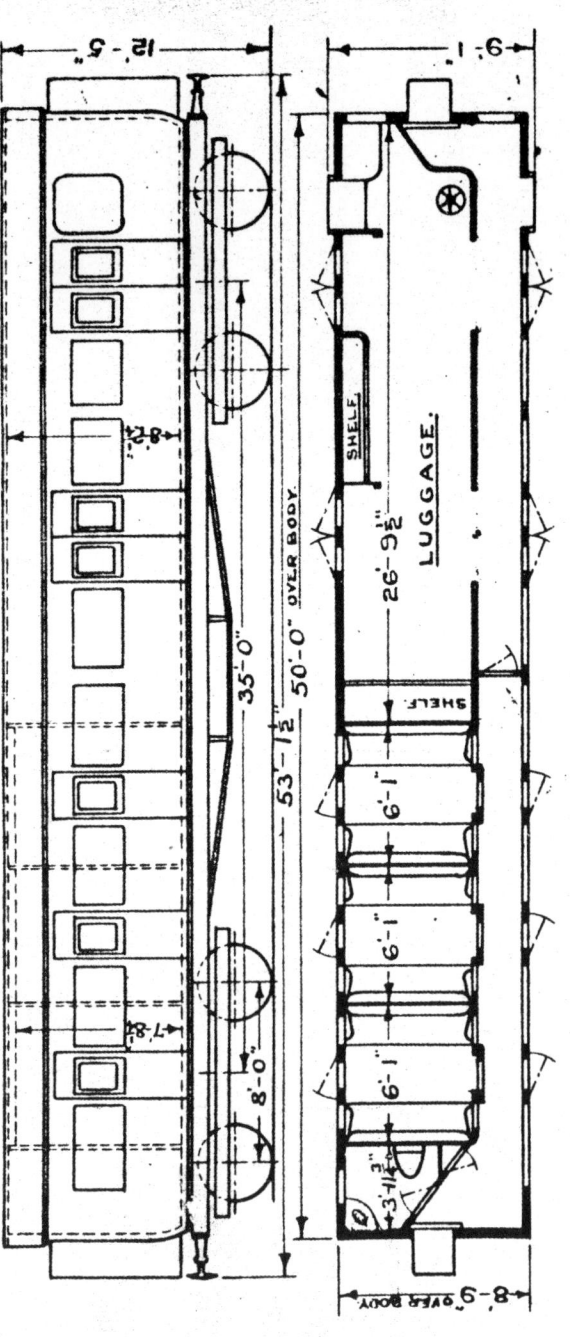

CODE Nº 6138.

DIAGRAM Nº 14600-527E.

L N E R

BRAKE THIRD CLASS CARRIAGE.

BUILT 1907.

12'-5"

7'-8½"

35'-0"

50'-0" OVER BODY

53'-1½"

8'-0"

7'-8½"

9'-1"

SHELF

LUGGAGE.

26'-9½"

SHELF

6'-1"

6'-1"

6'-1"

6'-1"

3'-4½"

8'-9" OVER BODY

TO SEAT 24 THIRD CLASS PASSENGERS.

TOTAL WEIGHT EMPTY   T. C. Q.
                      25-16-1.

"   LOADED   30-17-3.

G.A. Nº 15071E.

LUGGAGE LOAD 3½ TONS.

FITTED WITH ELECTRIC LIGHT. STEAM HEATING. VACUUM BRAKE.

GER bogie brake/third to diagram 527 for conductor-guard working.

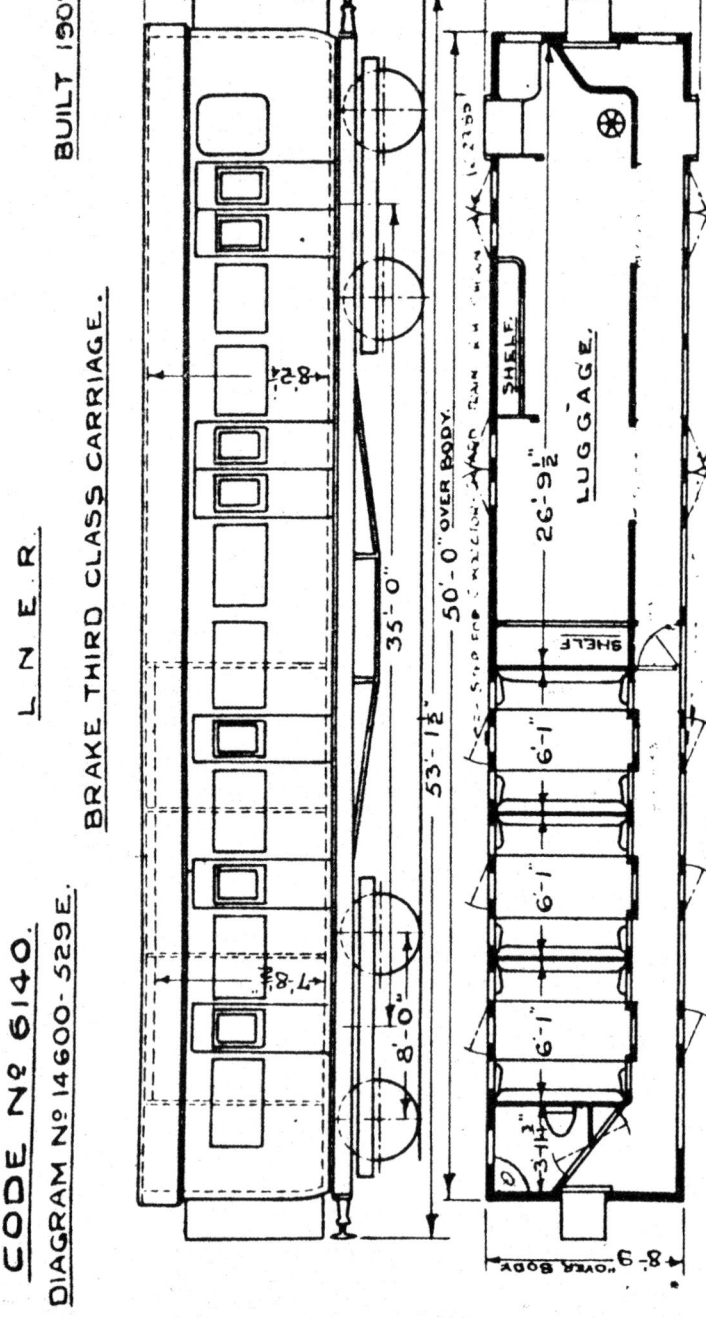

CODE Nº 6140. L N E R

DIAGRAM Nº 14600 - 529 E.

BRAKE THIRD CLASS CARRIAGE.

BUILT 1907.

TO SEAT 24 THIRD CLASS PASSENGERS.

TOTAL WEIGHT EMPTY 25-11-3. G.A. Nº 15071 E.
      "   LOADED 30-13-1. LUGGAGE LOAD 3½ TONS.

FITTED WITH ELECTRIC LIGHT, STEAM HEATING, VACUUM BRAKE.

GER bogie brake/third to diagram 529 for conductor-guard working.

The leading dimensions of the stock were:

GER diagram		246	248	440	552
Type		Composite	Composite	Third	Brake Third
Length over buffers		35 ft 1 in.	37 ft 4½ in.	37 ft 4½ in.	37 ft 4½ in.
Length over body		32 ft 0 in.	34 ft 6 in.	34 ft 6 in.	34 ft 6 in.
Height overall		11 ft 3¼ in.	11 ft 3 in.	11 ft 3 in.	11 ft 3 in.
Body height		6 ft 11 in.	7 ft 0 in.	7 ft 0 in.	7 ft 0 in.
Width over body		8 ft 0 in.	8 ft 0 in.	8 ft 0 in.	8 ft 0 in.
Width over guard's lookout		-	-	-	9 ft 3½ in.
Wheelbase		20 ft 0 in.	22 ft 6 in.	21 ft 0 in.	21 ft 0 in.
Seating	first class	12	12	-	-
	third class	16	32	43	24
Luggage		15 cwt	-	-	2 tons
Weight empty		13 tons 0 cwt	13 tons 0 cwt	13 tons 0 cwt	13 tons 0 cwt

The six-wheel stock remained in use on the Framlingham branch until 1940 when it was replaced by GER 50 feet bogie vehicles converted for conductor-guard working. It was usual for the branch train to be formed of a composite to diagram 227-1 and brake third to either diagram 527 or 529 and these remained in service until the passenger service was withdrawn on 1st November, 1952. Only a few specific vehicle numbers are known to have worked on the line, including composite E63612E and brake/third E62386E. Details of conversion of stock were:

Composite diagram 227-1	Converted from main line stock built in 1907/8, including four vehicles for the 'Norfolk Coast Express' (diagram 227), withdrawn between 1954 and 1957.
Brake third diagrams 527 and 529	Diagram 527 built for the 'Norfolk Coast Express' and 529 built for main line services, all built 1907. A total of nine vehicles converted and equipped with retractable steps. All coaches withdrawn 1954 to 1957.

The leading dimensions were:

GER diagram		227-1	527	529
Type		Bogie composite	Bogie brake third	Bogie brake third
Length over buffers		53 ft 1½ in.	53 ft 1½ in.	53 ft 1½ in.
Length over body		50 ft 0 in.	50 ft 0 in.	50 ft 0 in.
Height overall		12 ft 5 in.	12 ft 5 in.	12 ft 5 in.
Body height		8 ft 2¼ in.	8 ft 2¼ in.	8 ft 2½ in.
Width over guard's lookout		-	9 ft 1 in.	9 ft 1 in.
Width over body		8 ft 9 in.	8 ft 9 in.	8 ft 9 in.
Wheelbase		8 ft 0 in.*	8 ft 0 in.*	8 ft 0 in.*
Seating	first class	12	-	-
	third class	38	24	24
Luggage		-	3½ tons	3½ tons
Weight empty		26 tons 12 cwt	25 tons 16 cwt	25 tons 11 cwt

* Bogie wheelbase

The *GE Area Country Branch Carriage Working* for 1950 showed the Framlingham branch services being worked by a two-coach set formed of CKBS (corridor composite with British standard gangway) with two first and five third class compartments and a BTKBS (corridor brake third with British standard gangway) with three third class compartments. The 'conductor guard' set accommodating just 12 first class and 62 third class passengers and weighing 54 tons worked the branch on a daily basis.

Framlingham station, with buffer stops 91 miles 02 chains from Liverpool Street, showing a set of three Gresley corridor coaches at the platform forming a return Framlingham College special train from Liverpool Street. To the left and occupied by wagons is the 250 ft carriage dock road and to the far left the 270 ft cattle dock road. Behind the platform is the entrance to the up side goods yard served by 280 ft loading dock road.   *The late Dr Ian C. Allen*

'J15' class 0-6-0 tender locomotive No. 65467 is the allocated branch engine deputising for the non-availability of an 'F6' class 2-4-2 tank engine. Here the 0-6-0 sets off round the curve from Wickham Market Junction past Blackstock Wood with her two-coach train for Framlingham formed of a two-coach bogie conductor-guard set of ex-GER coaching stock, brake/third to diagram 529 and composite to diagram 227-1. Note with true branch line malpractice the engine is carrying the incorrect headcode for a stopping passenger service and has yet to receive her smokebox numberplate.   *The late Dr Ian C. Allen*

In the event of the GER conductor-guard brake vehicle not being available, a Gresley LNER brake third corridor coach was substituted on the train. As the coach had no steps for use at Hacheston Halt the guard invariably borrowed a step ladder from the Framlingham station master and held the steps against a compartment door so that intending passengers could alight from or join the train. If the substitution was for any length of time the brake/third corridor vehicles sent from Ipswich as substitutes were already equipped with a set of step ladders.

Conversion of passenger carrying stock from oil to gas lighting was almost completed by the early 1900s and charging of gas cylinders on carriages was carried out at Framlingham and Ipswich. For repairs and routine maintenance the coaching vehicles were returned to Ipswich, but if minor repairs were required an examiner or fitter travelled to either Wickham Market or Framlingham to attend to defective vehicles.

Wagon Stock

The wagons used by the ECR were wooden open vehicles with side doors and fitted with dumb buffers. Where grain, straw or merchandise were susceptible to wet weather, a tarpaulin sheet was utilised to cover the contents of the wagon. The brake van at the tail end of the train would have been a 10 ton vehicle. In the years prior to the turn of the century the GER utilised four-plank-bodied, open wagons with wooden frames, dating from 1882 for the conveyance of general merchandise and minerals. From 1887, these wagons were gradually superseded by five-plank, 9 ton capacity (later 10 ton) opens, to diagram 16 with 9 ft 6 in. wheelbase and measuring 15 ft 0 in. over headstocks. Later 10 ton, five-plank open wagons to diagram 17, with a length of 15 ft over headstocks and 9 ft 0 in. wheelbase, were also used. Another variation was the use of 10 ton, seven-plank opens to diagram 55, measuring 17 ft 0 in. over headstocks and 9 ft 6 in. wheelbase for vegetable and root traffic. For fruit and perishable traffic, 10 ton ventilated vans to diagram 15 were provided, measuring 16 ft 1 in. over headstocks, with 9 ft 0 in. wheelbase and overall height of 11 ft 0¾ in. Later covered goods vans to diagram 47 were also utilised. They measured 17 ft 3 in. over headstocks, had a wheelbase of 10 ft 6 in. and were 11 ft 2 in. in height. A third variation was the 10 ton-capacity covered goods wagon to diagram 72, which measured 19 ft 0 in. over headstocks whilst maintaining a 10 ft 6 in. wheelbase.

The extensive cattle traffic conveyed to and from Framlingham would have entailed the use of three types of cattle wagons on the branch. The first of 8 ton capacity was to diagram 5 and was 18 ft 7 in. over headstocks, had a 10 ft 6 in. wheelbase and was 10 ft 10¾ in. in height. The second to diagram 6 was of 9 tons capacity and measured 19 ft 0 in. over headstocks, with a 10 ft 6 in. wheelbase and overall height of 10 ft 10½ in. The third GE variant of cattle wagon to diagram 7 was of 10 tons capacity, 19 ft 3 in. over headstocks with 10 ft 6 in. wheelbase and overall height of 11 ft 2 in. At the tail of the train was usually a 20 ton four-wheel brake van to GE diagram 56 measuring 17 ft 6 in. over

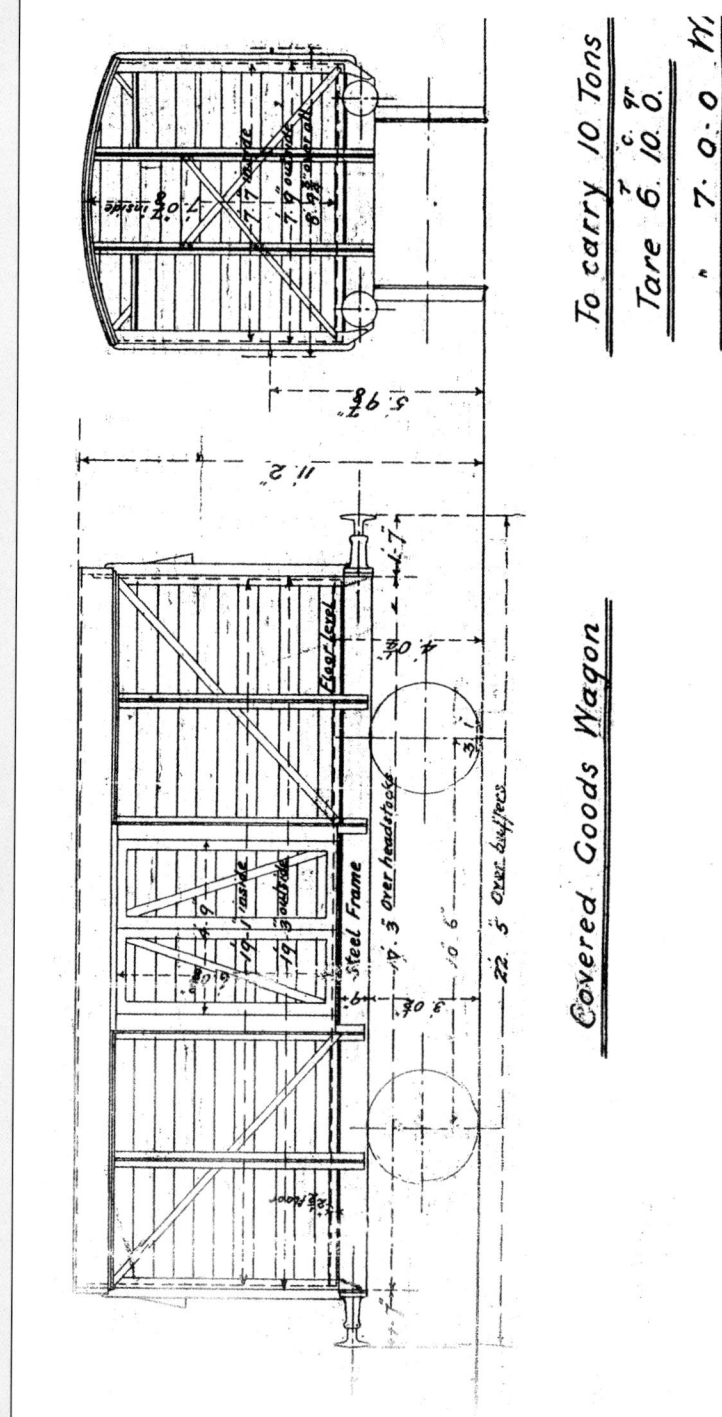

GER 10 ton covered goods wagon to diagram 47.

headstocks, a 10 ft 3 in. wheelbase and 3 ft 1 in. diameter wheels. In addition many wagons owned by other railway companies were used to deliver and collect agricultural and livestock traffic, whilst coal and coke supplies came in private owner coal wagons. These fell into two categories, those belonging to the collieries consigning the coal, and merchant and coal factors wagons, which were loaded at collieries.

After Grouping, the GER wagons continued to be utilised but gradually LNER standard designed wagons made an appearance. The most numerous were probably the 12 ton, five-plank opens with an 8 ft 0 in. wheelbase to code 2, and 12 ton, six-plank opens with 10 ft 0 in. wheelbase to code 91 built after 1932. Later variations included a 13 ton, seven-plank open wagon to code 162 measuring 16 ft 6 in. over headstocks and with a 9 ft 0 in. wheelbase. All were used on vegetable and sugar beet traffic. Fitted and unfitted 12 ton, 9 ft 0 in. wheelbase covered vans to code 16 conveyed perishable goods, fruit and malt and later some were designated for fruit traffic only. From 1934, 12 ton capacity vans to code 171, with steel underframe and pressed corrugated steel ends, were introduced whilst at the same time the wheelbase was extended to a length of 10 ft 0 in. Specific fruit vans with both 9 ft and 10 ft wheelbase also saw service on the Framlingham branch for malt traffic. Agricultural machinery destined for local farms was delivered on 12 ton 'Lowfit' wagons, with 10 ft wheelbase and overall length over headstocks of 17 ft 6 in. Larger machinery

'J15' class 0-6-0 tender locomotive No. 65389 shunts a train of vans and open wagons from the goods loop line back on to the main line at Framlingham as she prepares the 'bonus' freight for the return run to Ipswich. The goods shed is behind the train and granary road and back road sidings are behind the engine. *The late Dr Ian C. Allen*

Framlingham station facing the buffer stops on 27th September, 1952, with a 'J15' class 0-6-0 tender locomotive No. 65467 waiting to depart with an up train. A crane wagon occupies the carriage loading dock road.   *The late H.C. Casserley*

The 6 ton-capacity rail-mounted crane standing in Wickham Market goods yard on 31st July, 1961.   *John Watling*

would have arrived or departed on one of the ex-GER 14 ton, 25 ft 6 in. 'Mac K2' machinery wagons to diagram 75 and later LNER builds. LNER brakevans provided for branch traffic included 20 ton 'Toad B' to code 34 and 'Toad E' to code 64 vehicles with 10 ft 6 in. wheelbase and measuring 22 ft 5 in. over buffers. Later 'Toad D' brake vans to code 61 with 16 ft wheelbase and measuring 27 ft 5 in. over buffers were employed. After Nationalisation many of the older wooden wagons were scrapped and much of the traffic was conveyed in open wagons in the standard 16 ton all-steel mineral vehicles. Malt traffic was conveyed in 20 ton bulk grain wagons. For a number of years after World War II the allocated goods brake van for the branch was former Great Central Railway six-wheel vehicle No. E509451.

In GER days the body, solebars and headstocks of the open wagons were painted slate grey, whilst the ironwork below solebar level, buffer guides, buffers, drawbars, drawbar plates and couplings were black. The LNER wagon livery was grey for non-fitted wagons and covered vans, whilst all vehicles fitted with automatic brakes, including brake vans, were painted red oxide which changed to bauxite around 1940. Similar liveries were carried in BR days.

The maintenance of wagon stock used on the branch was carried out by the wagon repairs shops at Ipswich. In the event of the failure or defect of a wagon on the branch, a travelling wagon repairer carried out repairs locally.

Authority was granted for a propelling movement for goods traffic between Wickham Market and Marlesford, providing the train did not exceed six wagons, including brake van. For many years a path was show in the working timetable between the running of the booked passenger train service. In June 1949 the branch home signal is cleared at Wickham Market Junction to allow 'F3' class 2-4-2 tank locomotive No. 67127 to propel an open wagon and former Great Central branch van on such a working to Marlesford. The single line Train Staff had to be collected from the signalman at the junction to protect the movement. *The late Dr Ian C. Allen*

A Framlingham College special train soon after leaving Framlingham with 'B12/3' class 4-6-0 No. 61537 blackening the surrounding countryside near Hoggate Hill crossing. The train is formed of Gresley and Thompson ex-LNER corridor stock. *The late Dr Ian C. Allen*

Although 'D16/3' class 4-4-0 tender locomotive No. 62552 is carrying headlamps denoting an empty stock working she is in fact working a Framlingham College special train off the Framlingham branch and over the crossover to the up main line at Wickham Market Junction in 1954. The train is unusually formed on non-corridor ex-LNER Thompson suburban stock. *The late Dr Ian C. Allen*

Appendix One

Level Crossings

No.	Location	Mileage from Liverpool St m. ch.		Local Name	Status
Main Line					
41	Wickham Market & Wickham Mkt Jn	84	52	Hurrens	Occupation
42	Wickham Market & Wickham Mkt Jn	84	64	White House	Footpath
43	Wickham Market & Wickham Mkt Jn	85	17	Haywards	Occupation
44	Wickham Market & Wickham Mkt Jn	85	33	Blackstock	Public
Branch					
-	Wickham Market Junction & Marlesford	85	57	Gamekeeper	Footpath
1	Wickham Market Junction & Marlesford	86	09	Alder Carr	Footpath
2	Marlesford & Parham	86	25	Yarmouth Road A12	Public
3	Marlesford & Parham	86	37	Lime House/Cornish	Public
4	Marlesford & Parham	86	55	Marlesford Ford	Public
5	Marlesford & Parham	86	77	Decoy	Footpath
6	Marlesford & Parham	87	58	Hacheston	Public
7	Marlesford & Parham	87	70	Sandpit	Footpath
8	Marlesford & Parham	88	15	Parham Hall No. 1	Occupation*
9	Marlesford & Parham	88	20	Parham Hall No. 2	Occupation*
10	Marlesford & Parham	88	40	Church	Footpath
11	Marlesford & Parham	88	49	Parham Station	Public
12	Parham & Framlingham	88	79	Parham Wood No. 1	Footpath
13	Parham & Framlingham	89	06	Parham Wood No. 2	Footpath
14	Parham & Framlingham	89	35	Brick Lane/Sot's Hole	Public
15	Parham & Framlingham	89	73	Broadwater	Public
16	Parham & Framlingham	90	32	Hoggate Hill	Footpath
17	Parham & Framlingham	90	55	Kettleburgh Road	Public

* Level Crossings Nos 8 and 9 closed March 1917

The secondman of a BR/Sulzer type '2' diesel-electric locomotive opens the gates of Lime House level crossing No. 3 at 86 miles 37 chains to allow the passage of the branch freight train to Framlingham. The notice by the crossing denotes that the Yarmouth Road A12 road crossing by Marlesford station is 270 yards distant. After the withdrawal of passenger services all public road crossing gates on the branch were opened and closed by trainmen.   *The late H.N. James*

The 12.47 pm mixed train from Framlingham to Wickham Market is well loaded as 'J15' class 0-6-0 No. 65467 approaches Parham River Bridge No. 1104 at 89 miles 27 chains from Liverpool Street on 11th October, 1952. In the background is Brick Lane level crossing No. 14 at 89 miles 35 chains.

G.R. Mortimer

Appendix Two

Bridges

Bridge No.	Location	Mileage from Liverpool Street (m. ch.)	Local Name	Under or Over	Type	Spans	Square Span between abutments or supports (ft in.)	Skew Span between abutments or supports (ft in.)	Depth of construction (ft in.)	Distance from road or surface of water to rail (ft in.)	Construction
Main line											
438	Wickham Market & Saxmundham	84 49	Station	Over	Public road	1	38 0	50 4	3 1	17 1	Brick abutments, wrought-iron girders. Built 1901.
439	Wickham Market & Saxmundham	84 78	Buck's Head	Under	Public road	1	20 2	- -	2 4	17 1	Brick abutments, wrought-iron girders. Built 1901.
440	Wickham Market & Saxmundham	85 40	Blaxhall	Under (side)	Public road over diverted stream	1	14 2	- -	3 0	6 7	Brick abutments, brick arch and parapets.
Framlingham branch											
1102	Marlesford & Parham	86 77	Hacheston Culvert	Under	Stream	1	6 6	- -	3 2	6 7	Brick abutments, brick arch and parapets.
1103	Marlesford & Parham	87 42	Hacheston River Bridge	Under	River Ore	1	21 10	- -	2 5	8 11	Brick abutments, brick arch and parapets.
1104	Parham & Framlingham	89 27	Parham River Bridge	Under	River Ore	1	20 5	22 4	4 2	11 3	Brick abutments, brick arch and parapets.
1105	Parham & Framlingham	90 18	River Ore No. 1	Under	River Ore & Occupation Road	2	14 11 / 15 0	over river / over road	2 11 / 3 0	24 1 / 17 3	Brick abutments, brick arch and parapets.
1106	Parham & Framlingham	90 45	River Ore No. 2	Under	River Ore	1	15 1	- -	4 6	17 11	Brick abutments, brick arch and parapets.

Acknowledgements

The publication of this history would not have been possible without the assistance of many people. In particular I should like to thank:

The late A.R. Cox
The late W. Fenton
The late G. Woodcock
The late Dr I.C. Allen
John Watling
Dave Hoser
The late Bernard Walsh
John Petrie
Alan Keeler
R.H.N. (Dick) Hardy
The late Canon C. Bayes
The late G. Pember
The late P. Proud
Chris Cock
Robert Powell
The late R.C. (Dick) Riley

also staff of the former Ipswich motive power depot and many active and retired railway staff of the Ipswich district, some of whom worked on the Framlingham branch.

Thanks also to the National Archives, British Railways, Eastern Region, the House of Lords Record Office, the British Library Newspaper Library, Suffolk County Record Office and members of the Great Eastern Railway Society.

Side view of the ornate station building at Framlingham in 1998.   *Author*

Bibliography

General Works

Aldrich, C.L .   *GER Locomotives*
Allen, C.J.   *The Great Eastern Railway* (Ian Allan)
Gordon, D.I.   *Regional History of the Railways of Great Britain Volume 5,*
                         (David and Charles)
RCTS   *Locomotives of the LNER*

Periodicals

Bradshaw's Railway Guide
Bradshaw's Railway Manual
British Railways, Eastern Region Magazine
East Anglian Magazine
Great Eastern Railway Magazine
Locomotive Carriage & Wagon Review
Locomotive Magazine
LNER Magazine
Railway Magazine
Railway World
Railway Year Book
Trains Illustrated

Newspapers

East Anglian Daily Times
Framlingham Weekly News
Ipswich Journal
Suffolk Chronicle

Other Sources

The Minute Books of the East Suffolk Railway (Extracts)
The Minute Books of the Eastern Counties Railway
The Minute Books of the Eastern Union Railway (Extracts)
The Minute Books of the Great Eastern Railway
The Minute Books of the London & North Eastern Railway

Working Timetables   ECR, GER, LNER and BR (ER).
Appendices to Working Timetables   GER, LNER and BR (ER)

Index